PORTHOLE

GEOPOLITICAL, STRATEGIC AND MARITIME

TERMS AND CONCEPTS

The closer you 'look', the wider you 'see'

PORTHOLE

Geopolitical, Strategic and Maritime Terms and Concepts

Gurpreet S Khurana

National Maritime Foundation

PENTAGON PRESS

PORTHOLE: **Geopolitical, Strategic and Maritime Terms and Concepts**
Gurpreet S Khurana

First Published in 2016

ISBN 978-81-8274-863-7

Comments and suggestions will be valuable for revised editions in the future, and may be sent to the author at gurpreet.bulbul@gmail.com

Disclaimer

1. Towards the aim of simplifying the text contained in official documents, the author has made an attempt to interpret it in a simplified manner that best represents the 'spirit' of the original document. However, such interpretation may not comprehensively address the details of the concerned subject, for which, the original documents need to be consulted.
2. The views expressed in this publication are the author's own, and do not represent those of the National Maritime Foundation (NMF), the Indian Navy or the Government of India.

Published by
PENTAGON PRESS
206, Peacock Lane, Shahpur Jat,
New Delhi-110049
Phones: 011-64706243, 26491568
Telefax: 011-26490600
email: rajan@pentagonpress.in
website: www.pentagonpress.in

Branch:
Flat No.213, Athena-2,
Clover Acropolis,
Viman Nagar,
Pune-411014
Email: pentagonpresspune@gmail.com

Printed at Avantika Printers Private Limited.

National
Maritime
Foundation

FOREWORD

The vision to establish the National Maritime Foundation (NMF) in 2005 as the premier national maritime think-tank was premised on the need to provide a common platform for deliberations among various seagoing agencies and the academia, and generate awareness in India of 'matters maritime'. An attendant aim was to address the dynamics of international relations and related strategic developments that are closely enmeshed with the affairs of the sea.

The NMF caters for a number of stakeholders including several government ministries, the strategic community, the Indian Navy and other maritime forces, the merchant marine, the oil and gas industry, and educational institutions. The task to bridge the diverse spectrum of strategic analyses and maritime activity in conceptual terms is indeed challenging. It requires evolving a synergy among the policy-makers, the various implementing authorities and the users of the sea. For the endeavour to succeed, the foremost imperative lies in bringing all concerned to a common conceptual platform.

Towards this end, I am confident that Captain Khurana's effort to compile the essentials of geopolitical, strategic and maritime terms and concepts would be helpful to achieve a conceptual unison and resonance on issues pertaining to international relations, national strategy, and maritime and naval affairs.

Admiral DK Joshi
PVSM, AVSM, YSM, NM, VSM (Retd.)
Chairman, National Maritime Foundation
Former Chief of the Naval Staff

PREFACE

The prerequisite for academic and strategic analyses and articulation—both oral and through publishing—is 'communication'. The essence lies in the ability of an analyst to be understood by the 'audience'. The commonality of English language—or any other language—is not adequate. A particular term, along with the conceptual and contextual underpinning of its usage must be fully comprehended by the 'target audience'. This rationale is best exemplified by a military doctrine, whose key aim *inter alia* is to elucidate the operational terminology to enable the uniformed personnel at all levels of the chain of command to share a common conceptual platform, so that when the higher commander gives a directive using such terminology, it raises the same thought among all subordinates as that of the commander, and mirrors the commander's intent to achieve the military objective.

As a compendium, *Porthole* is a nascent endeavour to standardise the geopolitical, strategic, military-strategic and other maritime-related concepts and terms to facilitate effective communication within the strategic and academic community, and their onward communication with their larger audiences comprising *inter alia* the policy-makers, the practitioners, the media, the enlightened citizens and the broader world. I hope that it would also address the needs of young professionals of the sea-going services, and initiate them into the multifarious issues of the 'wider' maritime world that are so closely intertwined.

Porthole is inspired by the *Indian Maritime Doctrine*, 2009, which is primarily meant as a doctrinal guidance for naval practitioners and the government policy-makers who are functionally connected to 'matters-military'. In comparison, *Porthole* addresses the broader context, thereby also encompassing the civilian aspects of maritime activity, and the closely connected aspects of international relations. With the objective to make this document more comprehensive, it also includes the concepts and terms often used to expound on the various aspects at the national-strategic and military-strategic levels, which are closely linked to 'issues international' and 'matters maritime'. Furthermore, given the salience of international law in maritime affairs, a concerted endeavour has been made to address the aspects ranging from the legitimacy of the use of force in international relations, to relevant global treaty-based conventions such as the Law of the Sea.

All terms and concepts explained in *Porthole* are sequenced in alphabetical order, and listed in the 'Contents' section. The explanation of a term (or concept) often draws comparisons with other related term(s), which are *italicized* and explained in their respective alphabetical sequence. At times, the signification of two terms is so similar—through distinct—that these are often (erroneously) considered synonymous. The Compendium also explains the varying nuances of such terms.

As a compilation of relevant knowledge, *Porthole* is based upon a multitude of sources—ranging from the Constitution of India and official Indian documents to authoritative foreign publications and websites—which have been given at the end of this Compendium. The occasional inconsistencies—and even contradictions—among the various sources were expected, which I have tried to reconcile by according priority to primary sources and my informed judgment based on my experiences of *inter alia* contributing to the *Indian Maritime Doctrine*, 2009, and compiling the *Handbook on the Law of Maritime Operations*, 2013 for the Indian Navy.

Gurpreet Singh Khurana, PhD
Captain (Indian Navy)
Executive Director
National Maritime Foundation

ACKNOWLEDGEMENTS

My endeavour to write *Porthole* stems from my good fortune to be appointed at the *Institute for Defence Studies and Analyses* (IDSA) from 2003 to 2008. Fresh out of an operational tenure in the far-flung Andaman and Nicobar (A&N) Islands, the appointment as Research Fellow at the IDSA educated me, at least to 'become aware of what I didn't know' in the broader domain of international relations, military strategy and maritime affairs. The tenure made me realise that despite my fondness for reading, I still had not been able 'connect' my professional—largely tactical—expertise and experience with the 'conceptual underpinnings' of these higher aspects of learning, and the imperatives of national strategy and policy-making. During those years, I was fortunate to find a mentor in Commodore C Uday Bhaskar, who was also instrumental in my selection for the IDSA Fellowship. It was under his guidance that I developed the yearning for such a 'broader vision'.

In early 2009, I was appointed to the then newly instituted *Maritime Doctrine and Concept Centre* (MDCC), Mumbai. My five-year tenure at the MDCC under the *Flag Officer Doctrines and Concepts* (FODC) Rear Admiral (now Vice Admiral) Bimal K Verma and my Director Captain Arun Singh—and his successors Captain Rajiv Sharma and Captain Sanjay Bhalla—gave me a rare opportunity to fill my 'conceptual void'. I, therefore, acknowledge my gratefulness to them. At the MDCC, I undertook the vetting and production of the *Indian Maritime Doctrine*, 2009. Commodore Sanjay J Singh—who had prepared the revised draft of the Doctrine—helped me to clear the many 'cobwebs' that existed in my mind with regard to doctrinal issues. I owe gratitude to him for being 'indoctrinated' into naval doctrines.

I am particularly thankful to the *National Maritime Foundation* (NMF), for it is here that the 'ink' of my thoughts has eventually 'dried' on paper. I express thanks to Admiral DK Joshi, Chairman NMF and Dr. Vijay Sakhuja, Director NMF, for their immense support that triggered me to put my pen to paper and fulfil my long-time yearning to publish this Compendium. I also thank my colleagues at NMF for their inputs, particularly Captain Raghavendra Mishra, Commander Sandeep Bali and Ms. Abhiruchi Chatterjee. In fact, the title of the Compendium—*Porthole*—was Sandeep's bright idea over a drink.

Admiral Arun Prakash, Dr. Arvind Gupta, Vice Admiral Pradeep Chauhan, Vice Admiral Pradeep Kaushiva, Dr C Raja Mohan, Rear Admiral Raja Menon and Admiral Sureesh Mehta deserve special thanks for their guidance and encouragement, and so does the anonymous referee for reviewing my draft and providing inputs and suggestions. These inputs have been insightful and incorporating them in this publication has been a learning experience for me. I am also obliged to the inputs provided by various organisations and individuals cited in the end of this Compendium. While I am grateful to all these benefactors, I accept all accountability for any errors or voids in this Compendium, which I intend to address in its subsequent revised edition.

Last but not the least, I thank my parents, my wife Jayajeet and my daughter Veera for standing by me while I wrote this Compendium, without demanding my attention that they so much deserved.

CONTENTS

A

Active Deterrence

See *Conventional Deterrence* and *Compellance, and Deterrence by Punishment.*

Admiralty Law

A body of law that encompasses 'Private International Law' and domestic law on maritime aspects and offences. (It is distinct from *UNCLOS*, which is 'Public International Law'). Being Private International Law, it governs the relationships between private entities that operate vessels on the oceans, and deals with aspects like sea-borne trade and travel, shipping, navigation, salvage and seafarers. Admiralty jurisdiction pertains to a set of laws that regulate maritime conduct with regard to contracts, torts, injuries and offences, particularly those relating to shipping, and necessitates a court or tribunal administering maritime law by a procedure peculiar to it.

The genesis of the Admiralty Law in India is based on five Acts passed by the British in the 19th century, as follows:

- The Admiralty Offences (Colonial) Act, 1849.
- The Admiralty Jurisdiction (India) Act, 1860.
- The Admiralty Court Act, 1861.
- The Colonial Courts of Admiralty Act, 1890.
- The Colonial Courts of Admiralty (India) Act, 1891.

The aforesaid pre-independence British Acts stipulating Admiralty Law are still in force in India. These Acts draw legitimacy from Article 372 of the Indian Constitution, which states that "all laws in force in the territory of India immediately before the commencement of the Constitution shall continue in force therein until altered or repealed or amended by a competent legislation or competent authority. Accordingly, the High Courts at Kolkata, Mumbai and Chennai have Admiralty Law jurisdiction under the Admiralty Court Act, 1861.

ADMM and ADMM Plus

Towards the evolution of the 'ASEAN Security Community' (ASC), the first ASEAN Defence Ministers' Meeting (ADMM) was held in May 2006. The ADMM is the highest defence consultative and cooperative mechanism in *ASEAN*, which aims to promote mutual trust and confidence through greater understanding of defence and security challenges as well as enhancement of transparency and openness. All ten ASEAN member countries are members of the ADMM. The Chairman of the ADMM is the ASEAN Chair and its rotation follows the ASEAN chairmanship. The key initiatives of ADMM being implemented are cooperation in areas of *Humanitarian Assistance and Disaster Relief (HADR)* and *Peacekeeping Operations (PKO)*, and establishing the ASEAN Defence Interaction Programme, ADMM Logistics Support Framework and Direct Communications Link. The Link, when established, will address emergent contingencies, particularly relating to *Maritime Security*.

In 2010, the ADMM was expanded to constitute 'ADMM Plus' by including ASEAN's eight dialogue partners—Australia, China, India, Japan, New Zealand, Russia, South Korea and the United States—aimed at strengthening security and defence cooperation for regional peace and stability. The ADMM Plus agreed on five areas of practical cooperation—*maritime security*, counter-*Terrorism*, humanitarian assistance and disaster management, *Peacekeeping Operations (PKO)* and military medicine. To facilitate cooperation on these areas, five Experts' Working Groups (EWGs) were established. See *Association of Southeast Asian Nations (ASEAN)* and *Southeast Asia Nuclear Weapons Free Zone (SEANWFZ).*

Aframax (Ship)

See *Commercial Ship Sizes.*

African Union (AU)

The African Union (AU) is a *Continental Union* of 54 countries in Africa. The AU was established on 26 May 2001 in Addis Ababa (Ethiopia), replacing the Organisation of African Unity (OAU). The vision of the AU is formally stated as to achieve "an integrated, prosperous and peaceful Africa, driven by its own citizens and representing a dynamic force in the global arena".

The most important decisions of the AU are made by the Assembly of the AU, a semi-annual meeting of the Heads of State and Government of its member States. The other political institutions of the AU include the following:

- Executive Council comprising the Foreign Ministers, which prepares decisions for the Assembly
- Permanent Representatives Committee comprising the heads of missions to Addis Ababa (Ethiopia), which hosts the AU's secretariat called the AU Commission, and
- Economic, Social and Cultural Council (ECOSOCC) as a civil society consultative body.

The only African State that is not a member of the AU is Morocco. This is because it opposes the AU membership of Sahrawi Arab Democratic Republic (a State not recognised by Morocco and some other countries) that exercises jurisdiction over the disputed area of Western Sahara (claimed by Morocco).

Aircraft Carrier

A warship designed to support and operate aircraft—both fixed wing and rotary wing. With its ability to occupy a 'high-ground' or 'high-space' (in terms of the elementary laws of physics) a Carrier is crucial for early detection for defence or offence, and key to *Power Projection*. Aircraft carriers usually operate with a composite force (*Carrier Battle Group*), which includes multi-purpose *Destroyers*, *Frigates*, *Logistics Ships*, and possibly even *Nuclear Submarines*. The Carrier is a central part of a *Carrier Battle Group* (CBG), a self-sustained group capable of applying combat force in multiple dimensions for exercise of *Sea Control* and *Power Projection*. The Carrier is also a versatile platform for stand-alone employment in peacetime and short-of-war scenarios. It is designated by the letters 'CV'. If nuclear-powered, it is referred to as 'CVN'.

Although an aircraft carrier is of immense operational utility to enable a country's ability for *Power Projection*, it comes with a substantial financial cost, which not many countries can afford. Notably, since the end of the Second World War, the number of carrier-operating navies has increased incrementally from four to ten. These countries are Brazil, China, France, India, Italy, Russia, Spain, Thailand, and the USA.

Air Defence (AD)

The territorial Air Defence of a country (including its littoral areas and assets) is usually the responsibility of its Air Force. The navy's military task of *Anti-Air Warfare (AAW)* pertains to Air Defence of the forces at sea, including those under escort. This includes *Anti-Missile Defence (AMD)* to counter incoming missiles. In context of the *Carrier Task Force* (CTF), the concept of AD incorporates a layered defence through the employment of radar and electronic surveillance, carrier-borne interceptor aircraft, ship-borne anti-air missile and gun systems of varying ranges, and electronic counter-measures (ECM) like jammers and decoys. See *Anti-Air Warfare (AAW), Electronic Warfare (EW).*

Air Defence Identification Zone (ADIZ)

An area of airspace over land or water beyond a country's sovereign territory within which, it requires the identification, location, and air traffic control of aircraft in the interest of its national security. ADIZs are located primarily over waters of coastal States, and often include large swaths of airspace beyond their *National Airspace.*

While many countries have established one or more ADIZs, there is neither any international law that specifically governs ADIZs, nor any international agreement or consensus regarding the establishment of or the flight operations and air traffic procedures related to such airspace. Nonetheless, international norms do exist. The USA was the first country to establish an ADIZ in 1950. The justification for an ADIZ stems from the right of a State to establish reasonable conditions of entry into its *National Airspace.*

In the ADIZ, aircraft are required to comply with special identification and/or reporting procedures additional to those related to the provision of *Air Traffic Services* (ATS). ADIZ regulations may require filing of flight plans and periodic position reports. Some countries require all aircraft entering their ADIZ to comply with ADIZ procedures, whether or not they intend to enter *National Airspace.* See *Security Zone.*

Airborne Early Warning (AEW) and Control

A concept of detection of distant air threats (incoming hostile fighter aircraft, *cruise missiles* and drones), which alerts the defences of one's own force as early as possible before the threat materialises. Since *radar* detection range can be enhanced considerably if it is airborne, AEW entails the operation of long-range radars on airborne platforms (aircraft, helicopters or aerostats). AEW can also detect warship deployments and troop build-up deep inside enemy territory. The Russian Ka-31 operated by the Indian Navy is an AEW helicopter. The US 'E-2 Hawkeye' (Northrop Grumman) is a fixed-wing AEW aircraft capable of operating from *Aircraft Carriers.*

Modern aircraft designed for AEW missions are usually also capable of undertaking Control function for directing friendly fighter aircraft to neutralise a threat, leading to the acronyms AEW&C (Airborne Early Warning and Control) and AWACS (Airborne Warning and Control System). Modern AWACS are potent 'force multipliers' with a range of as much as 400 km. The Indian Air Force currently operates AWACS aircraft based on the IL-76 airframe, which is equipped with the Israeli 'Phalcon' system comprising the Elta EL/M-2075 AESA L-band radar.

Airlift and Airlift Capacity

Airlift is an organised delivery of military supplies or military personnel primarily via military transport aircraft. Strategic airlift involves moving men or material over relatively long distances (such as across a continent or an operational theatre). Tactical airlift involves the movement, by air, of men or material within an operational theatre. Airlift is not only essential for combat deployment and re-deployment to progress military operations, but may also be required in *Low Intensity Conflict* scenarios. The strategic IL-76 airlift of Indian paratroopers to Maldives in 1988 to quell an attempted coup d'état is a case in point. Airlift may also be required for undertaking benign missions such as *Humanitarian Assistance and Disaster Relief (HADR)*, *Non-Combatant Evacuation Operations (NEO)* and medical or casualty evacuation (MEDEVAC/CASEVAC).

The delivery of men or material to the objective area could be undertaken either by the aircraft landing in the area or by a mid-flight airdrop, based on various factors such as the type of mission, the prevailing security environment and the availability of a landing strip.

Airlift capacity is expressed in terms of number of passengers and/or weight/cubic displacement of cargo that can be carried at any one time to a given destination by the available aircraft. Also see, *Sealift and Sealift Capacity*, and *Expeditionary Operation.*

Air Traffic Services (ATS)

See *Flight Information Region (FIR).*

Alliance

See *Military Alliance.*

Amnesty

A legal guarantee that exempts a person or group of persons from being prosecuted for criminal or political offences. International law, however, prohibits grant of amnesty from criminal prosecution to perpetrators of *War Crimes, Crimes against Humanity and Genocide.*

Amphibious Operation

An offensive *Joint* operation that employs naval forces to project military power onto a hostile or potentially hostile shore. In a typical operation (amphibious assault), land forces embarked on naval *Sealift* platforms are transported via sea to the chosen *Littoral* area, and launched onto the shore though a landing operation using amphibious craft, amphibious vehicles and integral airlift. The land forces are thereafter sustained ashore from the sea for the duration of the operation, including through 'Naval-Gun Fire-Support' (NGFS).

Such an operation may be conducted to progress ongoing land operations in hostile territory, to capture or recapture a strategic area, to obtain a site for forward naval or air basing, or simply to deny the use of an area or facilities (like a port) to the enemy. An amphibious operation may also be undertaken in the form of an Amphibious Raid, or for 'distracting' or 'deceiving' the enemy.

At the *Operational Level,* an amphibious operation necessitates adequate *Amphibious Ships* for military sealift, even though such capacity could be supplemented by commercial ships (*STUFT*). *Manouevre* and *Littoral Sea Control* are also essential ingredients for such operations. Given the increasing advantage to the adversary defending its coast, the traditional method of securing a 'beach-head' to progress land operations inland is giving way to the concept of direct 'Ship-to-Objective Manoeuvre (STOM)', albeit with developing attendant capabilities.

At the *Tactical Level,* an amphibious operation necessitates a very high level of inter-service synergy (jointness), preparation and training. See

Expeditionary Operation, Mobile Landing Platform (MLP), Sealift and Sealift Capacity, and *Vertical Envelopment.*

Amphibious Ships

Warships designed for military sealift of a land-fighting force (called 'landing force') and their vehicles, weapons and stores for undertaking an *Amphibious* (or *Expeditionary*) *Operation*. Based on the strategic circumstances that a country encounters, and the imperatives of operational flexibility, such platforms vary in terms of capacity and facilities. By tradition, the abbreviations and nomenclature of these vessels follows an 'Inventory' system. Thus, the acronym 'LST (L)' expands to 'Landing Ship: Tank (Large)'—in other words, a ship that capable of 'landing operations' and carries large tanks. At the lower end of the spectrum, a 'Landing Craft: Utility' (LCU) can carry about a hundred troops along with a few wheeled vehicles or a single tracked armoured vehicle (tank). The 'Landing Ship: Tank' (LST) is a larger ship that can carry a few hundred troops but is specifically designed to carry tracked armoured vehicles (tanks and/or 'Infantry Combat Vehicles'). Such platforms are usually designed to 'beach' onto the shore to discharge the 'landing force', vehicles and stores, via a ramp.

Among the largest amphibious ships are 'Landing Platforms: Dock' (LPD) or 'Landing [Platform]: Helicopter [&] Dock' (LHD) that carry helicopters on their deck (or in their hangars), as well as smaller landing craft or 'Landing Craft: Air-Cushion' (LCAC) housed in a special floodable dock on board. The LPD/LHD is capable of 'stand-off' amphibious operation, wherein the 'ship-to-shore' movement of the 'landing force', vehicles and weaponry is undertaken using the helicopters (*Vertical Envelopment*) and smaller craft or LCAC. The Indian Navy inducted its first LPD, the Jalashwa (ex-USS Trenton) in 2007. See *Mobile Landing Platform (MLP).*

Amphibious Aircraft

Fixed-wing or rotary-wing aircraft that are designed to be able to use both the terrestrial and maritime realms to take-off and land, and rest for extended periods in both mediums through the inter-changeability of landing gear, comprising retractable wheels/skis for snow bound terrain and floats for landing-on or taking-off from water-bodies.

In terms of their utilisation for military missions, such aircraft—particularly the fixed-wing 'amphibians'—could contribute to operational logistics, and thus the sustenance of naval forces in distant seas. However, in terms of their optimal usage, these aircraft are mainly meant for purposes quite unlike the primary missions of the *Amphibious Ships*. Such fixed-wing aircraft are best suited for maritime surveillance around island territories, besides *Maritime Search and Rescue (M-SAR)*. Rotary-wing 'amphibians' (helicopters) have the advantage of being embarked aboard ships, and may be used for *Maritime Search and Rescue (M-SAR)*, *Maritime Salvage* or *Oceanography*.

Anti-Access/Area Denial (A2/AD)

Refers to a defensive military strategy appreciated by the USA to have been developed by China to sanitize its maritime periphery in the Western Pacific to prevent the forces of its potential adversaries to dominate a given area comprising international waters and super-adjacent airspace. Such a strategy is based on area denial weapon systems, and reinforced by a declaratory policy. In 2003, the US Center for Strategic and Budgetary Assessments (CSBA) defined 'anti-access' as "enemy actions which inhibit military movement into a theatre of operations", and 'area-denial' operations as "activities that seek to deny freedom of action within areas under the enemy's control".

The USA appreciates that China's A2/AD strategy is based on area denial weapons such as the *Anti-Ship Ballistic Missile (ASBM)*. The *Air Defence Identification Zone (ADIZ)* promulgated by China in the East China Sea is among its declaratory policies. See *Asymmetric Operations*.

Anti-Air Warfare (AAW)

Generally used in the maritime context, the AAW task is part of the navy's military role, and essential implies *Air Defence (AD)* of the surface units at sea. AAW seeks to neutralise enemy aircraft and airborne weapons, whether launched by air, surface or sub-surface platforms.

Anti-Ballistic Missile (ABM)

See *Ballistic Missile Defence (BMD)*.

Anti-Ballistic Missile (ABM) Treaty

A treaty signed between the United States and the erstwhile Soviet Union in 1972 (with a validity of 30 years) on the limitation of the Anti-Ballistic Missile (ABM) systems. Under its terms, each side was obliged to possess two ABM complexes, each limited to 100 ABMs. In 1997, the United States and Russia (along with a few other former Soviet republics) agreed to become successors of the treaty. However, in June 2002 (based on the 30-year validity-period), the United States withdrew from the treaty, leading to its termination. See *Anti-Ballistic Missile (ABM)* and *Strategic Arms Limitation Talks (SALT) Treaty.*

Anti-Fouling Systems (AFS) Convention

The International Convention on the Control of Harmful Anti-fouling Systems in Ships (AFS Convention), 2001 is an *International Maritime Organisation (IMO)* treaty, whereby countries agree to prohibit the use of harmful anti-fouling paints and other systems on ships' hulls. Such AFS contain chemicals whose leaching from the hulls cause severe adverse effects on marine ecology.

The Convention entered into force in September 2008. Presently, 70 countries, including India, have ratified it amounting to about 85 per cent of the world's shipping fleet. A *Flag State* that is party to the Convention is required to enforce the prohibitions on all ships flying its flag, and a Port State is similarly required to inspect—and where required detain—any non-compliant ship that enters its port, or berths alongside an *Offshore Terminal.* See *Arctic Marine Strategic Plan (AMSP)*, *Marine Biodiversity*, *Marine Pollution*, *Polar Code*, and *Sustainable Fisheries.*

Anti-Missile Defence (AMD)

See *Air Defence.*

Anti-Piracy and Counter-Piracy

'Anti-Piracy' is a comprehensive term used to describe a maritime-security response against *Piracy.* It ranges from enactment of anti-piracy legislations by the government of a country to the Ship Protective Measures and other actions adopted by merchantmen as part of *Best Management Practices (BMP).*

Counter-piracy is a 'subset' of Anti-Piracy. The term refers to active measures by *Maritime Security Forces* to deter and disrupt piracy, whether at sea or ashore. Deterrence patrols by navies and escort of merchantmen is a counter-piracy measure. See *Piracy: Activity, Approach, Attack, Hijack, etc.*, and *Piracy High Risk Area (HRA)*.

Anti-Piracy Best Management Practices (BMP)

See *Best Management Practices (BMP)*.

Anti-Ship Ballistic Missile (ASBM)

A *Ballistic Missile*—given its flight profile—can strike at large distances, even across continents, which makes it suitable for delivery of a nuclear warhead. At least theoretically, such a missile can be used for very long-range targeting of large ships. However, so far, these missiles have not been proved against mobile targets. Nonetheless, if an appropriate precision guidance system involving real-time updates could be incorporated into the ballistic missile during its re-entry into the earth's atmosphere, it could be an effective weapon against high-value warships, like *Aircraft Carriers*.

As part of what the US military calls China's *Anti Access/Area Denial (A2/AD)* strategy, China is known to be developing land-based ASBM technology since the late-1990s. Based upon the 1,500 km plus range DF-21D (CSS-5) ballistic missile, China's ASBM project incorporates a variety of land-based, air-borne and space-based sensors, such as over-the-horizon (OTH) radars, optical and radio imaging satellites, long-range *UAVs* and SIGINT/ELINT systems. These systems are meant to provide accurate, real-time targeting data. See *Asymmetric Operations*, *Ballistic and Cruise Missiles*, and *Electronic Warfare (EW)*.

Anti-Submarine Warfare (ASW)

A task or mission within the military role of naval forces, which utilises surface platforms and/or aircraft and/or submarines to locate, track and neutralise enemy submarines—whether conventionally propelled or propelled by nuclear power. The effectiveness of ASW depends on a mix of sensor and weapon technology, training and experience. While *Sonar* equipment and other sensors such as the Magnetic Anomaly Detector (MAD) are used for initial detection, the detected 'contact' needs to be tracked and classified before it is attacked. Attack is usually undertaken using torpedoes or depth charges. These weapons may be launched from the air, and/or from surface and/or underwater platforms. Since aircraft (including helicopters) are mostly immune to a submarine attack, airborne combatants are usually more effective for ASW missions. Further, since one's own submarines operate in the same hydrographic environment as those of the adversary, such aircraft are more suited as ASW platforms, particularly in choke-points and other high submarine-probability-areas.

The ASW protection of a force or the ASW sanitisation of an area of interest is a central task for the establishment of *Sea Control* and to counter *Sea Denial* by the adversary. 'Search and Attack Units' (SAU) and 'Air Search and Attack Units'(ASAU) are tactical groupings of ships and aircraft respectively, specially designated to search and destroy enemy submarines.

Anti-Surface Warfare (ASuW)

A task or mission, undertaken by naval forces within the 'military' role of navies, which seeks the *attrition* of enemy surface-forces. This mission is necessary to achieve *Sea Control.* Once *Surveillance* inputs detect and identify an enemy surface force, the latter is attacked by the delivery of ordnance, based on targeting data from integral sensors or those from a consort, often using *Over the Horizon Targeting (OTHT).*

The ordnance, comprising anti-ship missiles, projectiles, bombs and/ or torpedoes may be launched from ships and/or carrier/ship-borne aircraft and/or shore-based aircraft and/or submarines. If the operational imperative necessitates it, the *Task Force* commander may choose to detach a Surface Action Group (SAG) to neutralise the opposing force.

Australia-New Zealand-US (ANZUS) Security Treaty

A *Military Alliance* between Australia and New Zealand, and Australia and the United States of America. The ANZUS was established in 1951 as a tri-party pact. However, following a dispute between the US and New Zealand, in 1984, over visits to New Zealand by US warships carrying nuclear weapons, the pact between the two countries was annulled. Notably, however, after the US permitted New Zealand warships to visit its ports in 2000, the US and New Zealand resumed bilateral defence and security, albeit outside the ANZUS. The New Zealand Navy also resumed participation in *RIMPAC Exercises* in 2012.

Under ANZUS, the US and Australia hold annual meetings called 'Australia-United States Ministerial Consultation' (AUSMIN) in a 2+2 format (involving defence and foreign ministers and equivalents). Unlike *the North Atlantic Treaty Organisation (NATO)*, ANZUS has neither an integrated defence structure nor any dedicated military forces.

Aquaculture and Mariculture

Aquaculture refers to the farming of aquatic organisms—both freshwater and saltwater—including fish, molluscs, crustaceans and aquatic plants. The farming is done under controlled conditions with some sort of intervention in the rearing process to enhance production, such as regular stocking, feeding and protection from predators. Aquaculture may be contrasted with commercial fishing, which is essentially the harvesting of wild fish.

Mariculture is a specialised branch of Aquaculture involving the cultivation of marine organisms for both food and non-food products in the open ocean, an enclosed section of the ocean, or in tanks or ponds filled with seawater. An example of the latter is the farming of marine catch—both finfish and shellfish (such as prawns or oysters)—and seaweed in saltwater ponds. Non-food products produced by mariculture include fish-meal, nutrient agar, jewellery (cultured pearls, for example), and cosmetics.

Arab League

A regional organisation of Arab countries located in north and northwestern Africa, and southwest Asia. The League was established in 1945 with six member countries—Egypt, Iraq, Jordan, Lebanon, Saudi Arabia and Yemen—with the aim of strengthening and coordinating the political, cultural, economic, and social programs of its members, as also to mediate in disputes involving them. In 1950, the members signed an agreement on defence and economic cooperation.

At present, the Arab League has 22 members and 4 observers (Brazil, Eritrea, India and Venezuela). As per the 'Charter of the Arab League', the organisation's main goal is the "strengthening of the relations between the member states, the coordination of their policies in order to achieve co-operation between them and to safeguard their independence and sovereignty; and a general concern with the affairs and interests of the

Arab countries". These encompass economic, social and cultural issues, including issues relating to health, communication, transport and travel. The League has been proactive to resolve the long outstanding conflict between Palestine and Israel. It strives to resolve burning issues among the Arab countries, and to enhance the image of the Islamic countries. See *Gulf Cooperation Council (GCC).*

Arbitration

In general, the term Arbitration refers to a quasi-judicial method of settling disputes of a civil nature, without recourse to a court of law. It is a traditional method of dispute settlement. It entails a contract, wherein the parties involved enter into an agreement to submit their case to the decision of one or more arbiters (or arbitrators or an arbitral tribunal), which are selected by or on behalf of the parties and apply adjudicatory procedures to resolve the dispute. The arbiter is an authoritative and legitimate third party, superior in strength to the parties to the dispute. In the case of an arbitral tribunal, the parties to the dispute are usually free to agree to the number and composition of the tribunal.

As per the terms of the contract, the recommendation reached by a (neutral) arbiter is usually considered 'binding'. However, arbitration may also be 'non-binding', when the parties so decide, such as to use arbitration as an aid to the process of negotiation. Notably, the role of arbiter here is distinct from 'third-party facilitation'. In case of the latter, the parties maintain a three-way communication, but in arbitration, the disputing parties 'talk' to (and rely on) only the arbitrator. See *International Arbitration.*

Archipelagic Sea Lanes

See *Archipelagic Waters.*

Archipelagic Waters

Those waters enclosed by archipelagic baselines drawn in accordance with Article 47 of *UNCLOS*. The sovereignty of an archipelagic State extends to the waters enclosed by the baselines, regardless of their depth or distance from the coast, as well as the associated seabed, subsoil and airspace. These waters contain *Archipelagic Sea Lanes* (ASL), which are sea lanes and air routes designated by an archipelagic State as suitable for the continuous and expeditious passage of foreign ships and aircraft through and over the archipelagic waters and the adjacent territorial sea. *ASL* Passage means the exercise (in accordance with *UNCLOS*) of the rights of navigation and overflight in the normal mode through archipelagic sea lanes solely for the purpose of continuous, expeditious and unobstructed transit between one part of the *High Seas* or an *EEZ* and another part of the *High Seas* or an *EEZ*. All vessels and aircraft may exercise the right of *ASL* passage in the normal mode of operation observing the same conditions applicable to 'Transit Passage' through *International Straits*. *ASL* passage may not be suspended or obstructed by the archipelagic state.

Arctic Council

A high-level inter-governmental forum formed as a result of the 1996 Ottawa Declaration, which also defines its objectives. In broad terms, the Arctic Council seeks to promote cooperative interactions among the eight 'Arctic States' (Canada, Denmark, Finland, Iceland, Norway, Russia, Sweden, and the United States) on common Arctic issues relating to sustainable development and environmental protection, while involving Arctic inhabitants, including its indigenous communities of the region. The Council's ministerial meetings are held biennially. The activities of the Arctic Council are conducted through its subsidiary bodies comprising six permanents working groups, besides task forces and expert groups. The working groups cover specific areas of pollution, conservation of biodiversity, emergency response, marine environment and sustainable development. The working groups include experts from ministries and government agencies, and researchers. The Secretariat of the Arctic Council is located in Tromso (Norway).

Besides member 'Arctic States', the Council has 'Permanent Participants' comprising organisations representing the indigenous communities, and 'Permanent Observers' composed of non-Arctic States, relevant global and regional organisations, both inter-governmental and non-governmental. So far, 12 countries (including India) have 'observer' status in the Council. The 'observers' have no voting rights, but attend the ministerial meetings and, when invited, other meetings as well. They are also permitted to engage in working group activities, propose projects (through an Arctic State or a Permanent Participant) and make statements during meetings.

Decisions at all levels of the Council are taken by the Arctic States, based on consensus. Notably, the 2011 'Agreement on Aeronautical and Maritime SAR Cooperation in the Arctic' was the first legally binding treaty successfully negotiated by the Council. See *Maritime Search and Rescue (M-SAR).*

Arctic Economic Council (AEC)

An independent organisation created by the *Arctic Council* in 2014, whose objective is to facilitate sustainable economic development in the Arctic, including environmental protection and social development. It provides the members of the *Arctic Council* advice and business perspective on specific areas of economic activity ranging from mining and shipping to reindeer herding and aboriginal development activities. The mix of perspectives ensures the sustainability of economic endeavours.

The AEC's work is driven by three working groups. The first, 'Stewardship in the Arctic', deals with engagement with indigenous communities, including traditional knowledge and development of small/ medium enterprises. The second, 'Maritime Transportation' deals with issues and opportunities associated with commercial shipping, including maintenance of requisite safety standards for environmentally fragile areas. The third deals with 'Responsible Resource Development'. Also see *Arctic Marine Strategic Plan (AMSP)* and *Polar Code.*

Arctic Marine Strategic Plan (AMSP)

The AMSP is an overarching framework to guide the activities of the *Arctic Council* and to hereby protect Arctic coastal and marine ecosystems while promoting sustainable development, and to simultaneously address the interests of the regional inhabitants. It is prepared by the Protection of the Arctic Marine Environment (PAME) Working Group of the *Arctic Council.* The first AMSP was promulgated in 2004. The Arctic Marine Strategic Plan 2015-25 (AMSP) was promulgated in April 2015.

The AMSP is implemented by the Arctic Council working groups in coordination with Arctic member countries, observers and other relevant international and regional organisations. Actions under AMSP-2015 are aimed at meeting the following four broad 'Strategic Goals':

- **Goal 1.** Improve knowledge of the Arctic marine environment, and monitor and assess current and future impacts on Arctic marine ecosystems.

- **Goal 2.** Conserve and protect the ecosystem and *Marine Biodiversity*, so as to enhance resilience and provide for ecosystem services.
- **Goal 3.** Promote safe and sustainable use of the marine environment, factoring cumulative environmental impacts.
- **Goal 4.** Enhance the economic, social and cultural wellbeing of Arctic inhabitants, including the Arctic indigenous peoples and strengthen their capacity to adapt to changes in the Arctic marine environment. See *Polar Code.*

Area Denial

See *Anti-Access/Area Denial (A2/AD).*

Armed Conflict

See *War and Armed Conflict*

Armed Robbery at Sea

Any act of robbery involving the use or force or its threat against a vessel within the *Territorial Waters* of a state, and thus under the jurisdiction of the concerned state. See *Piracy.*

Asian Development Bank (ADB)

An *International Financial Institution (IFI)* established in 1966 as a regional development bank to facilitate economic development in Asia (not including West Asia). The ADB was modelled closely on the World Bank and has a similar 'weighted voting system' where votes are distributed in proportion to the capital subscriptions made by its members. The ADB is headquartered in Manila, the Philippines. At present, the ADB has 67 members, of which 48 are from within Asia and Oceania. The non-regional members—besides the US and Canada—are largely European countries. Japan holds the largest proportion of shares in ADB, followed by the US, China, India and Australia.

Asian Infrastructure Investment Bank (AIIB)

An *International Financial Institution (IFI)* proposed by China and launched in 2014 as a regional development bank to provide finance to infrastructure projects in Asia. The AIIB is seen as a rival to the *International Monetary Fund (IMF)*, the *World Bank* and the *Asian Development Bank (ADB)*, all three of which are dominated by the United

States and its allies. Almost all Asian countries and most major countries outside Asia had joined the AIIB, with the notable exceptions of the US, Japan (which dominate the ADB) and Canada.

Asia-Pacific Region

The term refers to a region whose geographical extent varies based upon the context. In terms of the sub-regional constituents of Asia-Pacific, the only 'constants' are East Asia, Southeast Asia and Oceania. In a somewhat restricted sense, the term 'Asia-Pacific' region refers to the littorals of the Western Pacific Ocean. On some occasions, however, it may span the area from South Asia to Russia (in the North Pacific), broadly coincident with the area of responsibility of the US Pacific Command (PACOM).

American strategic thinkers and writers would frequently use the term to imply the Asian part of the Pacific Ocean, while many Indian strategists used it to mean the whole of Asia and the whole of the Pacific (implying an expanse from the East coast of Africa to the West coast of the USA). In the context of the *Asia-Pacific Economic Cooperation (APEC)*, the term includes the East Pacific coast of the American continent. This lack of an objective geographic reference makes the term 'Asia-Pacific'—even as a 'functional region'—unsuited for strategic and academic analyses. The void is being filled by the increasing use of the alternative term, the '*Indo-Pacific*' or the 'Indo-Asia Pacific'.

Asia-Pacific Economic Cooperation (APEC)

A multilateral forum comprising 21 Pacific Rim economies, established in 1989 with the aim of promoting *Free Trade* in the Asia-Pacific region. Key drivers for setting up the APEC were the growing economic interdependence among the regional countries and the emergence of new *Free Trade Areas* in other parts of the world.

The criterion for APEC membership is that the member is a separate economy, and not necessarily a *nation-state*. As a result, its members include Taiwan (officially called 'Chinese Taipei'), and Hong Kong. India enjoys an 'observer' status within the APEC. The annual APEC Economic Leaders' Meeting is attended by the heads of government of all member countries (Chinese Taipei is represented by a minister). The APEC Secretariat is based in Singapore. The APEC leaders are currently examining a proposal to establish a '*Free Trade Area* of the Asia-Pacific' (FTAAP).

Association of Southeast Asian Nations (ASEAN)

The ASEAN is a political and economic organisation formed in 1967, which comprises ten Southeast Asian countries—Brunei, Cambodia, Indonesia, Laos, Malaysia, Myanmar, the Philippines, Singapore, Thailand and Vietnam. Notably, Timor L'Este is a Southeast Asian country, but is not a part of ASEAN. The genesis of ASEAN was a common fear of communism among its five founder countries—Indonesia, Malaysia, the Philippines, Singapore and Thailand—and their quest for economic development. This led to the five countries to sign the ASEAN Declaration in Bangkok.

The objectives of ASEAN include accelerating economic growth, social progress and cultural development among the countries and promoting regional peace and stability. Its longer-term objectives are broadly to evolve ASEAN integration based on the ASEAN Security Community (ASC), the ASEAN Economic Community (AEC), and the ASEAN Socio-Cultural Community (ASCC). On the economic front, ASEAN seeks to evolve from merely a *Free Trade Area* to a *Common* (single) *Market* ensuring a free flow of goods, services, investment and capital, and skilled labour.

After the 1997 financial crisis in East Asia, the Chiang Mai Initiative (a result of a Malaysian proposal) sought to enhance the integration of economies within ASEAN, and with those of China, Japan and South Korea, leading to formation of the grouping called 'ASEAN Plus Three (dialogue partners)'. In 2005, the grouping was enlarged to 'ASEAN Plus Eight (dialogue partners)' to include India, Australia, New Zealand, United States, and Russia under the rubric of the *East Asia Summit* (*EAS*).

Since the ASEAN Charter came into force in 2008, ASEAN Summit meetings are held bi-annually involving heads of governments, who also conduct meetings with other countries on the sidelines of the ASEAN meeting. EAS meetings are held annually after ASEAN Summit meetings. See *ADMM and ADMM Plus*, and *Southeast Asia Nuclear Weapons Free Zone (SEANWFZ)*.

ASEAN Plus Three

See *Association of Southeast Asian Nations (ASEAN)*.

ASEAN Regional Forum (ARF)

In 1994, the outreach of the ASEAN to its 'dialogue partners' led to the formation of the 'ASEAN Regional Forum (ARF)' as an official forum for multilateral consultation on peace and security issues in the *Indo-Pacific Region*. Besides the ASEAN-Ten, the ARF presently includes Australia, Bangladesh, Canada, China, the European Union (EU), India, Japan, North Korea, South Korea, Mongolia, New Zealand, Pakistan, Papua New Guinea, Russia, East Timor, United States and Sri Lanka. The ARF has adopted an evolutionary approach to security involving a three-stage process. The first stage comprises *Confidence Building Measures (CBM)*; the second is the development of preventive diplomacy; and the third is the development of common approaches to conflicts.

The ARF process is three-tiered comprising Track-1, Track-1½ and Track-2 structures. At the apex of Track-1 meetings is the annual ARF meeting at the level of Ministers, held in July or August of each year in the capital of the ASEAN Chair for that year. At the second level is the ARF Senior Officials' Meeting (SOM). At the third level is the Inter-sessional Support Group (ISG) on CBMs and Preventive Diplomacy (ISG on CBMs and PD).

ARF's Track-1½ tier engages in activities approved by the ARF Experts and Eminent Persons (EEPs) meetings that involve scholars and officials from member countries acting in their personal capacity. ARF's Track-2 tier provides for the *Council for Security Cooperation in the Asia-Pacific (CSCAP)* as a non-governmental forum for academics, scholars, and researchers who interact in their private capacity to develop structured regional processes. See *Association of Southeast Asian Nations (ASEAN)*.

Asylum

See *Refuge, Refugee and Asylum*.

Asymmetric Operations

Refers to unconventional means adopted by a State or non-State entity, which involves the application of dissimilar ways and means (strategy, tactics and capabilities) against an adversary to circumvent or negate the adversary's strengths and capitalise upon its weaknesses and vulnerabilities. The laying of crude sea-mines in a maritime choke-point against a high-value warship is an example. Cyber warfare is a more recent 'weapon' for the conduct of asymmetric operations. Another example is the employment of area-denial weapons such as the *Anti-Ship Ballistic Missile (ASBM)* known to be in the process of development by China as part of what the USA terms China's *Anti-Access/Area Denial (A2/AD)* strategy. Notably, the term 'asymmetric threats' refers not only to non-State actors using such applications, but also to State actors who may opt to use these to offset their inferiority in terms of conventional military power. See *Escalation Dominance* and *Mine Counter Measures (MCM)*.

Attrition

As a generic concept of *War and Armed Conflict*, it subscribes to the strategy of protracted conflict. Such a strategy may be employed when freedom of action is large, but the resources available are inadequate to secure a quick military decision. Attrition may also be used by a decisively superior force simply to wear down a weaker adversary. The aim of this strategy is to erode the military strength of the opponent, and thereby, the morale of the opposing forces.

Specifically in the maritime context, the concept has a slightly differing connotation. It is important to note that most maritime-military missions necessitate *Sea Control*, for which, it is usually necessary to erode the capability of the opposing naval forces. If so, attrition becomes essential to achieve and maintain *Sea Control*. Once a *Sea Control* mission is successful, naval forces are free to undertake follow-on missions. At this stage, the forces may resort to '*manoeuvre*', which represents a contrasting concept to 'attrition'. (Note: While the foregoing statement is meant to simply the concept of 'attrition' and distinguish it from the concept of 'manoeuvre', in actual practice, *Sea Control* mission also entails elements of 'manoeuvre'. At this stage, manoeuvre is essential for a sequential destruction of the enemy's forces, and also embodies elements of attrition). Attrition is also central to the concept of *Sea Denial*.

AUSINDEX (Naval Exercises)

AUSINDEX refers to *combined* naval exercises between the Royal Australian Navy (RAN) and the Indian Navy (IN). The first exercise was held in the Bay of Bengal in September 2015. See *Joint and Combined*.

Australia Group

An informal grouping of countries formed through an Australian initiative in 1985, following Iraq's use of chemical weapons in 1984 during the Iran-Iraq war. It sought to help member countries to identify and regulate the exports linked to proliferation of chemical and biological weapons (CBW). The group initially got 15 countries together at a meeting in Brussels (Belgium), in 1989. The membership has now expanded to 42, broadly encompassing the countries of North America and Western Europe, besides Australia, Brazil, Japan and New Zealand.

The countries of the Australia Group maintain a uniform list of items for export control, many of which are not prohibited for export under the *Biological Weapons Convention (BWC)* and the *Chemical Weapons Convention (CWC)*, but can nevertheless be used to manufacture CBW. The following are among the key norms being followed by the group:

- **'No-undercut' Requirement**. Any member country that seeks to export an item to any country that had already been denied the same by another member country must first consult with the latter member before doing so.
- **'Catch-all' Provision**. It requires member States to halt all exports that could be used to manufacture chemical or biological weapons, regardless of whether or not the export is on the group's control lists.

The countries of the Australia Group do not undertake any legally binding obligations, but support the objectives of the *Chemical Weapons Convention (CWC) and the Biological Weapons Convention (BWC)* by enhancing the effectiveness of their national export licensing mechanisms. The representatives of member countries meet in Paris (France) on an annual basis. The Secretariat of the group is managed by Australia.

Australian Maritime Identification Zone/System (MIZ/AMIS)

In December 2004, Australia promulgated a 'Maritime Identification Zone' (MIZ) around its territory extending out to 1000 *nautical miles* seawards from its coastline. The MIZ required all vessels seeking to transit the Australian *EEZ* or to enter Australian ports to identify themselves by providing information on their formal identity, cargo, routing, and so on. The Australian authorities declared that non-compliance by a vessel would entail its interdiction on the *High Seas*.

Australia's MIZ policy was driven by its pressing security challenge of *Illegal Immigration*. The concept was nevertheless unprecedented, and led to a host of questions and arguments on its legitimacy in terms of the principle of *Freedom of the Seas* embodied in the *UNCLOS*. Australia later reviewed and reformulated the MIZ into 'Australian Maritime Identification System' (AMIS), wherein vessels were only required to identify themselves on a voluntary basis.

Automatic Identification System (AIS)

Mandated by the *International Maritime Organisation (IMO)*, it is a system used by ships and *Vessel Traffic Services (VTS)* as a navigational aid and collision avoidance system. AIS data includes the unique identity of the vessel, its geographical position, course and speed. The AIS supplements sea-borne and coastal radar, which had hitherto been the only means of tracking vessels.

AIS is mandated by the *Safety of Life at Sea (SOLAS) Convention, 1974/1988.* Its revised Chapter V (Safety of Navigation) requires AIS systems—capable of automatically providing information about the ship to other ships and to coastal authorities—to be fitted aboard all ships of 300 *Gross Tonnes* and upwards engaged in international voyages, cargo ships of 500 *Gross Tonnes* and upwards not engaged in international voyages, and passenger ships (irrespective of their size) built on or after 01 July 2002.

The AIS operates in the VHF radio band involving a line-of-sight transmission of electronic data between ships, AIS base stations and sometimes, even satellites (in case of Satellite-AIS or S-AIS). S-AIS is different from *Long-Range Identification and Tracking (LRIT)*. In whatever form, AIS does not require any action from a vessel except that it must have its AIS system switched on. See *National AIS (NAIS) Network.*

B

Balance of Power

In the strictest sense, this refers to the erstwhile concept of a 'military-strategic' balance of power amongst countries, which enhanced regional and *National Security*. It referred to the theory of equilibrium involving the distribution of military capabilities in a manner such that no single country (or a group of countries, in case of a *Military Alliance*) would be strong enough to be an aggressor. Historical techniques to achieve balance of power have comprised, inter alia, the following:

- National Mobilisation, involving rearmament.
- Formation of alliances.
- Compensation, involving division of a country strategically located between major adversarial powers (e.g. division of Poland located between Germany and Soviet Union before the Second World War).
- Neutralisation, involving accepting the neutrality of a country strategically located between major adversarial powers as a 'buffer zone' (e.g. th Neutralisation of Belgium, sited between England, France and Germany before the First World War).
- Intervention, by military forces or intelligence agencies.
- Divide and Rule, to prevent two major powers from forming a military alliance, or seeking to create or exploit differences between two existing allies.
- Resort to war.

The term 'balance of power' continues to be in vogue in present times, albeit in a broader sense of the balance among two or more countries based on their *Comprehensive National Power (CNP)* such that no country can dominate another. See *Geopolitics*.

Ballistic and Cruise Missiles

Ballistic Missile is a missile that follows a ballistic trajectory to deliver its warhead on to its intended target. This ballistic trajectory may lie entirely within the earth's atmosphere, or, it may lie partially within and partially outside it. A ballistic missile is guided only for relatively brief periods of flight. Most of its trajectory is unpowered and governed by gravity and air resistance. These missiles are usually employed for strategic/nuclear targeting. India's 'Agni' and 'Prithvi' (and its naval version 'Dhanush') are ballistic missiles. Based on their ranges, such missiles may be categorised as follows:

- Inter-Continental Ballistic Missiles (ICBM) More than 5,500 km
- Intermediate-Range Ballistic Missiles (IRBM) 3,500 to 5,500 km
- Medium-Range Ballistic Missiles (MRBM) 1,000 to 3,500 km
- Short-Range Ballistic Missiles (SRBM) 1,000 km or less
- Tactical Ballistic Missiles About 150 to 300 km

In contrast, a cruise missile is aerodynamically guided and undertakes a powered flight completely within the earth's atmosphere. It produces 'lift' in much the same way as an aircraft does, and flies an essentially horizontal 'cruise-flight profile' for most of the duration of its flight between launch and its terminal trajectory to impact. Cruise missiles may be launched from aircraft, surface ships or submarines against enemy surface ships and aircraft. All anti-ship and anti-air missiles are cruise missiles. See *Missile and Rocket*, and *Land Attack Cruise Missiles (LACM).*

Ballistic Missile Defence (BMD)

An anti-missile missile capability developed by a few countries to counter incoming *Ballistic Missiles* through a BMD system, also called Anti-Ballistic Missile (ABM) system. A BMD system can intercept a ballistic missile in its boost, mid-course or terminal phases.

The US National Missile Defence (NMD) meant to protect continental United States is largely based on Patriot-3 missile system. For Theatre Missile Defence (TMD), the US relies on sea-based BMD based on Standard Missile-2 (SM-2) and Standard Missile-3 (SM-3) interceptors fired from Aegis destroyers. Russia's national defence is based on A-135 BMD system, although its land and sea-based S-300PMU1 and PMU2 systems can intercept short and medium range ballistic missiles. Israel's BMD is based on the Arrow missile system.

India has an active land-based BMD development program, which began in 1999 with the indigenous development radars integrated and anti-missile missiles, and their integration. Phase I of India's BMD program was completed in 2012. It is a two-tiered shield, comprising the Prithvi Air Defence (PAD) missile for high altitude (up to 80 km) interception, and the Advanced Air Defence (AAD) Missile for lower altitude (up to 30 km) interception. In 2006, India successfully tested the PAD, becoming the fourth country in the world to acquire such a capability, after the United States, Russia and Israel. (Both China and France successfully tested their BMD capability in 2010). In 2007, India successfully conducted the AAD Missile system. India's two-tier BMD system is likely to be deployable at short notice to protect at least two cities Delhi and Mumbai.

As part of Phase II, India's Defence Research and Development Organisation (DRDO) is developing a new Prithvi interceptor missile PAD Delivery Vehicle (PDV) designed to intercept missiles at altitudes above 150 km, since this would provide enhanced reaction time. The first PDV was successfully test fired in April 2014. See *ABM Treaty* and *Strategic Arms Reduction Treaty (START).*

Ballistic Missile Submarine (NATO designation: SSBN)

A submarine designed to launch *Submarine-Launched Ballistic Missiles* (*SLBM*) armed with nuclear warheads. The letter 'N' in 'SSBN', however, stands for the vessel being nuclear-propelled, which is an essential prerequisite for such a platform. A SSBN differs fundamentally from a *Nuclear Attack Submarine (SSN/SSGN)* in its purpose—while SSN (or SSGN) specialises in *Sea Denial* or even *Sea Control* and undertaking land-attack, the primary mission of SSBN is *Nuclear Deterrence* and *Nuclear Second Strike*. It is important to note that the planning SSBN force levels and their deployment is based on *National Strategic* (rather than *Military Strategic*) decisions. In other words, a SSBN is a national asset, and thus a 'political tool'; not one at the disposal of the navy, or even the country's *Joint* defence apparatus. See *Ballistic and Cruise Missiles*, and *Nuclear Attack Submarines (SSN/SSGN).*

Bathymetry and Hydrography

Originally referring to the 'ocean's depth relative to sea level', the term 'bathymetry' has come to mean 'submarine topography', or the depths and shapes of the underwater terrain. It involves mapping of underwater profile of the seas and oceans leading to the production of nautical charts for navigation by sea-going vessels, and for other purposes through the advancement of Earth Sciences. Notably, water covers 71 per cent of the Earth's surface, but only about 10 per cent of its seafloor has been adequately surveyed (to a resolution of 1 minute or better). Variations in sea-floor relief are depicted by colour and contour lines called depth contours or isobaths.

Bathymetry is a subset of Hydrography. Hydrography includes not only bathymetry, but also the shape and features of the shoreline, the characteristics of tides, currents, and waves, and the physical and chemical properties of the water itself. Hydrographic data is a critical necessity for navigation of *Submarines* and the effective operation of its *Sonar* sensors. See *Oceanography and Oceanology.*

Beaufort Scale

A scale indicating varying states of wind and sea, which was devised by Sir Francis Beaufort, an Irish officer serving as a hydrographer in the Royal Navy during the period 1829-55. The 'Beaufort Wind Force' scale varies from '0' (calm, with speed less than 1 *Knot*) to '12' (hurricane, with wind-speed over 64 *Knots*), with each successive numeral indicating a progressive increase in wind-speed.

A similar scale is used to indicate the state of the sea, based on the height of sea waves. It varies from '0' (glassy calm or flat sea) to '9' (phenomenal sea condition with the maximum wave height of over 16 metres).

Best Management Practices (BMP)

In the context of *anti-piracy*, these are recommendations and guidelines for shipping companies and Masters of merchantmen, particularly when transiting through a *Piracy High Risk Area* (HRA). These began to be issued by the *International Chamber of Shipping (ICS)* in response to the rampant piracy off Somalia and Gulf of Aden since 2005. Similar guidelines were later issued by the Piracy Reporting Centre (PRC) of the *International Maritime Bureau (IMB)* for anti-piracy measures in the Gulf of Guinea.

BMP guidelines comprise inter alia risk-assessment, voyage-planning, Self Protection Measures (SPMs)—including technological solutions—policy for switching on a vessel's *Automatic Identification System (AIS)*, use of armed guards, communication plan, ship-movement reporting-procedures, and, and post-incident reporting. These contain specific guidelines for vessels engaged in fishing. See *Piracy* and *Piracy: Activity, Approach, Attack, Hijack, etc*, and *Piracy High Risk area (HRA).*

BIMSTEC

A multi-lateral regional organisation involving countries largely located around the Bay of Bengal (Bangladesh, Bhutan, India, Myanmar, Nepal, Sri Lanka and Thailand). The organisation was formed in Bangkok in June 1997 under the name BIST-EC (Bangladesh, India, Sri Lanka, and Thailand Economic Cooperation). When Myanmar joined the group in December 1997, its name was changed to BIMST-EC. Nepal and Bhutan joined the group in 2003. During its first summit held in July 2004, the acronym BIMSTEC was expanded to 'Bay of Bengal Initiative for Multi-Sectoral Technical and Economic Cooperation'. BIMSTEC headquarters was inaugurated in September 2014 at Dhaka, Bangladesh.

Bill of Lading

A shipping term that evidences a contract of carriage by sea. It refers to a document that establishes the terms of contract between a *Shipper* and a *Ship-operator* (shipping company) of the carriage of goods by sea and the taking over or loading of goods by the *Carrier*, and by which the *Carrier* undertakes to deliver the goods against surrender of the document. The Bill of Lading is, therefore, like a receipt in the hands of the *Shipper*, indicating the quantity of goods, their condition, weight, number of packs, consignee, ports of loading and discharge, and so on. See *Cargo Manifest*, *Carriage of Goods at Sea* (*Laws and Rules*), and *Shipment, Ship-owner, Ship-operator, Shipper* and *Carrier.*

Biological Weapons Convention (BWC)

The 'Convention on the Prohibition of Development, Production and Stockpiling of Bacteriological (Biological) and Toxin Weapons and on their Destruction' (BWC), 1972 is an international treaty that prohibits the production and stockpiling of biological weapons, and aims to achieve the complete elimination of all types of biological weapons. The BWC was intended to supplement the 1925 Geneva Protocol, which prohibited the use but not the possession or development of chemical and biological weapons (CBW). The BWC entered into force in 1975. The treaty has 173 state parties—including India, which ratified the Convention in July 1974.

Notably, while acceding to the Convention, many countries—including India—formally expressed their reservation that the exemption (in the BWC) with regard to biological agents or toxins permitted for prophylactic, protective or other peaceful purposes could potentially create a loophole that countries may exploit to produce and possess biological and toxin weapons. The effectiveness of the BWC is also limited due to the lack of any formal verification regime to monitor compliance by countries. See *Australia Group* and *Chemical Weapons Convention (CWC)*.

Blockade

A concept of *War or Armed Conflict* at sea legally mandated under the *Law of Armed Conflict* (*LOAC*). Traditionally, belligerent states have been legally permitted to 'Blockade' as a means to prevent enemy (and neutral ships) from transporting personnel and goods (*Contraband*) to/from enemy ports. For this, the belligerent is required to declare a 'blockade' and publicise the cordon (barrier line) separating enemy waters from *International Waters*.

The relevance and legal justification of this provision has continued into present times, although in altered circumstances. Since a 'closed' blockade is not achievable today (due to technological advances in naval warfare), navies have begun resorting to *SLOC Interdiction*, which is also legally justified as a belligerent right and analogous to 'blockade'. Some analysts call *SLOC Interdiction* a form of 'distant blockade'. See *Visit, Board, Search and Seizure (VBSS) Operations*.

Blue Economy

Based on its genesis, the term is used in many contexts. However, in the contemporary context, the concept germinated in the island countries of the *Indian Ocean Region (IOR)*, and refers to the emerging imperative for countries to develop the various facets of their maritime-based economy encompassing various activities ranging from fishing to marine tourism, such that the subsistence activity does not conflict with large-scale commercial ventures, and the marine resources are tapped in a sustainable manner whilst preserving the *Marine Biodiversity* and eco-system. The underlying aim is to bolster their economic development through innovative means, including addressing *Marine Pollution* through *Oil Spills* and dumping of toxic industrial waste into the seas. See *Sustainable Fisheries*, and *Anti-Fouling Systems (AFS) Convention.*

Boarding Operation

See *Visit, Board, Search and Seizure (VBSS) Operations.*

Bulk Cargo

Commodity cargo that is transported unpackaged in large quantities, but not in packages or *Containers*. It refers to material in either liquid or granular, particulate form, as a mass of relatively small solids, such as cement, coal, crude oil, grain, ore and sulphur. Bulk freight is shipped loose in the hold of a ship without mark and count. A bulk-freight *Container*—with a discharge hatch in the front wall—may, however, be used to carry bulk cargo.

C

Cabotage

In the maritime context, this refers to the exclusive right of a country to prefer that its national vessels—rather than foreign-flagged ones—undertake its coastal trade or transportation of passengers within the country. Such a policy is intended to protect one's domestic shipping industry from foreign competition, preserve domestically-owned shipping infrastructure for national security purposes, besides ensuring safety in congested *Territorial Waters*.

Traditionally, India has exercised the right of Cabotage contained in its *Merchant Shipping Act, 1958*. The only exceptions are time-limited licenses issued to foreign *Ship-owners* by the *Directorate General of Shipping (DGoS)* when suitable Indian-flagged vessels are not available, and particularly during exceptional circumstances such as natural disasters when foreign vessels might be required to carry relief material. In the coming years, national Cabotage laws are likely to be relaxed to encourage international carriers to use Indian *Container* ports for India-bound cargo. The rationale is essentially 'competitiveness'. Eventually, the reorientation of this policy could enable Indian ports to become regional Container *Transhipment* 'hubs', thereby optimising the country's geo-strategic location and peninsular disposition.

Capacity Building and Capability Enhancement

The 'capacity' of a military force refers to its wherewithal in the limited context of its hardware. On the other hand, 'capability' refers to the ability of the force in a more comprehensive sense encompassing not only its physical capacity in terms of 'material' assets, but also the conceptual and human components including *Doctrines*, battle indoctrination and training. Therefore, 'capacity building' is most often used in the context of 'material' wherewithal, such as the provision of platforms, infrastructure, equipment or stores.

Capability enhancement, on the other hand, refers to the realisation of a potential 'aptitude' or 'ability' of a maritime force. In the naval context, it implies that the potential recipient has already developed adequate 'capacity' for a specific mission, and the addition accretion of capability is necessary for it to exploit such 'capacity' to undertake the mission effectively. Capability-enhancement may be achieved by many means such as assisting the development of skills through training and enabling optimum exploitation of platforms and systems through doctrine-development and *Maritime Domain Awareness (MDA).*

Navies often engage in 'capacity building' and 'capability enhancement' of the maritime forces of friendly countries as part of 'Constructive Maritime Engagement' (CME), so that they can help these forces to develop the capacity through Technical Military Assistance (TME), and their comprehensive capability to achieve security 'self-reliance' and/or to undertake *Combined* (or coordinated) *Exercises and Operations* with own forces.

Capesize (Ship)

See *Commercial Ship Sizes.*

CARAT Exercises

'Cooperation Afloat Readiness and Training' (CARAT) exercises are a series of annual bilateral exercises being conducted by US Navy Pacific Fleet with Southeast Asian navies (Brunei, Cambodia, Indonesia, Malaysia, the Philippines, Singapore, Timor L'Este and Thailand) and Bangladesh (Bangladesh joined in 2010). CARAT exercises began in 1995 with Thailand. These exercises are scheduled by the Commander-in-Chief, US Pacific Fleet, and also involve elements of the US Marine Corps and the US Coast Guard, and their equivalents of other participating countries. See *RIMPAC Exercises.*

Cargo Manifest

It refers to a document pertaining to the commercial shipping industry that lists all cargo carried on a specific vessel or voyage. This shipping document is required by *Customs* authorities to review the vessel's intended trip. It summarises all *Bills of Lading* that have been issued by the shipping company for that particular *Shipment.*

For example, a cargo manifest might be used for *Shipments* made by sea, air or land, and will generally show the *Shipment's* consigner (*Shipper*) and consignee, as well as list product details such as number, value, origin and destination of the consignment. See *Carriage of Goods at Sea (Laws and Rules)*, and *Shipment, Ship-owner, Ship-operator, Shipper* and *Carrier*.

Carriage of Goods at Sea (Laws and Rules)

The transnational nature of seaborne merchandise trade requires a set of international laws (and related rules) defining the responsibilities and liabilities of parties to the 'contract of carriage of goods'—primarily the *Shipper* and *Carrier*—which have evolved over time. The resort to transportation necessitated further development of these laws and rules.

- **Hague Rules.** The law governing international maritime shipping was first codified in the 'Hague Rules' of 1924, based on the International Convention for the Unification of Certain Rules Relating to *Bills of Lading*, 1924. The Convention was adopted to redress the imbalance between the dominant position of *Ship-owners* and the fragile situation of *Shippers*. These rules laid down the responsibilities of *Shippers* and *Carriers* with reference to the carriage of cargo under a *Bill of Lading*. Under these rules, the *Carrier's* liability was minimal vis-á-vis the Consigner (*Shipper*) and the Consignee. Subsequently, the rules were updated (Hague-Visby) and new rules developed (Hamburg and Rotterdam), which progressively increased the *Carrier's* liability.
- **Hague-Visby Rules.** The Hague Rules were updated through the 'Hague-Visby Rules', which were then promulgated through the Brussels Protocol, 1968. The update was mandated by currency depreciation necessitating a revision of liability-limits, and containerisation of trade. To protect the interests of the *Shipper*, the rules enhanced the obligations upon the *Carrier*. However, even under these rules, the *Carrier* is exonerated from liability if a loss of goods or damage is caused by the ship's seaworthiness or navigational error or fire not involving the actions of the *Carrier*. Also, these rules do not cover liability for delay. Further, these rules apply only when either the *Bill of Lading* or the port of loading is located in the country that is party to the Protocol. Many countries declined to adopt the Hague-Visby Rules and continued to follow the 1924 Hague Rules.

- **Hamburg Rules.** In 1992, the 'Hamburg Rules' came into being as a result of the UN Convention on the Carriage of Goods by Sea, 1978. The driving force of the Convention was the attempt by developing countries to level the playing field. The Hamburg Rules prescribe the minimum liabilities of the *Carrier* far more equitably than did the preceding laws, so as to correct the tilt against *Shippers*. The rules are based on a presumption of fault or negligence on the part of the *Carrier* for any loss or damage to the cargo, and for any delay in delivery, unless the *Carrier* proves that it and its agents took all measures that could be reasonably required to avoid it. The Hamburg Rules exempt a *Carrier* from liability in only two cases—those of fire and assistance to another vessel—but do not exonerate it on the basis of nautical fault. Also, as per these rules, the maritime phase of carriage of goods is not limited to the period of transport ('tackle to tackle'), but commences the moment the *Carrier* takes over the goods, and lasts until the time of delivery ('port to port'). In contrast to the Hague-Visby Rules, these rules ignore the place of issuance of the *Bill of Lading* since it may not be related to the voyage. Despite these merits, the Hamburg Rules have not received uniform support, since the increase a *Carrier*'s liability has also raised the cost of shipping, particularly of insurance, and most countries have adopted a hybrid of 'Hague' and 'Visby-Hamburg' Rules.
- **Rotterdam Rules.** Lately, a new set of rules, known as the 'Rotterdam Rules', have been proposed, which are based on the UN Convention on Contracts for the International Carriage of Goods Wholly or Partly by Sea, 2008. It will come into force once 24 countries ratify the Convention. At present, only three countries have done so. These rules factor technological and commercial developments in the maritime transport industry, namely the growth of containerisation and the development of electronic transport documents. These rules also address the requirement for door-to-door contracts, under which, receipt and delivery may be inland, and include the international sea leg under a single contract. Under the Hamburg Rules and the Rotterdam Rules, the *Carrier* is always liable for loss, damage or delay caused by fault of the *Carrier*, his servants or agents.

In India, the carriage of goods by sea is largely governed by the Indian Bills of Lading Act, 1856 and the Indian Carriage of Goods by Sea Act,

1925 (COGSA-1925), besides the *Merchant Shipping Act, 1958*. The Indian Bills of Lading Act, 1856 emphasises the negotiable and other characteristics of a *Bill of Lading*. The COGSA-1925 is based on the Hague Rules, which are applied to carriage of goods by sea "from any port in India to any other port whether in India or outside India". Notably, however, India never became a party to the 1924 Convention laying down the 'Hague Rules'. COGSA-1925 was based on the British 'Carriage of Goods by Sea Act, 1924' (which the United Kingdom repealed in 1971, when it incorporated the 'Hague-Visby Rules' adopted by the Brussels Protocol of 1968). COGSA-1925 (based on the 'Hague Rules') was in force until 1993, when it was amended by adding the 'Hague-Visby' limits under the Multi-Modal Transportation Act of 1993. See *Cargo Manifest*.

Carrier (Shipping)

See *Shipment, Ship-owner, Ship-operator, Shipper* and *Carrier*.

Carrier Battle Group (CBG) and Carrier Task Force (CTF)

A Carrier Battle Group (CBG) is a self-contained and composite balanced naval force comprising an *Aircraft Carrier* as its central element. A CBG is capable of undertaking the entire range of maritime-military operational tasks, including presence, surveillance, maritime strike, *Anti-Submarine Warfare (ASW), Anti-Surface Warfare (ASuW), Anti-Air Warfare (AAW)*, etc., and is essential for establishing *Sea Control*; and thereby, for *Power Projection* in times of peace, tension or conflict.

A Carrier Task Force (CTF) may be composed of one or more CBG. It may be recalled that in 1941, the erstwhile Imperial Japanese Navy was the first to assemble five carrier groups (then called 'Carrier Divisions') into a single task force, known as 'Kido Butai'. Today, however, since most carrier-operating navies possess only a single carrier, the term CTF is usually used interchangeably with CBG. The US, with its preponderance of aircraft carriers that are custom-designed for strikes on targets ashore, prefers the term Carrier Strike Group (CSG) instead of CBG. India's current maritime strategy envisages maintaining three CBGs, so as to support an operational capability of two CTFs. See *Task Force*.

Chemical Weapons Convention (CWC)

The 'Convention on Prohibition of Development, Production, Stockpiling and Use of Chemical Weapons and on their Destruction', 1993 is an international treaty that prohibits the production, stockpiling, and use of chemical weapons, and aims to achieve the complete elimination of all types of chemical weapons. The CWC was intended to supplement the 1925 Geneva Protocol, which prohibited the use but not possession or development of chemical and biological weapons (CBW). The CWC entered into force in 1997.

The 190 State-parties to the treaty have undertaken never to use chemical weapons as a means of warfare. The CWC is administered by the 'Organisation for the Prohibition of Chemical Weapons' (OPCW), which is an inter-governmental organisation based in The Hague (Netherlands). The treaty provides for an unprecedented procedure, whereby a State-party to the CWC that is in doubt about another party's compliance can request for a 'challenge inspection' based on the principle of 'anytime and anywhere', with no right of refusal.

India acceded to the Convention in September 1996. To implement its provisions, it enacted a national legislation called the 'Chemical Weapons Convention Act, 2000' and established the 'National Authority Chemical Weapons Convention' (NACWC). See *Australia Group* and *Biological Weapons Convention (BWC).*

Chinamax (Ship)

See *Commercial Ship Sizes.*

Clandestine and Covert Operations

These operations are usually conducted by *Special Operations* Forces. The two terms are distinct, but often used interchangeably. The difference between the two is that while a clandestine operation tries to conceal the operation, a covert operation has as its primary intent, the concealment of the sponsoring country. Hence, while the former operates at the *Operational* and *Tactical* levels, the latter plays out at the *Military-Strategic* and *National-Strategic* levels.

Coalition

An *ad hoc* arrangement among two or more countries that agree to take *Combined* or coordinated military action for the attainment of common objectives over the short-term. The US-led coalitions that were formed following the Iraqi aggression against Kuwait in 1990-91, or during the Gulf War 2003 are examples. Although most UN peace-support operations are undertaken through coalitions, a UN mandate is not a prerequisite for coalition operations. In a coalition, the differing character and priorities of countries contributing military forces pose significant challenges in terms of *Command and Control* (C^2), *Rules of Engagement* (RoE), and *Interoperability*. See *Alliance*.

Coastal Security and Coastal Defence

Coastal activities encompass all maritime activities within a coastal State's *Territorial Waters* and the *Contiguous Zone*, such as local fishing, coastal shipping and ferry operations, port operations and recreational activities. These are closely related to activities in the hinterland that comprises fishing villages, communities, landing points and ports. 'Coastal Security'—as a subset of *Maritime Security*— represents the ability of a coastal State to preserve these *National Security* interests in the coastal zone, mostly against low-intensity maritime threats faced in times of general peace, or tension. It encompasses multifarious facets such as maritime border management, island security, the maintenance of good order and law-enforcement in coastal zones, as also the security of ports, coastal installations, vessels and people engaged in marine activities.

'Coastal Defence' is a term used in context of both coastal security and national defence. Measures under coastal defence are activated under conditions of imminent attack. It represents the objective of the navy's military and constabulary roles towards preventing the ingress of either anti-national elements or 'traditional' (military) threats from seawards across the coastal zone. See *Low Intensity Maritime Operations*, *Offshore Security and Offshore Defence* and *Seaward Defence*.

Coastal Surveillance Network (CSN)

A *Maritime Domain Awareness (MDA)* system developed by the Indian Coast Guard, which integrates the surveillance information obtained from the country's static sensor chain, including coastal radars. At least 46 radar stations are located in nine coastal (provincial) states and the four coastal Union Territories, each of which relay a surface picture to six core centres located in Gandhinagar (Gujarat), Mumbai, Chennai, Port

Blair, Visakhapatnam and Kochi. See *ISLEREP*, and *Merchant Ship Information System (MSIS).*

Code for Unplanned Encounters at Sea (CUES)

Adopted by the *Western Pacific Naval Symposium (WPNS)* in April 2014, CUES is a code of conduct for the *De-confliction of* (unplanned) *Naval Encounters* between naval ships and aircraft. It is not a legally binding treaty, and does not apply to encounters within a country's *Territorial Waters*. In essence, it provides a common communication platform and guidelines for the maintenance of navigational safety and the avoidance of incidents at sea. For example, it establishes radio-communication frequencies and specifies English as the standard language. It defines terms based on the phonetic alphabets 'Alpha', 'Bravo', 'Charlie', and so on, which can be used by those not proficient in English to communicate their intentions via radio. 'Bravo', for example, means a ship is conducting weapons practice. The agreement also advises naval commanders to avoid actions such as shining lights upon a ship's bridge or an aircraft's cockpit, or simulating attacks by aiming guns, missiles or fire-control radar at another country's vessels. See *Confidence-Building Measures (CBM)* and *Incidents at Sea, 1972 (INSEA-72).*

Coercion

This involves presenting a credible military force to the adversary in a manner that signals one's own capability and intent of not permitting the adversary to continue on his chosen course of action. The force is kept poised and ready to be used (though its use is not intended), while psychological pressure is built upon the adversary based on the possibility that force could, indeed, be used. This aims to shake the opponent's confidence and will to continue in defiance of one's instructions or regulations. Coercive pressure may be calibrated, with the choice of alteration of behaviour being offered to the opponent at various stages, and with the pressure being eased or withdrawn upon acquiescence.

Traditionally, naval forces have been effectively used as tools of coercive diplomacy (commonly referred to as 'Gunboat Diplomacy'), as they signal political intent and military capability without being unduly offensive since they operate in *International Waters* and can be rapidly deployed and withdrawn without loss of face. Coercion is normally felt at the

Strategic Level of Warfare, even if it is applied at the *Operational* or *Tactical Levels*. See *Compellance and Deterrence by Punishment*, and *Persuasion and Dissuasion*.

Collective Security

See *Australia-New Zealand-US (ANZUS) Security Treaty*, *Collective Security Treaty Organisation (CSTO)*, *Gulf Cooperation Council (GCC)*, *Jus Ad Bellum*, *Military Alliance* and *North Atlantic Treaty Organisation (NATO)*.

Collective Security Treaty Organisation (CSTO)

A *Military Alliance* acting as counterpart to the *North Atlantic Treaty Organisation (NATO)*, established in 2002. The genesis of the CSTO lies in a treaty signed in Tashkent in May 1992 (also called 'Tashkent Pact') by six countries of the Commonwealth of Independent States (CIS)—Russia, Armenia, Kazakhstan, Kyrgyzstan, Tajikistan, and Uzbekistan—formed after the fall of the Soviet Union. Three other former Soviet countries—Azerbaijan, Belarus, and Georgia—signed the treaty in 1993. The treaty took effect in 1994. In 1999, six of the nine—all except Azerbaijan, Georgia, and Uzbekistan—agreed to renew the treaty for five more years, and in 2002, these six agreed to create the CSTO as a military alliance. Uzbekistan rejoined the CSTO in 2005 but again withdrew in 2012. The CSTO commits its member-countries to 'collective security' and conducts *Combined Exercises* periodically. Under the terms of the treaty, Russia has the right to veto the establishment of new foreign military bases in the member-countries.

COLREGS and Rules of the Road

The International Regulations for Preventing Collisions at Sea, 1972 (COLREGS) are published by the *International Maritime Organisation (IMO)*. COLREGS specify the navigation rules—called 'Rules of the Road' (RoR) in maritime parlance—to be followed by vessels at sea, including warships, to prevent collisions among them. The RoR comprises a set of 38 such rules. These rules apply in all international waters (comprising *High Seas*, *EEZ* and *Contiguous Zone*), and also in *Territorial Waters*, *Archipelagic Waters* and *Internal Waters* of coastal States, except where the concerned coastal State has specifically established and promulgated different rules. See *Traffic Separation Scheme (TSS)*.

Combined Exercises and Operations

See *Joint and Combined.*

Combined Maritime Forces (CMF)

A US-led multi-national naval coalition instituted to promote *Maritime Security* in the north-western Indian Ocean, including the contiguous seas, an area encompassing the world's most important *International Shipping Lanes (ISL)*. The CMF is composed of navies of about 30 countries, and is divided into three *Task Forces.*

- **Combined Task Force (CTF) 150.** It operates in the Red Sea, Gulf of Aden, Indian Ocean, Persian Gulf and the Gulf of Oman, and is also mandated for counter-*Terrorism.* CTF-150 was established after the terrorist attacks of September 2001.
- **Combined Task Force (CTF) 151.** It operates in the Gulf of Aden and off Somalia, with a particular emphasis on *Counter-Piracy* mission, including policing the Internationally Recommended Transit Corridor (IRTC) in the Gulf Aden. Its operations are coordinated with those of the *EU NAVFOR/ATLANTA*, *North Atlantic Treaty Organisation (NATO)* and independently deployed naval ships from other countries. CTF-151 was established as a multi-national *Task Force* in January 2009. Its Command is rotated among the navies of participatory countries on a three to six monthly basis.
- **Combined Task Force (CTF) 152.** Its operations are confined to the Persian Gulf, and are planned and executed in coordination with the maritime forces of the *Gulf Cooperation Council (GCC)* countries. CTF-152 was established in March 2004.

The CMF is commanded by a US Navy Vice Admiral, who also serves as Commander US Navy Central Command (CENTCOM) and US Navy Fifth Fleet, and is headquartered in Bahrain. The contributions from various participating navies range from positioning a liaison officer at CMF headquarters to providing warships and land-based maritime reconnaissance aircraft to the *Task Forces.*

Command and Control (C^2)

This term is usually used in the context of military forces, and refers to system empowering the designated personnel to exercise lawful authority and direction over assigned forces for the accomplishment of missions and tasks. See *Peace Enforcement Operations* (*PEO*), *Rules of Engagement* (*RoE*), and *Sea Basing*.

Command of the Sea

See *Sea Control.*

Commercial Ship Sizes

The global shipping fleet comprises commercial ships of different sizes, categorised by capacity and limiting dimensions. The latter categorisation is related to the ability of these vessels to transit through restricted waters such as straits and canals (including canal locks). The sizes of cargo vessels range from a modest 'Handysize' carrier (10,000 to 30,000 DWT) to a giant *Ultra Large Crude Carrier* (*ULCC*) upwards of 500,000 DWT.

Traditionally, 'Panamax' referred to the relatively smaller vessels of 50,000 to 80,000 *DWT* (mostly tankers) that usually operated off Latin America, and were the largest ships capable of sailing through the Panama Canal. Following the implementation of the Panama Canal Expansion Project, the specifications of 'Panamax' vessels are being changed progressively. The vessel specifications are published by the Panama Canal Authority. The current *Deadweight Tonnage* limit of 'New PANAMAX' vessels has been enhanced to 120,000 DWT. Its TEU limit is now 13,000 TEU. Ships that do not fall within the Panamax-sizes are called 'post-Panamax'.

'Suezmax' are medium-to-large sized ships (usually *Oil Tankers*) of 120,000 to 200,000 *DWT*, whose dimensions permit them to pass through the Suez Canal in a fully-laden condition. The current depth of the Canal allows for a maximum draught (the portion of ship that remains underwater) of about 20 metres and a beam (the ship's maximum width) of 50 metres. Notably, the dimensional limits of 'Suezmax' have been changing over the years, along with the deepening of the Canal.

'Aframax' vessels are mid-sized cargo carriers. The term 'AFRA' stands for 'Average Freight Rate Assessment'. Hence, 'Aframax' represents a medium-sized (80,000 to 120,000 *DWT*) vessel. An Aframax *Oil Tanker* is capable of carrying about a million barrels of crude-oil, and is primarily used in regions of lower crude production (non-*OPEC* countries), since the ports and waterways through which these countries export oil are unsuited to handle larger tankers (*ULCC*s, *VLCC*s or even Suezmax).

Hence, these tankers generally ply in the European waters of the Black Sea. Aframax vessels also ply as cargo *Container* vessels in the Mediterranean Sea, the North Sea and the Caribbean Sea.

Other key terms pertaining to commercial ship sizes are 'Malaccamax' (largest dimensions to be able to pass through the Malacca Strait), 'Capesize' (bulk carriers too big to pass through the Suez Canal, and thus need to sail around the Cape of Good Hope), and 'Chinamax' (vessels able to use a number of harbours while fully laden).

Common Heritage of Mankind

This refers to a principle of international law, which holds that defined territorial areas and elements of humanity's common heritage (cultural and natural) should be held in trust for future generations and be protected from exploitation by individual countries or their corporations. Whereas the spirit of term finds its origin in the Latin term 'Res Communis' derived from ancient Roman Law, and has been applied in various treaty-based laws, such as the 1954 'Hague Convention for the Protection of Cultural Property in the Event of Armed Conflict' and the 'Outer Space Treaty' of 1967, the term itself was first mentioned in the 1970 UN General Assembly Resolution 2749 on the 'Declaration of Principles Governing the Seabed and Ocean Floor'. See *Global Commons* and *Seabed Mining*.

Common Market, Single Market and Unified Market

These are terms commonly used in the field of economics. A 'common market' is built upon a *Free Trade Area* with relatively free movement of goods, services and capital, but not so advanced in reduction of the rest of the trade barriers. Examples would include *Mercosur* and *Association of Southeast Asian Nations (ASEAN)*. A 'common market' is usually the first stage towards the creation of a 'single market'. For example, the former European Economic Community (EEC) led to the formation of European Union (EU), as a 'single' market'.

A 'single market' is a type of a *Free Trade Area* in which, most barriers for trade in goods have been removed, and largely common policies exist on the free movement of capital, labour, enterprise and services. The physical (borders), technical (standards) and fiscal (taxes) barriers among the member states are removed to the maximum extent possible. The

Gulf Cooperation Council (GCC) and the European Union are current examples of single markets.

A 'unified market' is the last stage and the ultimate goal of a 'single market' with a totally free movement of goods, services (including financial services), capital and people, and is akin to a federation of states, such as the United States of America (USA). See *Excise Duty and Custom Duty*, *Foreign Trade*, *Free Trade Agreement (FTA) and Free Trade Area*, and *Non-Tariff Barriers (NTB)*.

Compellance, and Deterrence by Punishment

'Compellance' refers to the process of compelling an opponent—through the actual use of military force against it—to take a certain action. It entails the use of escalatory force upon the opponent (such as through the use of limited precision strikes) by effecting damage and destruction, with the threat of its continued use until the opponent acts as directed. The concept differs from *Coercion*, which only presents a credible threat of the use of force (and not its actual use), to achieve the same effect.

Deterrence by Punishment, too, entails use of escalatory force, but seeks to check an opponent's inimical posture or behaviour. This form of deterrence is also referred to as 'Active Deterrence', and contrasts with the more common 'Passive Deterrence'. Given the ability of naval forces to control escalation, naval power is inherently suited for both Compellance, and Deterrence by Punishment. See *Deterrence* and *Land Attack*.

Comprehensive National Power (CNP)

The term sums up the comprehensive power of a *Nation-State*. It includes both tangible and intangible constituents. Its tangible constituents include geography, demography, natural resources, economic capacity, science and technology base, administrative organisation and military power. Its intangible constituents encompass national character (emanating from inter alia historical, psychological and sociological factors), political system, leadership and national morale. See *Balance of Power*.

Comprehensive Nuclear Test Ban Treaty (CTBT)

An international treaty concluded with the objective of banning all nuclear tests involving explosions in all environments, for both military and civilian purposes. It was adopted by the UN General Assembly in 1996, but has not entered into force. This requires the signature and ratification of all 44 countries listed as nuclear technology capable. At present, eight of those countries are yet to join, with India, Pakistan and North Korea being amongst the non-signatories.

Although India has not signed the CTBT, it has been supportive of its objectives ever since Prime Minister Jawaharlal Nehru's famous initiative in 1954 for a "standstill agreement" on nuclear testing. After its 1998 nuclear tests, India has been observing a unilateral moratorium on nuclear testing, indicating that it is not averse to the spirit of CTBT. See *Non-Proliferation Treaty (NPT)* and *Nuclear Suppliers Group (NSG)*.

Confidence-Building Measures (CBM)

These are measures that countries adopt—either bilaterally or multilaterally—to enhance mutual trust and stability in their international relations. CBMs could operate at the *National-Strategic* (political) level, the military-strategic level, or even at the operational level across land and maritime frontiers of the countries. An agreement prohibiting an attack on nuclear facilities is an example of a CBM at the *National-Strategic* level. A CBM at the military-strategic level may be exemplified by the requirement to provide advance notice (by each country) of a major exercise scheduled by its military forces. At the *Operational Level* involving maritime forces, CBMs could involve an agreement for *De-Confliction of Naval Encounters*, setting up of 'hot-lines' between the apex theatre commanders, periodic talks between the local commanders, and other agreements—such as those for the conduct of coordinated operations against maritime crime or for a speedy repatriation of each other's fishermen arrested for violation of an established or agreed maritime boundary. See *Incidents at Sea Agreement, 1972 (INSEA-72)* and *Code for Unplanned Encounters at Sea (CUES)*.

Container

A truck trailer body that can be detached from the chassis for loading onto a vessel, a railway car or stacked in a container depot, and meant for the multi-modal (sea, road and rail) transportation of merchandise. A container may be 20 feet, 40 feet, 45 feet, 48 feet or 53 feet in length, 8 feet or 8.5 feet in width, and 8.5 feet or 9.5 feet in height. Since the smallest standard container is 20 feet in length, container capacity is measured in multiples of TEU (Twenty-foot Equivalent Unit).

Containers may be ventilated, insulated, refrigerated, flat rack, vehicle rack, open top, bulk liquid or equipped with interior devices. A 'Reefer' is a container meant for refrigerated cargo. A Bulk-Freight container, with a discharge hatch in its front wall, is used for the transportation of *Bulk Cargo*. The place where loaded and/or empty containers are loaded or discharged into or from a means of transport is called a 'Container Terminal'.

Container Ship

A merchant ship designed to transport containerised cargo. Its hull is divided into cells that are accessible through large hatches into which the *Containers* fit. Most container ships lack integral cranes and are hence dependent upon shore cranes for loading and unloading of *Containers*. Specialised types of container ships are the *Lighters Aboard Ship (LASH)* and *Sea Barge (SeeBee) Ships*, which carry floating *Containers* (or 'lighters'). Presently, the largest container ships have a capacity of 19,224 TEUs (Twenty-foot Equivalent Units).

Container Security Initiative (CSI)

This US initiative is a product of the anxiety over 'transportation-security' following the September 2001 terrorist attack on the USA (9/11). The CSI was launched in January 2002, and was driven by the fear that terrorists could smuggle *Weapons of Mass Destruction (WMD)* concealed within shipping *Containers* into the US.

The CSI involves the screening of all *Containers* at foreign ports by US *Customs* officials in concert with their host-nation counterparts, before being shipped to US ports. The rationale is to extend the security perimeter of the USA outwards so that its borders become the last—rather than the first—line of defence. The process involves the use of intelligence, automated information, advanced detection technology (X-ray imaging and radiation detection equipment) and 'smart' (tamper-proof) *Containers*.

The US authorities have stipulated that their ports of the USA's trading partners need to be CSI-compliant, viz. installed with necessary non-intrusive and automated screening and detection equipment; failing which, their exports would have to be re-routed through CSI-compliant *Transhipment* ports, which could lead to delays, disruptions due to congestion in these ports, increase of costs, and ensuing losses, including in terms of competitiveness. Nhava Sheva was the first Indian port to become CSI-compliant. See *Maritime Terrorism*.

Contiguous Zone

This maritime zone lies beyond the *Territorial Waters* of a coastal State up to a distance of 24 nautical miles from the *Maritime Baselines*. Within this zone, the State may exercise such control as is necessary to prevent infringement of its *Customs*, fiscal, immigration or sanitary laws and regulations. It must, however, be noted that this zone comprises *International Waters*, wherein ships and aircraft enjoy the '*High Seas* freedoms of navigation and overflight'.

Continental Shelf and Legal Continental Shelf (LCS)

The term 'continental shelf' is used in the geological (scientific) context. It refers to the underwater landmass which extends from a continent, resulting in an area of relatively shallow water known as the shelf sea. Beyond the continental shelf, the underwater geology slopes steeply ('continental slope'), and then flattens due to the sediment cascading down the slope ('continental rise') before meeting the deep ocean floor. The 'continental slope' and 'continental rise' are together called the 'continental margin'.

The *UNCLOS* provides the legal context to the continental shelf, calling it the Legal (juridical) Continental Shelf (LCS). Through the LCS concept, *UNCLOS* permits a coastal country to exercise *Sovereign Rights*, not only over the continental shelf proper (as geologically defined) but also the 'slope' and 'rise' ('continental margin'). The LCS of a coastal country thus comprises the sea-bed and subsoil of the natural prolongation of its land territory extending up to the outer edge of the continental margin, or to a distance of 200 *nautical miles* from the coastline (baseline), whichever is greater. If the natural prolongation of its land territory extends beyond 200 *nautical miles* ("extended continental shelf"), the coastal country is required to submit its claim to the UN 'Commission on the Limits of the Continental Shelf' (CLCS).

The LCS claim is validated based on twin criteria of 'constraint line' and 'formula line'. As per the former criterion, the outer limit of LCS may extend to a distance of 350 *nautical miles* from the coastline, or 100 *nautical miles* seawards of 2,500 metre depth contour (isobath), whichever is greater. However, the qualifying requirement of the 'formula line' criterion restricts this maximalist extent. As per the 'formula line' criterion, the 'constraint line' is tempered by the isobath at the 'foot of the (continental) slope' (FoS) plus 60 *nautical miles* seaward, or the 'Gardiner Line', whichever is greater. The 'Gardiner Line', which is named after a 1978 proposal to the UN by PR Gardiner, according to which the outer limit of the 'rise' could be defined in direct proportion to the thickness of the sediments. It connects all points where thickness of sedimentary rocks is one per cent of the distance to the 'foot of the slope'. The detailed methodology of delineating the LCS is contained in the 'Manual on Technical Aspects of the Law of the Sea' (TALOS) published by the International Hydrographic Bureau (IHB) and various scientific documents issued by the UN 'Division of Ocean Affairs and Law of the Sea' (DOALOS).

Continental Union

An inter-governmental supranational union of sovereign *Nation-States* (short of a *Federation* within a sovereign *Nation-State*) located in the same continent, or close to it. The concept is relatively new in the evolution of human governance, which began in historic times at the local level of tribes and city-states, and then graduated to larger areas comprising river basin habitations, and then to larger empires, and thereafter to the concept of *Nation-State*. The advent of *Globalisation* necessitated and facilitated the coalescing of sovereign states at the sub-regional and continental levels. It began with European countries forming the 'European Community' in the middle of the 20th century. Other examples of a continental union are the *African Union (AU)* and the 'Union of South American Nations' established since the beginning of the 21st Century. See *Common Market, Single Market and Unified Market*, and *Mercosur*.

Contraband

In context of *War and Armed Conflict*, 'contraband' is defined as those goods which are ultimately destined for territory under the control of the enemy that a belligerent considers objectionable because these goods may assist the enemy in the conduct of the war. Its origin lies in the Medieval French term 'contrebande' that denoted any item which, due to its nature, was illegal to possess or be sold. As an element of *Customary International Law* pertaining to *Blockade*, the genesis of the term lies in the *Declaration of Paris*, 1856. *Customary International Law* recognises three types of goods, as follows:

- **Absolute Contraband.** Goods that consist of articles of warlike or military characteristics such as arms, ammunition, military clothing, camp equipments and machinery for manufacture of ammunition.
- **Relative Contraband.** Dual-use goods that can be used for civilian use as well as war such as food, fuel and rolling-stock.
- **Free Goods.** Goods not susceptible to any military use in the war, such as glass, chinaware and paints. Free goods are not declared as contraband.

Contraband, along with the merchant vessel carrying it may be seized as prize for adjudication in a *Prize Court*. The purpose of a declaration of 'contraband' is to enable belligerents to inflict damage upon the economy of the enemy. As per the *Law of Armed Conflict* (LOAC), belligerents are required to declare a 'contraband list' at the initiation of hostilities to notify neutral nations of the type of goods considered to be 'absolute' or 'conditional' contraband, as well as those not considered to be contraband at all, that is, 'free goods'. The precise nature of a belligerent's contraband list may vary according to the circumstances of the conflict. Also see, *SLOC Interdiction*.

Conventional Deterrence

Conventional Deterrence is achieved either through 'passive' means by denying the gains to the potential adversary, regardless of the cost (deterrence by 'denial') or through 'active' means by raising the costs (deterrence by 'punishment'). Passive deterrence involves maintaining an implicit, though credible military capability, strategy and readiness. Active deterrence requires the possession (or its demonstration, if necessary) of a strong retaliatory military capability and an overt politico-military posture that assures the potential aggressor of unacceptably high costs. In case passive deterrence (through 'denial') is not credible or effective, a country could opt for deterrence through 'punishment'. See *Compellance and Deterrence by Punishment*, and *Deterrence*.

Conventional Submarine (NATO designation: SS/SSG)

An underwater combat platform that uses diesel-engines when on surface, and electric-propulsion when dived. It effectively exploits its stealth characteristics and the relative opacity of the underwater environment to interdict enemy surface units, by using anti-ship torpedoes and, in case of SSG, guided missiles. It possesses enormous one-on-one superiority over a surface combatant due to difficulty of detection by the latter, since water is not a consistent medium for the generation and receipt of sound waves in terms of the temperature gradient. However, this superiority does not give a submarine the ability for Sea Control, unless it is a *Nuclear Attack Submarine (SSN).*

A conventional submarine is particularly suited for *Sea Denial* missions, particularly in choke-points and in the approaches to harbours. Although electric propulsion make it very quiet, its relatively low dived speeds and the compulsion to come to the surface periodically to recharge their batteries make it vulnerable to detection. The Air Independent Propulsion (AIP) technology being used lately enhances the underwater endurance of a conventional submarine from a few days to up to three weeks, thereby reducing its vulnerability to quite an extent. A conventional submarine can also be used for 'Scouting Operations' involving *Search, Patrol, Tracking and Reconnaissance.* It is often the option of choice for mine-laying, the insertion of *Special Operations* Forces and *land attack* (if armed with *Land Attack Cruise Missiles* [LACM]). See, *Ballistic Missile Submarine* (SSBN) and *SLOC Interdiction.*

Co-operative Engagement Capability (CEC)

In the maritime context, CEC involves the sharing of sensor information amongst the diverse platforms of a naval force. It allows all available information from sensors such as radars, sonars and electronic support measures (ESM) of all platforms to be fused to effectively counter the threats in all dimensions. By linking all CEC-equipped sources, a common, consistent and highly accurate picture of the prevailing air, surface and sub-surface threat environments can be developed, using which, all individual defensive or offensive capabilities of the various elements of the composite force can be brought to bear on the threat. In other words, CEC enables effective engagement of a target by the designated platform, using target-information provided by another platform. See *Network Centric Operations (NCO).*

Corvette

Corvettes are relatively small surface-combatants, usually of 500-2,500 tonnes *Displacement*. However, the displacement varies widely. For instance, the Indian Navy's ASW Corvettes of the Kamorta Class have a displacement tonnage of about 3,000 tonnes. Corvettes are often optimised for specific military tasks, such as *Anti-Surface Warfare (ASuW)*, *Anti-Submarine Warfare (ASW)* or *Anti-Air Warfare (AAW)*. This specificity notwithstanding, corvettes are frequently fitted with a wide array of weapons and sensors to undertake both offensive and defensive operations within their designed roles.

Council for Security Cooperation in the Asia-Pacific (CSCAP)

See *ASEAN Regional Forum (ARF).*

Counterforce and Countervalue Targeting

These concepts usually refer to concepts of nuclear strategy, but are also used in Air Force conventional-warfare doctrines governing the military use of air power. Within nuclear doctrine, 'Counterforce' refers to striking targets of military value relating to the adversary's nuclear weapons capability. Such targets comprise the nuclear weapons themselves, their delivery systems (such as land-based launchers or nuclear-capable air squadrons) or nuclear *Command and Control* infrastructure. Such a strategy aims to deliver a decapitating strike against an adversary to disable or disrupt his capability to deliver a nuclear (usually retaliatory) strike. Countervalue refers to a nuclear strike against the adversary's high-value civilian targets such as a city with a high density of population or an economic hub. Usually, countervalue targeting is meant to be a *Nuclear Second-Strike* option. See *No First Use (NFU)* and *Nuclear Deterrence.*

The extrapolation of the concepts of nuclear doctrine—Counterforce and Countervalue—to conventional warfare is, at best, of limited use. Since conventional warfighting is circumscribed by the principle of 'military necessity' under the *Law of the Armed Conflict (LOAC)*, conventional military strikes would largely fall in the ambit of Counterforce targeting. Countervalue targeting can rarely be legally justified but may be used against an enemy's oil shipments, for example.

Country of Origin and Country of Provenance (Shipping)

These are terms used in the commercial shipping industry. A 'Country of Origin' is one in which the goods concerned have been produced or manufactured. Ascertaining the 'country of origin' is necessary for the *Customs* authorities to ascertain duties applicable to the goods under prevailing preferential tariff programmes, or to regulate the import of specific goods from specific sources. A 'Certificate of Origin' provides the proof of the country of original production of the goods that are shipped.

A 'Country of Provenance' is one from where the goods or cargo are sent to the importing country. See *Bill of Lading*, and *Shipment, Ship-owner, Ship-operator, Shipper and Carrier.*

Crimes against Humanity

See *War Crimes*, and *Crimes against Humanity and Genocide.*

Criminal Jurisdiction

Public international law permits a state to establish jurisdiction over criminal offences and prosecute alleged offenders based upon the following five principles.

- **Territorial Jurisdiction.** For offences committed within the State's territory, including in *Territorial Waters* and aboard vessels flying its flag.
- **Nationality Jurisdiction.** For offences committed anywhere by its own nationals.
- **Protective Jurisdiction.** For offences considered prejudicial to national security.
- **Passive Personality Jurisdiction.** For offences that have harmed its nationals.
- **Universal Jurisdiction.** For offences—such as *Piracy*—that have been declared to be *Crimes Against Humanity.*

Indian domestic criminal law (contained in the Indian Penal Code, 1860 and Code of Criminal Procedure, 1973) is explicit on 'Territorial' and 'Personality' principles. Nonetheless, if circumstances warrant, 'Objective Jurisdiction' ('Protective' or 'Passive Personality') could be established. The *Anti-Piracy* legislation is based on the principle of 'Universal Jurisdiction'.

Cruise Liner and Ocean Liner

These are two broad categories of passenger ships. A Cruise Liner (or cruise ship) is used for tourism or pleasure voyages, meant to cater for the experience of passengers in terms of the voyage itself, the ports of call and the ship's amenities. Since such ships are not intended for the 'transportation' of passengers, and usually follow a 'round-trip' routeing, finally disembarking passengers at their original port of embarkation. In contrast, the primary purpose of an Ocean Liner is the transportation of passengers from one port to another, and thus such vessels typically do 'line voyages'.

Although the functional difference between Cruise Liners and Ocean Liners is narrowing, the two categories remain distinct in terms of their construction and amenities. A typical Ocean Liner meant for trans-oceanic transit would be constructed with more passenger-carrying capacity, and a larger capacity for fuel, victuals, and other stores.

Cruise Missiles

See *Ballistic and Cruise Missiles.*

Customary International Law

'Customary International Law' arises where there is a uniform, consistent and general repetition of similar acts by competent State authorities, and the recognition by countries that such practice is binding upon them as law. A rule of customary law in international relations is thus created by a normative State practice coupled with what is known as '*opinio juris*', viz. a widespread belief that an action must (or must not) be carried out because it is a legal obligation to do so. Over the period of time, the common practices have attained a certain regularity leading to a general consensus among countries of their obligatory nature, and have thus assumed the form of customary law.

The existence of 'Customary International Law' is dependent upon 'general agreement', and not 'unanimous agreement'. Thus, a country is bound by a treaty that expresses customary law, even though it is not a party to that treaty. It is important to note that although much of international law has now been codified in treaties, many important aspects of maritime activity, especially naval warfare, continues to be regulated by customary law. The link between customary law and treaty law is established by the 'Martens Clause', which emanates from a declaration adopted at the 1899 Hague Conference (it is named after Fyodor Fyodorovich Martens, a Russian jurist and delegate to the first of The Hague Conferences, 1899-1907). As per the Clause, insofar as the treaties are silent on a specific issue, customary international law continues to govern the situation. As a corollary, some act that is not expressly forbidden by the treaty law, is not necessarily permitted.

Customs

The department of the Civil Service that deals with the levying of duties and taxes on goods imported from foreign countries. It also regulates the export and import of goods, in terms of the allowed quota and prohibited goods, etc.

Customs Act, 1962

A national legislation meant to prevent illegal import and export for various reasons, inter alia *National Security* considerations, preventing tax evasion, conservation of foreign exchange, preventing shortage of goods or resources in the country, protecting patents and copyrights, protecting national treasures of heritage value to issue notifications declaring the export or import of certain goods as restricted or prohibited, etc. It also regulates the entry and exit of carriers, passengers and goods by notifying the ports, airports and inland *Container* depots which alone shall be '*Customs* Stations'. The Act stipulates that except in cases of emergencies, the commander of a vessel or aircraft shall not call or land at any place other than a '*Customs* Stations'. The *Customs* ports, customs airports and land stations are notified through circulars issued periodically by the 'Central Board of Excise and *Customs*'.

D

Dead Weight Tonnage (DWT)

A measure of a commercial ship's capacity to carry cargo, DWT refers to the number of tons of cargo, stores, spare-parts, provisions, fresh water and bunker fuel that a merchant vessel can transport, when loaded to its maximum draught as applicable under the circumstances. It is the difference between the number of tons of water the empty vessel displaces and the number of tons it displaces when submerged to the 'load line' (carrying its maximum load). In contrast, *Displacement Tonnage* (of warships) applies only to the vessel, not to its cargo. While *Gross Tonnage (GT) and Net Tonnage (NT)* relate to merchant ships, these are based upon the internal volume of the vessels, rather than upon their mass.

De-confliction of Naval Encounters

Naval ships and aircraft may meet with their foreign counterparts in international waters (and the super-adjacent airspace) as per a planned schedule agreed upon by their respective national command authorities. However, cases of unplanned encounters in international space often arise. In certain scenarios, particularly when two countries have adversarial postures, such encounters bear risks of escalation arising from misperception or misinterpretation of the other's action/intent. Traditionally, these have been known by the term 'Incidents at Sea'.

In such scenarios, certain actions by one side (such as certain manoeuvres, signalling or collection of pictorial or acoustic data of the other side) could lead to a military *escalation*. Such encounters, therefore, need to be 'de-conflicted' based on international norms, and preferably reinforced by standing agreements; or at least, codes of conduct such as the WPNS *Code for Unplanned Encounters at Sea (CUES)*. See *Incidents at Sea Agreement, 1972 (INSEA-72)*.

Deep Seabed Mining

See *Seabed Mining*.

Deep Submergence Rescue Vehicle (DSRV)

See *Submarine Rescue.*

Demersal Fish

Fish that live and feed on (or near) the sea bottom. See *Fishing Methods and Gear* and *Pelagic Fish.*

Destroyers and Frigates

The traditional dividing line between destroyers and frigates primarily lay in their role. Destroyers were capable of multi-dimensional engagement, but primarily tasked to destroy enemy surface forces. (*Anti-Surface Warfare* task). Frigates were meant for a specific uni-dimensional task such as *Anti-Submarine Warfare* (ASW) or *Anti-Air warfare* (AAW), and deployed as escorts to protect high-value naval and commercial platforms.

However, this distinction has gradually blurred with both destroyers and frigates now capable of undertaking multi-dimensional missions. The key difference today lies in their *Displacement Tonnage* (size). In the Indian Navy, warships of 6,000 to 7,500 tons *Displacement* are termed as destroyers, whereas those between 3,000 and 5,000 tons are classified as frigates.

Deterrence

Deterrence is meant to prevent military aggression against one's own country by convincing a potential aggressor that resorting to force is not a viable option. A country's deterrence strategy operates at two levels. The concept of *Strategic Deterrence* operates at the national-strategic level, and includes *Nuclear Deterrence.* To develop deterrence, it synergises and leverages all elements of national power—diplomatic, economic, informational and military—and international influence.

The concept of *Conventional Deterrence* operates at the military-strategic level. At that level, deterrence could be achieved either though 'active' or 'passive' means. A possession of a credible military capability is among the passive means of deterring the adversary. If such passive deterrence is not effective (or credible), 'deterrence by punishment' may be resorted to as an active means of deterrence. It would entail infliction of escalatory punishment upon the opponent till the opponent alters its inimical posture or behaviour.

Strategic Communication is a valuable instrument available to shape perceptions for reinforcing the credibility of national deterrence. See *Compellance and Deterrence by Punishment*, and *Persuasion and Dissuasion*.

Diaspora, NRI and PIO

A Non-Resident Indian (NRI) is an Indian citizen who has 'temporarily' emigrated to another country for more than six months for employment, residence, education or any other purpose. On the other hand, a Person of Indian Origin (PIO)—also called 'overseas Indian' or 'expatriate Indian'—is the citizen of another country who is of Indian origin or ancestry.

The term 'Diaspora' encompasses both categories. Having originated from Greek language and meaning "scattering" or "dispersion", the term refers to a scattered population with a common origin in a specific geographic locale. India has the second-largest Diaspora in the world after China. The Diaspora contributes much to the advantage for country of origin, not only in terms of the flow of *Remittances*, but also in many other intangible ways, including serving a 'bridge' for the country to propagate influence, and access knowledge, expertise, resources and markets.

Directorate General of Shipping (DGoS)

A statutory maritime authority established by the Government of India under the *Merchant Shipping Act, 1958*. DGoS (commonly called DG Shipping) is an attached office of the Indian Ministry of Shipping, mandated to implement the provisions of the Act, and formulate shipping policy and legislation in coordination with the *International Maritime Organisation (IMO)*. It periodically issues Merchant Shipping (MS) notices and circulars to convey information, guidelines and instructions on nautical matters relevant for the shipping community. The MS notices/circulars include advisories ranging from the risks of *Piracy* to offshore resource activity in Indian maritime zones. In March 2012, for example, the DGoS issued a notice advising all merchant ships to take note of dense fishing activity up to 50 *nautical miles* from the Indian coast, so that the ships' armed security guards do not mistake the fishing boats for pirate boats. See *Offshore Development Area (ODA)*, *Vessel Protection Detachment (VPD)* and *Private Maritime Security Companies (PMSC)*.

Disabling Fire

Fire directed at a vessel, aircraft or vehicle so as to impair its manoeuvrability, but not its survival. Disabling fire is commonly resorted to at sea while conducting *Low Intensity Maritime Operations (LIMO).*

Displacement Tonnage

Also referred to as merely 'displacement', it is used to denote the size of a warship in terms of the number of tons of water it displaces. It is calculated by dividing the volume of water displaced by the warship (along with her fuel tanks full and stores embarked) in cubic feet by 35, the average density of sea water. It differs from the use of the terms *Gross Tonnage (GT) and Net Tonnage (NT)* for commercial ships, which are a function of the ship's volume, and not its mass.

Dissuasion

See *Persuasion and Dissuasion.*

Djibouti Code of Conduct

A Code supported by the *International Maritime Organisation (IMO)* on 'Repression of Piracy and Armed Robbery against Ships in the Western Indian Ocean and the Gulf of Aden' signed since January 2009 by Djibouti, Ethiopia, Kenya, Madagascar, Maldives, Seychelles, Somalia, Tanzania and Yemen (original signatories), Comoros, Egypt, Eritrea, Jordan, Mauritius, Mozambique, Oman, Saudi Arabia, South Africa, Sudan and the UAE (a total of 20 countries). The signatories to the Code agree to co-operate to implement the provisions of the UN Security Council resolutions concerning *Piracy* in the area, and on various other *Anti-Piracy* measures, inter alia coordination of counter-piracy operations with multi-national naval forces, legal measures, information-exchange, rescue of victims and *Capacity Building* of the concerned countries.

Doctrine

The word originated from the Latin word 'doctrina', which refers to 'a code of beliefs' or 'a body of teachings'. A doctrine thus provides a framework of beliefs and teachings that guide a group in its actions. In the military context, doctrine provides a common reference point, language and purpose to an armed force (or service), and guides its actions in the way it organises, equips, trains, fights and sustains itself in pursuit of national objectives. While it does not direct how a problem is to be solved, a doctrine provides a shared way of thinking, including towards the solution. Doctrine thus differs from *Strategy*.

Drug Trafficking

See *Maritime Crime*.

Duty Free Port

An international port (or an area within an international port) wherein the crew, passengers, baggage, cargo, mail and stores may be disembarked or unloaded, may remain and may be transhipped, without being subjected to any customs charges or duties. However, the persons and material may be checked, for example, to meet security or narcotics control requirements. See *Special Economic Zone (SEZ)* and *Transhipment*.

E

Earth Summit

See *United Nations Framework Convention on Climate Change (UNFCCC).*

East Asia Summit (EAS)

See *Association of Southeast Asian Nations (ASEAN).*

Electronic Intelligence (ELINT)

See *Electronic Warfare (EW)*

Electronic Warfare (EW)

A military task or mission of naval forces that aims to exploit the electromagnetic spectrum, so as to ensure effective use of the spectrum by one's own forces, gain information on the enemy, and prevent or degrade the use of the spectrum by the opponent. It encompasses Electronic Support Measures (ESM), Electronic Counter Measures (ECM), Electronic Counter Counter Measures (ECCM), and Electronic Intelligence (ELINT).

ESM is the interception of enemy *Radar* and radio transmission using passive (i.e. non-transmitting) electronic equipment and is therefore, a method by which targets can be detected. ECM essentially involves 'disrupting' (jamming) or 'deceiving' the opponent's EW sensors. ECCM is meant to counter the use of ECM by the opponent. ELINT involves collection of Communication Intelligence (COMINT) and Signal Intelligence (SIGINT). See *Intelligence.*

Emission Control Areas and Special Areas

See *MARPOL 73/78.*

Energy Security and Security of Energy

Energy Security implies safeguarding for national use the availability of requisite quantities and types of energy from any kind of disruption—physical or economic. The degree of Energy Security possessed by a country is the excess of actual, or assured, availability of energy supplies over demand, at an acceptable price.

Security of Energy is a subset of Energy Security. It implies the assured availability of energy supplies in the event of a conflict. It encompasses military and quasi-military means adopted to address the vulnerabilities of energy supply, particularly for ensuring safety and security of energy assets in the *Littoral*, lines of communication of imported and indigenous sources, as also its storage and distribution networks.

Enforcement of Sanctions

This usually refers to 'military' enforcement of international sanctions imposed upon a State (in addition to diplomatic, trade and other sanctions), though not involving the use of force. Authorised under Article 41 (Chapter VII) of the UN Charter, it usually involves employment of coercive measures to interdict the movement of certain types of designated items into or out of a State or a specified area.

Escalation

Whenever military forces are employed against the adversary's forces in a conflict situation (ranging from *Short of War Scenarios* to *War and Armed Conflict*), there is a risk of escalation. It can be vertical or horizontal. 'Vertical' escalation involves an increase in the level of violence (in quantity, or by the introduction of new categories of weapons such as chemical or nuclear weapons or even by the inclusion of targets that had been spared). 'Horizontal' escalation is the expansion of the combat geographically to new theatres or environments. This leads to the concepts of *Escalation Control* and *Escalation Dominance*. See *Limited War*.

Escalation Control

To meet its political objectives in a *Short of War Scenario*, a country may opt to 'demonstrate' its military force (such as in case of *Coercion*) or 'use' such force (such as in case of *Compellance*). These measures would usually be taken concurrently with politico-diplomatic measures. In such cases, it is essential to control military escalation to prevent the outbreak of armed conflict. Due to the international medium where navies operate and their versatility to alter their posture, naval forces are inherently suited to control escalation in a *Short of War Scenario*. Escalation Control is also required during armed conflict to keep conventional warfighting within the space between conflict initiation and the nuclear threshold. See *Limited War*, *Escalation*, and *Escalation Dominance*.

Escalation Dominance

It is essentially a factor of balance between opposing military forces in the operational theatre, with the superior force possessing the advantage for Escalation Dominance, unless the weaker side can offset the conventional military balance through *Asymmetric Operations*. See *Limited War*, *Escalation*, and *Escalation Control*.

EU NAVFOR/ATLANTA

Refers to European Union (EU) Naval Force constituted in December 2008 under the 'European Common Security and Defence Policy' (CSDP) for *Anti-Piracy* off the Horn of Africa and the western Indian Ocean, including the conduct of counter-piracy operations through the EU Naval Task Group's 'Operation Atlanta'. EUNAVFOR operates the Maritime Security Centre, Horn of Africa (MSC-HOA) for dissemination of *Piracy*-related information. Its operational headquarters is located at Northwood in the UK.

The mission was triggered by the need to protect Somalia-bound vessels and shipments belonging to the 'World Food Programme' (WFP) and the 'African Union Mission in Somalia' (AMISOM) against *Piracy*. In 2012, the scope of EU NAVFOR was expanded to include Somali *Territorial Waters* and *Internal Waters* so as to co-ordinate *Counter-Piracy* operations with Somalia's 'Transitional Federal Government' (TFG) and regional administrations. The same year, the charter of EU NAVFOR was expanded in its regional and functional scope for *Capacity Building* of regional navies to counter *Piracy* and other maritime crimes under 'EUCAP Nestor'. EU NAVFOR coordinates its operations with Combined Task Force (CTF) 151 of the US-led *Combined Maritime Forces (CMF)*.

Expeditionary Operation

Expeditionary Operation is a means available to a State that seeks to project military power overseas to ensure security and stability in the distant neighbourhood, which may be linked to its own national security interests. It entails distant deployment of one's own airlift and/or sealift assets, and their operational sustenance via sea-borne or airborne means. Although airborne forces are endowed with quick response that may be valuable to cater for certain contingencies, sea-borne forces provide the enduring presence that is usually essential for the poise and calibrated use of force, as may be necessary.

For a maritime expeditionary capability, the three essential prerequisites are adequate amphibious sealift capacity, a landing force integral to the sealift platforms and a comprehensive logistic support, either through overseas facilities or sea-based logistic platforms. Also, the sealift platforms need to possess adequate sea-based Command, Control and Communication (C-3) facilities and integral vectors (landing craft and airlift assets) for ship-to-shore movement of the landing force and logistic supplies. On occasions wherein a military opposition is expected, a capability to achieve *Sea Control* may also be necessary. See *Command and Control* (C^2), *Lilypad*, *Mobile Landing Platform (MLP)*, *Sea Basing*, *Sealift Capacity*, *Airlift Capacity*, and *Amphibious Operation*.

Exclusion Zones

Exclusion zones have been declared at sea in many naval wars in the past. The concept emanates from State practice during wars, rather than from international law. The promulgation of such zones is not explicitly permitted by international law. Its legal validity may, nonetheless, be justified under the clause of 'right to self-defence' (Article 51 of the UN Charter). It is pertinent to note the ruling of the Nuremberg International Military Tribunal on the subject after the Second World War. The Tribunal held that establishment of exclusion zones wherein the neutral merchant ships incorporated into the belligerent war effort were subjected to a 'sink on sight' policy was illegal. Nevertheless, the Tribunal implicitly accepted the legitimacy of such zones.

The most notable example of the establishment of exclusion zones was by the United Kingdom (UK) and Argentina during the Falklands War of 1982. During the conflict, a temporary *Maritime Exclusion Zone* (MEZ) established by the UK eventually became a *Total Exclusion Zone* (TEZ). A few years later, during the Iran-Iraq war, the United States Navy declared a five-mile "moving bubble" exclusion zone around its warships in the Persian Gulf requiring aircraft and vessels to identify themselves before entering this bubble.

Exclusion zones may be perceived to interfere with *High Seas* freedom of navigation and overflight. However, these could be interpreted more broadly to cater for the right of belligerents to conduct naval operations on the *High Seas*, along with their obligation to constrain the conflict and avoid drawing in neutrals into the effects of the conflict. Hence, declaring exclusion zones may be seen as an operational imperative, not only for easing the dilemma of identification at sea, but also as a measure of protection and reassurance for the neutral shipping, in consonance with the underlying principles of Law. However, the relevant provisions of the law with regard to the promulgation of such zones must be observed. See *Security Zone* and *Air Defence Identification Zone* (ADIZ).

Exclusive Economic Zone (EEZ)

This maritime zone lies beyond the *Territorial Waters* up to a distance of 200 nautical miles from the *Maritime Baseline* of the coastal State. With a *sui generis* character, the rights granted to coastal States in this zone are limited to those that primarily relate to exploitation of the economic resources. In this zone, the coastal State has *Sovereign Rights* for exploring and exploiting, conserving and managing the living and non-living natural resources in both the water column and in its seabed.

Excise Duty and Custom Duty

Excise duty is the tax collected from a manufacturer on the goods produced or sold within the country. It also includes the tax on licenses issued within a country for specific activities. Levied along with 'Sales Tax' or 'Value Added Tax' (VAT), excise duty constitutes the largest proportion of taxes in the price of a commodity.

Custom duty is a 'tariff' levied on the goods that are imported from other country and are meant to be sold in the country. Based on commodity-specific codes developed by World Customs Organisation (WCO), a country decides the rate of custom duty for a particular commodity being imported.

Both excise and custom duties constitute 'indirect' taxes levied by the government of a country. Unlike 'direct' taxes (like income tax), these are indirect taxes as they are passed on to the citizens (as consumers) by adding them in the costing chain.

See *Common Market, Single Market and Unified Market, Foreign Trade, Free Trade Agreement (FTA) and Free Trade Area, Non-Tariff Barriers (NTB)*, and *World Trade Organisation (WTO).*

Export Processing Zones (EPZ)

See *Special Economic Zones (SEZ).*

Eyes in the Sky (EiS)

Coordinated air surveillance patrols over the Straits of Malacca and Singapore involving the three littoral countries—Indonesia, Malaysia and Singapore—and Thailand. The initiative was mooted by the Deputy Prime Minister of Malaysia during the Shangri-la Dialogue July 2005 in Singapore to complement *MALSINDO* (coordinated naval patrols), and launched in August 2005 in response to the increasing pirate attacks and other *maritime crimes* in the Straits. It features the conduct of maritime air patrol by the armed forces and maritime enforcement agencies of the littoral and invited international participating nations. EIS is an open arrangement that may involve the participation of other countries on a voluntary basis, if deemed necessary by the littoral states. Countries participating in the program provide their respective air assets to conduct operations involving flight profile, pre-flight administration, operation centres, monitoring and action agencies, and communications.

F

Failed State

See *Fragile State and Failed State.*

Federation and Federal State

The two terms are synonymous. They represent a political entity characterised by the union of partially self-governing provincial States under a central (federal) governing authority. In a federation, the self-governing status of the component provincial States, as well as the division of power between them and the central government, are typically constitutionally entrenched and cannot be altered by a unilateral decision of either party, the States or the central (federal) authority.

Fishing Methods and Gear

The equipment used for fishing. In the context of basic fishing methods in use worldwide, fishing gear may be divided into three broad categories. These are encircling technique gear, towed gear and static gear. The first two are optimised to catch either *Demersal Fish* (living close to sea bottom or shore) or *Pelagic Fish* (living away from sea bottom or shore). See *Sustainable Fisheries.*

- **Encircling Technique Gear**
  - Ring Net, operated by surrounding a shoal of with a "wall" of netting, often operated by two boats. It is meant to catch *Pelagic Fish.*
  - Purse Seine Net, used to surround a shoal of fish, the bottom of which is then drawn together to enclose them. It is meant to catch *Pelagic Fish.*
  - Beach Seine Net, shot from a small boat then drawn ashore by ropes. It is meant to catch *Pelagic Fish.*

    - Anchor Seine Net, shot in the open sea using very long ropes to lay out the net and ropes on the seabed prior to hauling from a boat at anchor. It is meant to catch *Demersal Fish.*
    - Scottish Seine Net, shot in the open sea using very long ropes to lay out the net and ropes on the seabed prior to towing the net closed and hauling from a boat under its own power. It is meant to catch *Demersal Fish.*
- **Towed Gear** (for *Demersal Fishing)*
    - Beam Trawl, towed on the seabed in which, the net is held open by a wood or steel beam.
    - Otter Trawl, towed on the seabed, held open by a pair of otter boards (trawl doors). It is usually a much larger net than a beam trawl.
    - Pair- or Multi-Rig Trawl, involving towing two or more otter trawls side by side.
    - Dredge, a rigid structure towed on the seabed, usually for shellfish.
- **Static Gear** (for traditional fishing)
    - Fixed Nets, comprising sheets of thin netting anchored in the water to catch fish by enmeshing or entangling them.
    - Drift Nets, comprising sheets of thin netting allowed to drift with tide or current to catch fish by enmeshing or entangling them.
    - Long Lines, anchored or drifting, with numerous baited hooks.
    - Traps, involving innovative structures into which, fish are guided or enticed through funnels that encourage entry but limit escape.

Flag Follows Trade

A concept that relates to the overseas investments, acquisitions or activities of business companies in a country (the 'trade'). It implies that while such 'trade' is driven by commercial drivers autonomous of government oversight and control, due to the country's strategic imperatives, it is supported by the government and its agencies (the 'flag') and constitutes an integral component of the country's foreign policy. Some countries even afford State protection to such 'commercial' activity overseas. The provision of counter-piracy *Vessel Protection Detachment (VPD)* aboard merchant ships flagged by some European countries is a case in point.

Flag State

As per international law, all merchant ships are required to be registered in a country. Flag State is the country under whose laws a commercial ship is registered and who has granted the right to the ship to sail under its flag. Over such vessels, the Flag State is empowered with the authority and responsibility to exercise legislative and enforcement jurisdiction with regard to its domestic laws, including those relating to safety and *Marine Pollution* control inspection and certification. This is best signified by the metaphor that a ship is a piece of 'floating territory'. If a vessel is involved in a case involving *Admiralty Law*, the domestic laws of its Flag State apply. However, the exclusiveness of Flag State's jurisdiction is not absolute. For example, in case of a collision between two ships of different nationalities, or an incident onboard a ship involving a foreign national, concurrent jurisdiction applies, which would be based on the specifics of the case. In some cases, such as *Piracy*, a third country may share jurisdiction with the Flag State. See *Flags of Convenience* and *Registration of Ships*.

Flags of Convenience (FoC)

The term describes the global commercial shipping practice of registering a merchant vessel in a country other than that of the *ship-owner* ('open registry' countries), and flying that country's flag on its mast. The practice is driven by the commercial incentive to reduce costs or avoid the regulations of the owner country. The initial fees for registration of a ship in a FoC country and the annual *Gross Tonnage* fees are much lower. The registration formalities involve minimal paperwork; sometimes the process is transacted over facsimile, and concluded in a matter of hours. Also, taxes on the shipping company's profits are very low, or do not exist at all.

The FoC practice began in the 1920s when the US government began to permit American *ship-owners* beset by high labour cost and stringent regulations to register their ships to Panama. Following the 'Flag Right Declaration' of 1921, even land-locked countries were legally permitted to register merchant vessels. Panama is currently the world's largest *Flag State*, with almost a quarter of the world's ocean-going tonnage registered in the country.

The practice of FoC poses significant challenges for *Maritime Security*. Since it makes it difficult to establish the link between the *ship-owner* and the *Flag State*, it could complicate the response against maritime crimes like *Piracy*, *Human Smuggling and Trafficking*, and trafficking of arms and drugs. Besides, 'open registry' countries typically have more lenient regulations with regard to the preservation of marine environment. See *Registration of Ships*.

Fleet Support Ships

See *Operational Logistics*.

Flight Information Region (FIR)

A defined area of airspace within which flight-information and alerting services are provided. The FIRs are established by the *International Civil Aviation Organisation (ICAO)* for the safety of civil aviation, and encompass both 'national' and 'international' airspace. Military aircraft on routine point-to-point flights through *International Airspace* usually follow *ICAO* flight procedures and utilise FIR services. Exceptions to this policy include military contingency operations, classified or politically sensitive missions, and routine *Aircraft Carrier* operations or training activities. When military aircraft do not follow *ICAO* flight procedures, they are required to navigate 'with due regard' for the safety of civil aviation.

Pursuant to Article 37 of the Convention on International Civil Aviation (Chicago 1944), contracting States like India are required to provide Aeronautical Information Service (AIS). In conformity with the promulgated standards and recommended practices of the ICAO, the Directorate General Civil Aviation (DGCA) and Airports Authority of India (AAI) provide AIS in respect of entire territory of India as well as the areas in which India is responsible for Air Traffic Services (ATS) outside its territory, viz. the FIRs. The air space allocated to India to provide ATS is divided among Delhi, Mumbai, Kolkata and Chennai FIRs. All these FIR nodes are required to maintain air plots, and also cater for *Maritime SAR (M-SAR)* in their respective FIRs. The information is disseminated through Aeronautical Information Publication (AIP), AIP Supplements and Amendment, Notices to Airmen (NOTAM) and Aeronautical Information Circulars (AIC).

Floating Armouries

See *Private Maritime Security Companies (PMSC).*

Force Majeure

Literally, it means 'superior force". In the military context, it refers to an abnormal circumstance beyond one's control that leads to a compulsion for a military unit to deviate from the laid down *Law of Armed Conflict (LOAC).* For example, based on the Law of Neutrality, a belligerent warship (one involved in an Armed Conflict) is not permitted to enter the *Territorial Waters* of a 'neutral' country. However, in case of a breakdown or accident (based on 'force majeure'), humanitarian considerations permit such entry, albeit under some restrictions.

Force Majeure also refers to a usual provision in a commercial contact, particularly one pertaining to insurance, which frees the contract parties from a liability until the circumstances of 'force majeure' prevail. The circumstances include war or other forms of violence, or various forms of natural calamities grouped under the legal lexicon of "Act of God".

Force Protection

Actions taken to prevent or mitigate hostile actions against one's own forces, encompassing all personnel (including their family members), platforms/resources, infrastructure/facilities, and critical information. The concept is being largely used in context of the asymmetric threat to military forces posed by non-state entities. It does not include actions to defeat the enemy or protect against natural or man-made disasters/ accidents, weather, or disease. See *Asymmetric Operations.*

Foreign Policy

A nation's policy meant and tailored to preserve its *National Interests* in the realm of international relations. India's Foreign Policy is derived from the Constitution of India and amplified through political directions in various forms. According to the 'Directive Principles of State Policy' enunciated in the Indian Constitution (Article 38), "The State shall endeavour to promote international peace and security; maintain just and honourable relations between nations; foster respect for international law and treaty obligations in the dealings of organised peoples with one another; and encourage settlement of international disputes by *Arbitration*".

Foreign Trade

Also referred to as 'international trade', it refers to the exchange of capital, goods and services across political boundaries of countries. While commodity trade among human settlements, communities and civilisations flourished in the ancient times, more recent developments such as industrialisation, technological advancements in transportation and *Globalisation* have changed the character of global trade, which has become a crucial driver for economic development of countries world-wide.

Foreign trade is premised on the fact that no country is self-contained in terms of resources to be able to generate adequate goods, services or raw materials for its needs, and must, therefore depend upon each other. In this sense, it is fundamentally similar to 'domestic trade'. However, foreign trade ipso facto involves different monetary currencies, and is regulated by varying laws, rules and regulations of the countries involved, leading to attendant complexities. Also, foreign trade entails higher financial expenses than domestic trade, since the border transit of goods imposes additional costs such as tariffs, time costs, and costs associated with country differences such as language, the legal system or culture.

Foreign trade consists of 'exports' and 'imports', thus leading to the alternative term 'EXIM Trade'. Export involves sale of goods and services to other countries. Import consists of purchases from other countries. A larger value of imports relative to exports leads to a 'trade deficit'. The term 'balance of trade' refers to the difference.

India's Foreign Trade is governed by the 'Foreign Trade (Development & Regulation) Act', 1992 and five-yearly formulations of Export-Import (EXIM) Policy. Payments for EXIM transactions are regulated by the 'Foreign Exchange Management Act', 1999. The physical movement of trade is regulated by the 'Customs Act', 1962. The quality of exports is ensured by the 'Exports (Quality Control and Inspection) Act', 1963. In 1982, India established the Export Import Bank of India (EXIM Bank) as its premier export finance institution to enhance exports and integrate Foreign Trade with the country's economic growth. Over the years, the EXIM Bank has played a major role in boosting the export potential of Indian industries, particularly the Small and Medium Enterprises (SME).

See *Common Market, Single Market and Unified Market, Excise Duty and Custom Duty, Free Trade Agreement (FTA) and Free Trade Area, Non-Tariff Barriers (NTB)*, and *World Trade Organisation (WTO)*.

Five Power Defence Arrangements (FPDA)

A 'loose consultative political framework', which replaced the 1957 Anglo-Malayan Defence Agreement following the 1971 withdrawal of UK's armed forces east of Suez and the termination of its guarantees for defence of Malaysia and Singapore. The FPDA involves a set of bilateral defence and security relationships among Australia, Malaysia, New Zealand, Singapore and the United Kingdom (UK) established in 1971, whereby the five countries will consult each other "immediately" in the event of external aggression or threat of attack against Malaysia or Singapore "for the purpose of deciding what (response) measures should be taken jointly or separately". There is no specific commitment for collective security. The FPDA is headquartered in Butterworth (Penang, Malaysia).

The most visible element of FPDA is the 'Integrated Air Defence System' (IADS) based at the Royal Malaysian Air Force (RMAF) station Butterworth, which provides for air defence of peninsular Malaysia and Singapore. The station is under the command of an Australian Air Vice-Marshal—although administered by the RMAF—and hosts rotating detachments of aircraft and personnel from all five countries. See *Military Alliance.*

Fragile State and Failed State

There is no consensus on the precise authoritative definition of these terms that are drawn from common parlance, for use in the geopolitical context. In broad conceptual terms, a 'fragile State' is a low-income country with a weak state capacity and/or legitimacy that is susceptible to internal and external shocks, and domestic and international conflicts. The US-based think-tank 'Fund for Peace' promulgates an annual 'Fragile States Index' classifying countries from least to most fragile under the broad categories of 'Sustainable', 'Stable', 'Warning' and 'Alert', and their sub-categories.

The term 'failed State' refers to a condition of 'State collapse' due to the inability of the sovereign government to meet its fundamental obligations towards security and governance of the country. The level of failure of a government to 'qualify' as a 'failed State' is a subjective issue that varies with individual perspectives. Nonetheless, a failed State may be characterised as one that has been unable to:

- Exercise control over its territory, including through monopoly of force;
- Wield legitimate decision-making authority;
- Provide public services and
- Conduct international relations.

The declaration of a State having "failed" is generally contentious, and when such a statement is made authoritatively, it is usually driven by geopolitical motives rather than objectivity. Notably, the 'Fragile States Index' was earlier called 'Failed States Index'. Evidently, the change in nomenclature was needed to avoid controversy. See *Responsibility to Protect (R2P)*.

Freedom of the Seas

A principle that the *High Seas* in time of peace are open to all countries and are not subject to national sovereignty. Its genesis lies in the theory of '*Mare Liberum*' (Latin for 'free sea') proposed in a book of same name by the Dutch jurist and philosopher Hugo Grotius in 1609. In the book, Grotius proposed the principle that the sea was international territory and all nations were free to use it. While Grotius asserted *Innocent Passage* across both 'land' and 'sea' for trade, he postulated that the 'ocean' was akin to 'air in a manner that it is not susceptible to occupation or possession, and is thus adapted for the use of all, whether for navigation or of fisheries. The concept of 'freedom of the seas' is also closely related to the concept of *Global Commons*.

The concept of 'freedom of the seas' later became an accepted principle of international law. In November 1947, a UN General Assembly Resolution entrusted the regime of *High Seas* to the International Law Commission (ILC). According to the ILC, *High Seas* comprised all area beyond the *Territorial Waters*, wherein 'freedom of high seas' comprises inter alia freedom of navigation, freedom of fishing, freedom to lay submarine cables and pipelines, and freedom to fly over high seas. The list could not be made exhaustive since new ocean technologies were constantly developing.

Eventually, the principle of 'freedom of the seas' became the basis of negotiations at United Nations Conferences on the Laws of the Sea. The 1958 'High Seas Convention' made additions to the list of *High Seas* freedoms, such as freedom to undertake scientific research and exploit the sub-soil of the *High Seas*. The ensuing treaty *UNCLOS*, 1982, broadly retained the principle of 'freedom of the seas', but also provided for *Sovereign Jurisdiction* of varying degrees over substantially increased areas of the maritime realm, such as the *Contiguous Zone* and the *Exclusive Economic Zone (EEZ)*. Notably, *High Seas* freedoms do not include *Seabed Mining*, which is regulated by the *International Seabed Authority (ISA)*.

Hence, after coming into force of *UNCLOS*, the ILC's definition of '*High Seas*' was altered. The *EEZ* was no longer a part of the *High Seas*. Nonetheless, the concept of '*High Seas* freedoms' in all *International Waters* (beyond *Territorial Waters*) continues to be valid. In contemporary context, the principle of 'freedom of the seas' encompasses both the freedom of navigation and over-flight in *International Waters*; and in spirit, is relevant to both vessels and aircraft, commercial or military. However, restrictions exist on such freedoms in specific circumstances based on the interpretation of the prevailing international laws by individual States. See *International Waters*.

Free/Foreign Trade Zone (FTZ)

See *Special Economic Zones (SEZ)*.

Free Trade Agreement (FTA) and Free Trade Area

An agreement between two or more countries to reduce trade barriers (import quotas and tariffs), and to increase trade of goods and services. The establishment of FTAs among a group of countries in an area may lead to development of a geographic economic grouping in the form of a 'Free Trade Area', wherein the barriers to trade—tariffs (tax on imports and exports) and *Non-Tariff Barriers (NTB)*—are reduced or eliminated among the participating countries. See *Excise Duty and Custom Duty*, *Foreign Trade*, and *World Trade Organisation (WTO)*.

Free Trade Area

See *Free Trade Agreement (FTA)*.

Frigate

See *Destroyers and Frigates*.

G

Geneva Conventions, 1949

See *International Humanitarian Law (IHL).*

Genocide

See *War Crimes,* and *Crimes against Humanity and Genocide.*

Geoeconomics

A branch of *Geopolitics,* which refers to the study of the spatial, temporal and political aspects of economies and resources.

Geopolitics

In a broad context, it refers to the utilisation of geography in the service of national governments. This definition may be applied in three senses.

The most prevalent connotation of 'Geopolitics' is the interplay among countries—bilateral and multilateral—based on their relative *Comprehensive National Power (CNP),* which is conditioned by the spatial, temporal, political, economic, security and legal aspects of international relations. Often referred to as 'power politics', this connotation is closely related to the erstwhile concept of (military) *Balance of Power,* that continues to be in vogue in present times, albeit in a broader sense of both 'hard' and 'soft' (including economic) power.

The term 'Geopolitics' is also used as a synonym for 'applied political geography'; or more loosely, to designate national policy as affected by the natural environment. See *Geoeconomics.*

Global Commons

Denotes all international and supranational domains like the oceans beyond national jurisdiction, the continent of Antarctica, the atmosphere, the outer space and the cyber-space. Every resource contained within this domain is referred to by the term *Common Heritage of Mankind.* See *Freedom of the Seas.*

Globalisation

The perpetual process of national and popular integration worldwide arising from the increasing flows of *Foreign Trade* and travel, and exchange of information. The process has been the cause for the growing global interdependence and broader awareness. In the contemporary times, the salient contributors to globalisation are the technological advances in transportation, telecommunications and cyber connectivity, and also the evolution of international legal frameworks and multilateralism. See *Global Undersea Communications Cable Infrastructure (GUCCI).*

Global Maritime Distress and Safety System (GMDSS)

A global communications service based upon automated systems, which is the technological 'backbone' of *Maritime Search and Rescue (M-SAR).* The core objective of GMDSS is to alert the SAR authorities ashore and ships in vicinity whenever a ship is in distress, so that SAR assistance can be provided with minimum delay. The system also provides urgency and safety alerts, and broadcasts Maritime Safety Information (MSI) on weather report and navigation warnings.

As per the *Safety of Life at Sea (SOLAS) Convention, 1974/1988*, the GMDSS operation is divided into sea areas where it is defined by the governments and uses the criteria recommended by the *International Maritime Organisation (IMO).* The GMDSS enables a ship in distress to sound an alert using many radio systems—both satellite-based and terrestrial—leading to a high probability of it being received by shore stations and the ships in vicinity. See *International Ship and Port Security Code (ISPS)*, and *Maritime Satellite Communications.*

Global Maritime Partnership Initiative

See *Thousand Ship Navy (TSN).*

Global Undersea Communications Cable Infrastructure (GUCCI)

As a critical international infrastructure, GUCCI consists of a global web of underwater cables that underpin the internet connectivity across the world, carrying 99 per cent of all intercontinental digital communications traffic, and thereby also playing a major role in the global economy and other facets of *Globalisation.* Notably, the growing need for bandwidth for inter-continental communications—to enable rapid transfer of high-capacity data—can be met only by undersea cables, not by the space (satellite)-based Information and Communications Technology (ICT).

Given India's central geographic location in the Indian Ocean and its peninsular disposition, a significant proportion of these cables stretch across India's maritime zones, with more than a dozen (and increasing) GUCCI interfaces connected to India. In accordance with the *UNCLOS* (Articles 58 and 113), India plays an important role in enhancing the resilience of GUCCI by facilitating the entry of specialised ships into Indian maritime zones to undertake periodic repairs of the cables.

Grand Strategy

See *National Strategy*.

Group of Twenty (G-20)

An international forum of the heads of governments and central bank governors from 19 major economies and the European Union (EU) for global cooperation on international economic and financial issues. The G-20 operates as a forum and is not a multilateral institution like *World Bank*, *International Monetary Fund (IMF)* or the United Nations. It does not have any secretariat or administrative structure.

The G-20 was founded in 1999 following the Asian financial crisis of 1997, with the aim of consultations and coordination between the developed countries and the emerging economies, who had begun to play a major role in the international economic and financial system. Following the global financial crisis of 2008, the G-20 was upgraded from being a forum for finance ministers to the level of heads of state (India is represented by the Prime Minister). In 2009, the G-20 replaced the Group of Eight (G-8) as the principal economic council of wealthy nations.

The salient objective of the G-20 is to coordinate policies for strengthening and regulating the international financial architecture, so as to prevent a global financial crisis; while concurrently promoting economic growth and sustainable development. It also seeks to achieve transparency of fiscal policy, and adopt internationally recognised standards with regard to global tax network, and combating money laundering and financing of terrorism. Although the decisions taken by the G-20 are not legally binding, the members usually commit to compliance, which it monitored through a 'Mutual Assessment Process (MAP)'.

Since 2011, the G-20 summits have been held annually. Up to five non-member countries also invited to attend the summit meetings. G-20 maintains close coordination with regional multilateral organisations, which are frequently represented in the G-20 working group meetings.

Gross Tonnage (GT) and Net Tonnage (NT)

Gross tonnage (GT) is a unit-less index related to a ship's 'overall' internal volume. It is calculated based on the moulded volume of all enclosed spaces of the ship, and is used as determining factor for ship's manning regulations, safety rules, registration fees, and port dues. In 1994, Gross Tonnage (GT) replaced the term 'Gross Registered Tonnage' (GRT), which was a ship's overall internal volume expressed in 'register tons', each of which equals 100 cubic feet.

Net tonnage (NT) is a unit-less index related to the total volume of the ship's 'cargo spaces', determined by using a mathematical formula. NT replaced the earlier term 'Net Register Tonnage' (NRT), which denoted the volume of the ship's revenue-earning spaces in 'register tons', each of which equals to 100 cubic feet. NT is used to calculate the port duties and is usually taken as 30 per cent of the ship's GT.

Both GT and NT are defined in the 'International Convention on Tonnage Measurement of Ships', which was adopted by the *International Maritime Organisation (IMO)* in 1969. Notably, the two terms are not a measure of the ship's displacement (mass) and should not be confused with terms such as *Dead Weight Tonnage (DWT)* or *Displacement Tonnage* (for warships). See *Flags of Convenience (FOC).*

Gulf Cooperation Council (GCC)

A sub-regional multilateral organisation comprising six Arab countries of the Persian Gulf—Bahrain, Kuwait, Oman, Qatar, Saudi Arabia and the UAE. All GCC countries are monarchies. While Saudi Arabia and Oman are absolute monarchies, Qatar, Kuwait and Bahrain are constitutional monarchies, and the UAE is a federal monarchy (comprising seven states with their own emir). Notably, Iraq is an Arab country, but is not a GCC member since it has a republican form of government. Jordan and Morocco (both being constitutional monarchies) have been seeking to join the GCC.

The GCC is envisaged to be a political and economic union. Among its salient objectives are to develop similar policies with regard to religion, legislation, administration, science, finance, trade and *Customs*, and eventually a common currency and a unified military. GCC already has a *Common Market* since 2008, with plans to realise a fully integrated *Single Market*. It also has a collective security mechanism in force through a joint military force called the 'Peninsula Shield Force' established in 1984, and a joint military command formed in 2013.

H

Hague Code of Conduct (HCoC)

The 'Hague Code of Conduct against Ballistic Missile Proliferation' (HCoC) was established in 2002 to regulate unrestricted access to *Ballistic Missiles* that can potentially deliver *Weapons of Mass Destruction (WMD).* Presently, the HCoC is the only dedicated multilateral instrument relating to *Ballistic Missiles*. The Code does not ban such missiles, but it does call for restraint in their production, testing, and export. Presently, 134 countries have signed the HCoC, which do not include China, India and Pakistan. See *Missile Technology Control Regime (MTCR).*

Hague Conventions, 1907

See *International Humanitarian Law (IHL).*

Hague Rules (Shipping)

See *Carriage of Goods at Sea (Laws and Rules).*

Hague-Visby Rules (Shipping)

See *Carriage of Goods at Sea (Laws and Rules).*

Hamburg Rules (Shipping)

See *Carriage of Goods at Sea (Laws and Rules).*

High Seas

All sea areas seaward of the coastal State's *Exclusive Economic Zone (EEZ)*, wherein the more comprehensive concept of *Freedom of the Seas* applies. It is, however, important to note that '*High Seas* freedom of navigation' applies in all maritime zones beyond the *Territorial Waters* that constitute *International Waters*.

In November 1947, a UN General Assembly Resolution entrusted the regime of *High Seas* to the International Law Commission (ILC).

The ILC defined the term 'high seas' to mean all parts of the sea that are not included in the *Territorial Waters* or the *Internal Waters* of a country. However, after the coming into force of *UNCLOS* in 1994, the *Exclusive Economic Zone (EEZ)* of coastal countries no longer formed a part of 'high seas'.

Historic Waters

Refers to the maritime space—bay, pool, strait or even the sea—over which, a country is legally accorded *Sovereignty* as its *Internal Waters* owing to historical evidence. For being accorded such a status, the country's claim needs to be rooted in history, and backed with adequate evidence that the country has always claimed and maintained sovereignty over the given maritime area due to its vital interests, irrespective of the dynamism of international legal regimes over maritime delimitation.

An example is the Palk Bay that comprises waters from Adam's Bridge to Palk Strait. Since India and Sri Lanka—as British 'possessions'—have exercised jurisdiction over Palk Bay for many centuries, the Bay is considered as a 'historic bay', and delimited though treaty signed between the two countries in 1974.

Hot Pursuit

The concept of maritime 'hot pursuit' recognises the right of a coastal state to pursue onto the *International Waters* a foreign vessel that has violated its laws in waters within its jurisdiction. The same is codified in *UNCLOS*. If a good reason exists to believe that the foreign vessel has violated India's national laws in its maritime zones, and it fails to stop and submit to law enforcement action, Indian maritime forces may undertake 'Hot Pursuit' of the vessel into *International Waters* beyond the zone where the violation has occurred. The pursuit may be commenced when the foreign vessel or one of its boats is within India's *Internal Waters*, *Territorial Waters*, *Contiguous Zone*, *EEZ*, *Continental Shelf* or *Safety Zones* around *Continental Shelf* installations, and has violated the law relevant to the specific zone. The pursuit must be continuous, either visually or through electronic means. The right of 'Hot Pursuit' ceases as soon as the foreign vessel enters the *Territorial Waters* of its own country or of a third country.

Humanitarian Assistance and Disaster Relief (HADR)

Material, personnel and services provided to an affected area to meet the needs of those affected by a disaster, either natural or man-made. In India, disaster-response is steered by the 'National Committee on Disaster Management', which was established in 1999 under the 'Ministry of Home Affairs' (MHA). In 2005, India adopted the 'Disaster Management Act'. It provides for a 'National Disaster Management Authority' (NDMA), and such authorities at the state and district levels, and the 'National Executive Committee', which includes the Defence Secretary and the Chief of the Integrated Defence Staff of the Chiefs of Staff Committee. Although HADR would usually involve a multi-faceted response, military forces, by virtue of their inherent attributes, are usually the 'first responders' in such contingencies. Accordingly, the conduct of HADR operation in the maritime-littoral environment is among the important peacetime 'benign' roles of naval forces.

The area affected by a disaster may be within India or in a friendly country. In case of the former, the parameters of the naval mission are well laid out within the ambit of national laws, and hence, the operational imperatives would largely pertain to organisational and material capacity. However, in case of HADR assistance to a foreign country, international law is inadequate. The impediments range from the lack of bilateral coordination in distribution of relief supplies to the affected state even declining the assistance involving foreign military forces due to sensitivities based on national security and geopolitical reasons. Nonetheless, a notable effort has been made to develop a framework called 'International Disaster Response Law (IDRL)' Guidelines, which was adopted by the state parties to the Geneva Conventions and the International Red Cross and Red Crescent movements in November 2007. See *Tropical Cyclone* and *Tsunami*.

Human Rights Law (HR Law)

Whereas *International Humanitarian Law (IHL)* regulates the conduct of State *vis-à-vis* State, HR Law regulates the conduct of State *vis-à-vis* individuals. While under IHL, the right to protection is vested in the State (not in the individual), but under HR Law, as a radical transition of international law, the protection flows to the individual directly, and theoretically protects individuals from their own State. This implies that

Human Rights Law applies in all situations—*International Armed Conflicts (IAC)*, *Non-International Armed Conflicts (NIAC)* and even other internal low-intensity isolated and sporadic conflicts, such as riots and counter-piracy situations—that have not crossed the NIAC 'threshold'.

It is important to note that the body of laws pertaining to *NIAC* and other intra-State conflicts (sub-NIAC), including the *Customary International Law* on these aspects, continues to be under-developed, and largely based on *Human Rights Law*, which began developing only in the middle of the 20th century. See *International Criminal Court (ICC)*.

Human Smuggling and Trafficking

Two forms of *Maritime Crime*, represented by distinct terms that are not synonymous. 'Human Smuggling' provides the means of transportation for *Illegal Immigration*, and is undertaken with the consent of the person(s) being smuggled, who usually pay money to be transported discreetly when other options of immigration are not tenable. The payment may be made to the smugglers before the transportation begins, or after facilitating illegal entry.

In case of 'Human Trafficking', the person(s) are victims, who are forced, coerced (actual, perceived or implied) or deceived. Unlike 'Human Smuggling', monetary benefits accrue mostly from the exploitation of the victim, rather than his/her transportation. See *Australian Maritime Identification Zone/System (MIZ/AMIS)* and *Refuge, Refugee and Asylum*.

Hydrography

See *Bathymetry and Hydrography*.

I

IBSAMAR (Naval Exercises)

Combined exercises among the Indian Navy (IN), the South African Navy (SAN) and the Brazilian Navy. The first IBSAMAR was held off South Africa in 2008.

Illegal Immigration

The migration of people across national boundaries in search for better employment opportunities and standard of living, or for other reasons, in a manner that violates the immigration laws of the destination country in terms of its national government policies to regulate immigration of people and other aspects of citizenship. See *Australian Maritime Identification Zone/System (MIZ/AMIS)* and *Human Smuggling and Trafficking*.

Illegal, Unreported, and Unregulated (IUU) Fishing

In broad terms, Illegal Fishing refers to fishing activities conducted by national or foreign vessels within maritime zones of a country, without its permission, or in contravention of its laws and regulations, or its international obligations. Unreported and Unregulated Fishing refers to fishing activities within the country's maritime zones or beyond, which have not been reported, or have been misreported to the relevant national authority, in contravention of the country's laws and regulations, and international obligations. Hence, globally, IUU fishing takes many forms both within nationally controlled waters and on the *High Seas*. It is a major contributor to declining fish stocks and marine habitat destruction. It is estimated that IUU fishing accounts for about 30 per cent of all fishing activity worldwide. See *Maritime Crime*, and *Sustainable Fisheries*.

Incidents at Sea, 1972 (INSEA-72)

In 1972, the USA and the erstwhile USSR entered into a legally binding agreement "on the Prevention of Incidents on and over the *High Seas*" (INSEA-72) to reduce the chances of an incident at sea between the two countries, and—in the event that one occurred—to prevent it from escalating.

Premised on the geopolitical environment prevailing in the Cold War era, INSEA-72 provided for various steps to avoid ship collisions and non-interference in the operational activities of the other force. In addition, both sides agreed to provide advance notice of three to five days of any projected actions to the contrary, establishment of communication channel between the naval attachés reciprocally assigned to diplomatic missions, and holding annual meetings to review the implementation of the agreement. See *Confidence Building Measures (CBM) Code for Unplanned Encounters at Sea (CUES)* and *De-confliction of Naval Encounters.*

Indian Bills of Lading Act, 1856

See *Carriage of Goods at Sea (Laws and Rules).*

Indian Carriage of Goods by Sea Act, 1925

See *Carriage of Goods at Sea (Laws and Rules).*

Indian Search and Rescue Region (ISRR)

See *Maritime Search and Rescue (M-SAR).*

Indian Ship Reporting System (INDSAR)

See *Maritime Search and Rescue (M-SAR).*

Indian Ocean Naval Symposium (IONS)

A voluntary grouping of maritime forces of the *Indian Ocean Region (IOR)* with a multilateral construct similar to the *West Pacific Naval Symposium (WPNS).* The IONS was launched in February 2008 based on an initiative by the Indian Navy. It seeks to increase co-operation among the countries by providing an open and inclusive forum for discussion of regionally relevant maritime issues. In the process, it endeavours to generate a flow of information between naval professionals that would lead to common understanding and possibly cooperative solutions on the way ahead.

Currently, the IONS has 22 member countries and 4 observer countries. The members are Australia, Bangladesh, France, India, Indonesia, Iran, Maldives, Mauritius, Mozambique, Myanmar, Oman, Pakistan, Saudi Arabia, Seychelles, Singapore, South Africa, Sri Lanka, Tanzania, Timor L'este, United Arab Emirates (UAE), and the United Kingdom (UK). The observers are China, Japan, Madagascar and Malaysia.

'Indian Ocean Naval Symposiums' and a 'Conclave' of the Chiefs-of-Navy are held every two years, with Chair and Secretariat being rotated. 'Preparatory Workshops' are held in the intervening years. IONS Seminars are also conducted on various occasions, sometimes in conjunction with the Symposium and the 'Preparatory Workshops'. At the 2014 'Conclave of Chiefs', the members agreed to the IONS 'Charter of Business'. The Charter lays down the objectives and principles of IONS, and defines its purpose.

Indian Ocean Region (IOR)

The region comprising the countries littoral to the Indian Ocean, including its contiguous seas like the Red Sea and the Persian Gulf (the ocean area encompassing the Indian Ocean is stipulated in the publication of the International Hydrographic Organisation (IHO) titled, 'Limits of Oceans and Seas'). Notably, France considers itself to be an IOR littoral country due to its island possessions in the region. See *Asia-Pacific Region*, *Indian Ocean Rim Association (IORA),* and *Indo-Pacific Region.*

Indian Ocean Rim Association (IORA)

Earlier known as the 'Indian Ocean Rim Association for Regional Cooperation' (IOR-ARC), it is a multilateral organisation launched in March 1997 (as 'Indian Ocean Rim Initiative') comprising the littoral countries of the Indian Ocean Region (IOR) as 'members'. The IORA is based on the principles of Open Regionalism. Its objective is to promote socio-economic and *Maritime Security* co-operation among the member countries. It current priority areas are: Maritime Safety and Security; Trade and Investment Facilitation; Fisheries Management; Disaster Risk Management; Academic, Science and Technology; and Tourism and

Cultural Exchange. In addition, it pays particular attention towards the growth of *Blue Economy*.

The IORA includes 20 member countries and 6 'dialogue partners'—China, Egypt, France, Japan, the UK and the US. The apex body of IORA is the Council of (Foreign) Ministers (COM). The meeting of the COM is preceded by the meetings of the Indian Ocean Rim Academic Group (IORAG), Indian Ocean Rim Business Forum (IORBF), Working Group on Trade and Investment (WGTI), and the Committee of Senior Officials (CSO). The Secretariat of IORA is located at Ebene, Mauritius. See *Indian Ocean Region (IOR)*.

Indian Register of Shipping (IRS)

An Indian ship classification society, founded as a non-governmental organisation (NGO) in 1975. On behalf of the Ministry of Shipping of the Indian Government, IRS establishes technical standards and formulates rules for the construction and operation of merchant vessels and offshore structures. Besides validating that construction is according to these standards, IRS undertakes regular inspections to ensure compliance with the standards. Globally, the counterparts of IRS include *Lloyd's Register* of the UK, American Bureau of Shipping (ABS) of the United States, Det Norske Veritas of Norway, Bureau Veritas (BV) of France, Nippon Kaiji Kyokai (NK) of Japan and Germanischer Lloyd (GL) of Germany.

For registration of a commercial ship in India, in accordance with the *Merchant Shipping Act, 1958*, a survey by IRS or the Mercantile Marine Department (MMD) of the *Directorate General of Shipping (DGoS)* is mandatory. Although the mandate of IRS largely pertains to commercial shipping, it has also formulated 'Rules and Regulations for Construction and Classification of Indian Naval Combatant Ships', which was released in June 2015. See *Registration of Ships*.

Indo-Pacific Region

The term 'Indo-Pacific' refers to the region stretching from the littorals of East Africa and West Asia, across the Indian Ocean and Western Pacific Ocean, to the littorals of Northeast Asia. Since circa 2010, the term is being used increasingly in the geo-political and strategic contexts. It was first used in 2007 (by the author) in a research paper titled 'Security of

Sea Lines: Prospects for India-Japan Cooperation', published in the January 2007 issue of 'Strategic Analysis' journal.

The term 'Indo-Pacific' seeks to address the lack of an objective geographic reference in the term *'Asia-Pacific' Region*. It has been averred that the new concept of 'Indo-Pacific' may lead to a change in popular "mental maps" of how the world is understood in strategic terms. Notably, since 2014, the US official discourse has incorporated the term "Indo-Asia Pacific", which would enable the USA to maintain its geographic inclusiveness and relevance in the new coinage of 'Indo-Pacific'. See *Asia-Pacific Region*, and *Indian Ocean Region (IOR)*.

INDRA (Naval Exercises)

Combined exercises between the Indian Navy and the Russian Navy. INDRA is an acronym derived from 'INDia and RussiA'. The INDRA series of bilateral exercises commenced in 2003. See *Joint and Combined*.

Information Management and Analysis Centre (IMAC)

See *National C^3I Network (NC^3IN)*.

Information Operations

See *Strategic Communication*.

Inmarsat/INMARSAT

A British satellite communications company that offers global mobile services, including telephony and data services to users worldwide, via portable or mobile terminals which communicate to ground stations through 11 geo-stationary telecommunication satellites.

The name 'Inmarsat' is sourced from 'INMARSAT', an abbreviation for the International Maritime Satellite Organisation formed in 1979 as an inter-governmental organisation to establish and operate a satellite communications network for the maritime community. It was the first international satellite organisation to be privatised. See *Global Maritime Distress and Safety System (GMDSS)* and *Maritime Satellite Communications*.

Innocent Passage

Innocent passage entitles a foreign warship to traverse a coastal State's *Territorial Waters* 'continuously and expeditiously'. This tenet of international law is codified in the *UNCLOS*, and is based on the principle of *Freedom of the Seas*. The passage is innocent as long as it is not prejudicial to the peace, good order or security of the coastal or island state. Foreign submarines are required to navigate on the surface and to show their flag. The coastal State can temporarily suspend innocent passage in specific areas for security reasons.

In Indian *Territorial Waters*, all foreign ships other than warships (including submarines) enjoy the right of innocent passage. Warships may enter/pass through the *Territorial Waters* after 'prior notification'. However, owing to security considerations, the entry of all or a specific type of foreign vessels may be disallowed or circumscribed, which is notified in the Indian Official Gazette.

Notably, some countries—mostly major maritime powers—do not insist on any notification or authorisation for a foreign warship to exercise its right of innocent passage through its *Territorial Waters*. During *UNCLOS* negotiations, all countries in South Asia—including India—opted for 'prior authorisation' for innocent passage. India later changed its stance to only 'prior notification', while the other countries have continued to insist on 'prior authorisation'. See *International Waters*.

INSPIRES (Position Reporting System)

Indian Ship Position and Information Reporting System (INSPIRES) is a ship position reporting system coordinated by the Indian Navy for enhancing *Maritime Domain Awareness (MDA)*. All ships above 100 *Gross Tonnage (GT)* operating in the Arabian Sea and Bay of Bengal are encouraged to report their identity and movements to Indian naval authorities on a voluntary basis. See *Coastal Surveillance Network (CSN)*, *Indian Maritime Search and Rescue (INDSAR)*, *ISLEREP*, *National Command Control Communication and Intelligence Network (NC³IN)*, and *White Shipping Information*.

Intelligence

A branch of military discipline that exploits a number of information-collection and information-analyses approaches to provide guidance and direction to commanders to support their decision-making, either for planning or execution of military operations. This is achieved through an assessment of available data from a wide range of sources. Intelligence includes Technical Intelligence (TECHINT), Signal Intelligence (SIGINT) and Human Intelligence (HUMINT). TECHINT refers to intelligence on the material capacity of foreign military forces. At the *national-strategic* level, TECHINT is usually referred to by the related term 'Scientific and Technical Intelligence'. In context of maritime-military operations, Intelligence is a critical enabler for *Maritime Domain Awareness (MDA)*. See *Electronic Warfare (EW)*.

Inter-Continental Ballistic Missiles (ICBM)

See *Ballistic and Cruise Missiles.*

Intergovernmental Panel on Climate Change (IPCC)

A scientific inter-governmental body established in 1988 by the UN's World Meterological Organisation (WMO) and the United Nations Environmental Programme (UNEP) to support the 1992 *United Nations Framework Convention on Climate Change (UNFCCC)*. At present, the panel has 195 member countries. The IPCC work program is decided upon at its plenary meetings, wherein the member governments participate.

The IPCC produces reports that help to understand the scientific basis of the risk of climate change induced by human activity. It provides the related technical and socio-economic information on the impact of climate change and the response options, including adaptation and migration. These reports are based on research by external experts and scientists, and are discussed and approved by member countries during the review meetings. See *Kyoto Protocol 1997*, *Lilypad*, and *Treaties for Protection of Ozone Layer*.

Intermediate Range Ballistic Missiles (IRBM)

See *Ballistic and Cruise Missiles.*

Internal Waters

Internal waters lie landward of the *Maritime Baseline* of a coastal State, except in case of an archipelagic State. It may include lakes, rivers, lagoons, some bays, harbours and canals. Within its *Archipelagic Waters*, the archipelagic State may draw baselines only across the mouth of rivers, bays and ports for the delimitation of internal waters. Since these waters have the same legal character as the land territory and super-adjacent airspace, national laws can be constructed by a State that would empower it to interdict a vessel within its internal waters. Foreign vessels have no right of passage within internal waters. See *Territorial Waters*.

International Airspace

In contrast to the term *National Airspace*, it is the airspace over the *Contiguous Zone*, the *Exclusive Economic Zone*, the *High Seas*, and territories not subject to national sovereignty.

International Arbitration

International *Arbitration* is a method for settlement of a dispute between two countries arising from international commercial agreements and other inter-state transactions through an arbitral tribunal (or *Arbitration* tribunal). In the Indian context, international commercial arbitration is governed by the '*Arbitration* and Conciliation Act, 1996' (the Act also governs arbitration between Indian parties). It is based on the 'Model Law on International Commercial *Arbitration*' adopted by the United Nations Commission on International Trade Law (UNCITRAL) in 1985.

The *UNCLOS*, 1982 also provides for international *Arbitration* to settle disputes concerning the interpretation or application of the Convention. Besides the *International Tribunal for the Law of the Sea (ITLOS)*—located at Montego Bay, Jamaica—provided for by *UNCLOS* Annex VI, Annex VII provides for *Arbitration* through other tribunals, such as the *Permanent Court of Arbitration (PCA)* located at The Hague, Netherlands.

International Armed Conflicts (IAC)

In terms of *International Humanitarian Law* (IHL), armed conflicts are divided into International Armed Conflicts (IAC) and *Non-International Armed Conflicts (NIAC)*. The former relates to inter-State conflicts, which have traditionally been more frequent necessitating greater global attention in terms of preventing them and their adverse effects on humanity. Hence, the *Law of Armed Conflict (LOAC)*—including those codified in *Hague Conventions*, 1907 and *Geneva Conventions, 1949*—were originally developed in the context of war between States. See *International Criminal Court (ICC)*.

International Atomic Energy Agency (IAEA)

See *Nuclear Non-Proliferation Treaty (NPT)* and *Zangger Committee.*

International Bargaining Forum (IBF)

A term related to the global commercial shipping industry. Formed in 2003, IBF serves as a platform for biennial negotiations between shipping employers and seafarers. The former group comprising *ship-owners* and manning agents is represented by the Joint Negotiating Group (JNG). The seafarers are represented by the *International Transport Workers' Federation (ITF)*. The JNG comprises the *International Maritime Employers' Committee (IMEC)* and a couple of similar organisations at the national level. As part of the Collective Bargaining Agreement (CBA), the IBF 'Framework Total Crew Cost (TCC) Agreement' formulates the 'baseline' entitlements for seafarers in social, professional and financial terms.

International Chamber of Shipping (ICS)

The principal trade association for the global shipping industry, representing *ship-owners* and *ship-operators* in all sectors and trades. Established in 1921, it aims to promote the interests of *ship-owners* and *ship-operators* in all matters of shipping policy and ship operations, and deals with all technical, legal, employment and policy issues relating to international shipping. ICS membership comprises various national ship-owners' associations across Asia, Europe and the Americas, whose member shipping companies operate over 80 per cent of the world's merchant fleet. ICS represents the *ship-owners* at the *International Maritime Organisation (IMO)*. See (Anti-Piracy) *Best Management Practices (BMP)*, and *Piracy High Risk area (HRA)*.

International Civil Aviation Organisation (ICAO)

See *Flight Information Region (FIR).*

International Criminal Court (ICC)

A permanent court established by the 'Statute of the International Criminal Court' (ICC), 1998—also called the Rome Statute—which entered into force in July 2002. The mandate of ICC is to probe and prosecute individuals accused of the most serious violations of

International Humanitarian Law (IHL) and *Human Rights Law (HR Law)*, such as *War Crimes, Crimes against Humanity and Genocide.* Unlike the International Court of Justice (ICJ), whose jurisdiction is restricted to States, the ICC considers criminal cases against individuals. The establishment of the ICC was catalysed by the special international tribunals that were set up to try IHL and HR Law offences committed in the Former Yugoslavia (1991) and Rwanda (1994). Unlike these special tribunals, the jurisdiction of ICC is not situation-specific and is not retroactive. The ICC is located in The Hague, Netherlands.

The ICC could establish jurisdiction over an alleged crime if it is committed in the territory or by national of a country that is party to the ICC Statute, 1998. The ICC may also establish jurisdiction if a country that is not a party to the Statute accepts such jurisdiction. India is not a party to the ICC Statute. See *International Armed Conflicts (IAC)* and *Non-International Armed Conflicts (NIAC).*

International Financial Institution (IFI)

A financial institution that has been established through an agreement involving more than one country. IFIs are major sources of financial and technical support for developing countries. The common goal of these institutions is to promote economic and social progress in developing countries by helping raise standards of living and productivity to the point of which development becomes self-sustaining. The major shareholders of IFIs are national governments. Most IFIs follow a weighted voting system where votes are distributed in proportion with members' capital subscriptions. Hence, the amount of share-holding capital contributed by a country in an IFI translates into the leverage it possesses in its policy formulation.

The best known IFIs are the Bretton Woods Institutions like the *World Bank* and the *International Monetary Fund (IMF)* that were established after the Second World War to assist in the reconstruction of Europe and provide mechanisms for international cooperation in managing the global financial system. Among the other IFIs are regional development banks—such as the *Asian Development Bank (ADB)*, the *Asian Infrastructure Investment Bank (AIIB)* and the European Investment Bank (EIB)—and bilateral development banks, set up by one country to finance development projects in another (usually a developing) country and its emerging market.

International Humanitarian Law (IHL)

A set of rules which seek, for humanitarian reasons, to place limits on the conduct and effects of *War and Armed Conflict* by balancing 'military necessity' and 'humanity'. It protects persons who are not or are no longer participating in the hostilities by restricting the means and methods of warfare. The edifice of IHL rests on a set of five 'pillars', viz. military necessity, distinction, proportionality, unnecessary suffering and reciprocity. Another important purpose of IHL is to provide immunity from prosecution to combatants who adhere to it. IHL is sometimes synonymously referred to as the *Law of Armed Conflict (LOAC)*. However, the scope of IHL is much broader than LOAC as it covers obligations *beyond International Armed Conflicts (IAC)*—such as the treatment of Prisoners of War (PoW)—and includes *Non-International Armed Conflicts (NIAC)*.

IHL is derived from *Hague Conventions, 1907* (which bear the have the status of *Customary International Law*) and *Geneva Conventions, 1949*. The *Hague Conventions, 1907*, are concerned essentially with the actual conduct of military operations including the methods and means of combat. It is essentially based on the principle that the right of the parties to a conflict to choose the methods and means of warfare is not unlimited. The *Geneva Conventions, 1949*, on the other hand is concerned with the protection of persons not involved in a conflict such as civilians, prisoners of war, and the sick and wounded. It is essentially based on the principle that persons rendered 'hors de combat' (out of combat) and those not directly participating in hostilities shall be respected, protected and treated humanely.

The latest codification of the Law for maritime warfare is contained in the 'San Remo Manual on International Law Applicable to Armed Conflicts at Sea', 12 Jun 94. Published by the 'International Institute of Humanitarian Law', the manual is a contemporary restatement of IHL, and takes into its fold the technological developments in naval warfare since the authoritative Hague and Geneva Conventions came into being. It also incorporates the proviso of the UN Charter and conventional State practices with regard to these issues. While most of it covers the currently applicable law, it also contains some aspects of legal evolution. The San Remo Manual, prepared jointly by naval practitioners and legal experts, does not wield legal authority, but nonetheless serves as a useful operationally relevant guide. See *International Criminal Court (ICC)* and *Human Rights Law*.

International Maritime Boundary Line (IMBL)

The limits of a country's promulgated maritime zones, over which it exercises *Sovereign Jurisdiction*. In case of geographically adjacent or opposite countries, the IMBL needs to be delineated (through a treaty) based on the principles contained in *UNCLOS* (or *Customary International Law* in case a country is not party to *UNCLOS*). India has delineated its IMBL with all its maritime neighbours, except Pakistan. Notably, India shares maritime boundaries with more countries than those with which it shares land borders. It has six land neighbours, but seven maritime neighbours (Pakistan, Maldives, Sri Lanka, Bangladesh, Myanmar, Thailand and Indonesia). When India's *Continental Shelf* claim is accepted, Oman may become India's eighth maritime neighbor.

International Maritime Bureau (IMB)

A specialised division of the 'International Chamber of Commerce' (ICC), the world's largest non-governmental business organisation. The IMB is one of the three divisions of the Commercial Crime Services (CCS) arm of the ICC. It was established in 1981 to enhance the security of international sea trade through identification, investigation and information exchange against all types of maritime crime and malpractice. One of the IMB's focal areas is the suppression of *Piracy*, which led to the creation of the IMB Piracy Reporting Centre (PRC) in 1992, which provides updated information to merchant mariners about pirate activity world-wide. See *MALSINDO*, *Maritime Crime* and *Private Maritime Security Companies (PMSC)*.

International Maritime Employers' Committee (IMEC)

An employers' organisation pertaining to the global commercial shipping industry. Based in London, the IMEC represents over 130 companies located all over the world that operate over 7,500 ships and employ over 185,000 seafarers of all nationalities. The IMEC works with employers mainly on issues relating to the seafarers' pay rate, employment conditions, and recruitment and training. Its genesis lies in the London Committee of Asian Seamen set up in 1940 by *ship-owners* employing seafarers from the Indian sub-continent. It was re-branded in 1992 as IMEC and commenced bargaining with the *International Transport Workers' Federation (ITF)* in 1998.

International Maritime Organisation (IMO)

A specialised agency of the United Nations responsible for safety and security of shipping and the prevention of *Marine Pollution* by ships. (Its motto is "Safe Ships and Clean Seas"). IMO maintains a comprehensive regulatory framework for shipping. Its mandate includes safety, environmental concerns, legal matters, technical co-operation, *Maritime Security* and the efficiency of shipping. Nearly all UN member States are also members of the IMO, with the few exceptions being land-locked States. IMO is governed by an Assembly of members, and its work is conducted through five committees. It functions through a permanent secretariat in London (UK) headed by a Secretary-General, who is periodically elected by the Assembly. The Secretarial comprises various divisions such as those for marine safety and environmental protection. See *MARPOL 73/78*, *Particularly Sensitive Sea Area (PSSA)*, and various maritime-related treaties/conventions in this Compendium.

International Mobile Satellite Organisation (IMSO)

An inter-governmental body established to ensure that *Inmarsat* continues to meet its public service obligations, including obligations relating to the *Global Maritime Distress and Safety System (GMDSS)*. Headquartered in London, it has about 100 member States. It aims to guarantee that services are provided by *Inmarsat* free from any discrimination and in a peaceful way to all persons living or working in locations that are inaccessible to conventional, terrestrial means of communication. It also ensures that the principles of fair competition are observed. See *Maritime Satellite Communications.*

International Monetary Fund (IMF)

An *International Financial Institution (IFI)*, borne out of the Bretton Woods Conference in 1944, as a supervisory institution for coordinating the efforts of member countries to achieve greater cooperation in the formulation of economic policies. The IMF's primary role is to foster monetary cooperation among member countries for global financial stability. It helps to promote exchange stability and orderly exchange relations among its members. The IMF also maintains and analyses statistics relating to the economies of its member to suggest improvements. It presently has 188 member countries. The US holds the maximum shareholding. The IMF is headquartered in Washington DC. See *World Bank*.

International Seabed Authority (ISA)

In consonance with the principle of '*Common Heritage of Mankind*', *UNCLOS*, 1982 creates an innovative legal regime for controlling mineral resource exploitation in deep seabed areas beyond national jurisdiction, which underlie most of the world's oceans. Part XI of *UNCLOS* has established the International Seabed Authority (ISA) as an inter-governmental body based in Kingston, Jamaica. The *UNCLOS* defines the international seabed area under ISA jurisdiction as "the seabed and ocean floor and the subsoil thereof, beyond the limits of national jurisdiction". The ISA is mandated to regulate seabed exploration and *Seabed Mining* in these areas. The ISA operates by contracting with private and public corporations and other entities, authorising them to explore, and eventually exploit, specified areas on the deep seabed for mineral resources. See *Global Commons*.

International Ship and Port Security (ISPS) Code

It is essentially an amendment to the *Safety of Life at Sea (SOLAS) Convention, 1974/1988* on minimum security arrangements for ships, ports and government agencies. Having come into force in 2004, it prescribes responsibilities to governments, shipping companies, shipboard personnel, and port/facility personnel to detect security threats and take preventative measures against security incidents affecting ships or port facilities used in international trade. It includes the installation of 'Ship Security Alert System' (SSAS) installed onboard ships in conjunction with *Inmarsat* equipment for satellite-based communications. Besides routine reports made to the ship's administrative authority and the concerned Maritime Rescue Coordination Centre (MRCC), the ship's SSAS beacon can be activated in case of emergencies like a pirate attack.

Among the provisions of ISPS Code is the mandatory requirement of *Pre-Arrival Notification* (*PAN*), sometimes referred to as Pre-Arrival

Notification of Security (PANS). In India, the *Directorate General of Shipping (DGoS)* of the Ministry of Shipping periodically issues guidance on ISPS compliance for vessels for entry into Indian ports. As per the prevailing guidelines, the masters of ships, *ship-owners, ship-operators* and ship agents are required to submit the information contained in their *Pre-Arrival Notification (PAN)* also to the Indian Navy and Indian Coast Guard. See *Maritime Search and Rescue (M-SAR).*

International Shipping Lanes (ISL)

Those shipping routes that are normally traversed by merchant shipping, whilst transiting from one point to another. These routes are determined by a variety of factors, primarily geography, navigational ease and safety, and minimisation of sailing distance for commercial profitability. 'Security' is not a factor in determination of these fixed routes. For example, if a pirate attacks increase in a sea area enclosing an ISL, the ISL does not change. The merchant ships plying the ISL either take appropriate anti-piracy precautions or use an alternative ISL. ISL differs from SLOC, which bears a military-strategic connotation. See *Piracy* and *Best Management Practices (BMP).* See *Sea Lines of Communication (SLOC).*

International Straits

Maritime choke-points overlapped by *Territorial Waters* that connect two segregated parts of *International Waters.* In these 'straits used for international navigation', *UNCLOS* bestows all ships and aircraft the right of 'Transit Passage', which implies that these platforms enjoy the freedom of navigation and overflight for the purpose of transit in their *normal modes* of operation. The term 'normal mode' indicates, for example, that a submarine may undertake the passage in dived mode, or warships may stream in formation, or launch/recover aircraft. *UNCLOS* restricts the authority of coastal state to both regulate such transit and intervene by stating that the passage for vessels" shall not be impeded (and) there shall be no suspension of transit passage". This tenet of international law codified in the *UNCLOS* is passed upon the principle of *Freedom of the Seas.* See *Innocent Passage.*

International Transport Workers' Federation (ITF)

A global trade union federation of transport workers' unions based in London. The federation comprises about 700 unions in 150 countries, encompassing merchant shipping, fisheries, inland navigation, road, rail, civil aviation and tourism services. In the shipping domain, the ITF seeks to protect the interests and rights of seafarers through regulation of the shipping industry. The federation engages in mitigating risks of *Piracy*, abandonment, non-payment of wages, and unsafe and poorly maintained vessels. It negotiates with the maritime employers forming the Joint Negotiating Group (JNG) at the *International Bargaining Forum (IBF)* on issues such as the *Piracy High Risk Area (HRA)*. The JNG is composed of inter alia the *International Maritime Employers' Committee (IMEC)* and a couple of similar organisations at the national level.

International Tribunal for the Law of the Sea (ITLOS)

See *International Arbitration*.

International Underwriting Association (IUA)

See *Joint War Committee (JWC)*, *Lloyd's Register and Lloyd's of London*, *P&I (Protection and Indemnity) Clubs*, *Underwriting*, and *War Risk Insurance*.

International Waters

All ocean areas not subject to the sovereignty of a nation. All waters seaward from the *Territorial Waters* are international waters in which *High Seas* freedoms of navigation and overflight are reserved to the international community. International waters include *Contiguous Zones*, *Exclusive Economic Zones (EEZ)*, and the *High Seas*. This tenet of international law is codified in *UNCLOS*, and is based upon the principle of *Freedom of the Seas*. See *Innocent Passage* and *Transit Passage*.

Interoperability

The ability of making systems and organisations work together (inter-operate). The term originated in context of information technology or systems engineering to allow for information-exchange. In the military context, interoperability is defined by the *North Atlantic Treaty Organisation (NATO)* as the ability of the forces of two or more nations to train, exercise and operate effectively together in the execution of assigned missions and tasks. At the strategic level, interoperability among defence forces of various countries seeks to harmonise their world views, *Strategies*, *Doctrines*, and force structures, and thus enables coalition building. Interoperability at the operational and tactical levels may also be referred to by the terms 'Operational Compatibility' and 'Tactical Compatibility'. Such compatibility flows from the fungibility or inter-changeability of force elements and units, and is driven by technological parity. A high level of 'tactical and operational compatibility' could lead to *Co-operative Engagement Capability* (CEC).

ISLEREP (Position Reporting System)

Island Reporting (ISLEREP) is a ship position reporting system coordinated by the Indian Coast Guard for enhancing *Maritime Domain Awareness (MDA)*. Based on voice communications, it is used voluntarily by all vessels closing within 20 *nautical miles* of India's island territories, viz. the Andaman and Nicobar, and Lakshadweep groups of islands. See *Coastal Surveillance Network (CSN)*, *INSPIRES*, *National Command Control Communication and Intelligence Network (NC³IN)*, and *White Shipping Information.*

J

JIMEX (Naval Exercises)

Japan-India Maritime Exercise (JIMEX). *Combined* naval exercises between the Indian Navy and the Japan Maritime Self-Defence Force (JMSDF). Although the two forces have been exercising together since 2007 under the *Malabar* series along with the US Navy, JIMEX was institutionalised at the bilateral level only in 2012. See *Joint and Combined.*

Joint and Combined

The term 'joint' is often incorrectly used where the term 'combined' is more appropriate. An example is, "India-US *Malabar* 'joint' (incorrectly used) naval exercises". The term 'joint' connotes operations, other activities (like exercises) and organisations, in which elements of two or more military services of the same country participate. In contrast, the term 'combined' refers to activities and organisations (only in case of military alliances) involving the military forces of more than one country. Hence, the correct phrase would be "India-US *Malabar* 'combined' naval exercises".

Joint Exercises and Operations

See *Joint and Combined.*

Joint War Committee (JWC)

It comprises members from both the Lloyd's Market Association of London and International *Underwriting* Association of London (IUA)—an entity that represents companies that trade in the London insurance market outside Lloyd's. It usually meets every quarter to assess the insurance risks for *War Risk Insurance* and issues circulars on "Listed Areas (for) Hull War, *Piracy*, *Terrorism* and Related Perils" (commonly referred to as "*War Risk Zones*") and the related "navigation limitations". See *Lloyd's Register and Lloyd's of London*, and *P&I (Protection and Indemnity) Clubs.*

Jus Ad Bellum

A Latin word for 'right to war', it refers to the right of countries to use armed force in international relations. The same is codified in the Charter of the United Nations. It essentially says that while countries must use peaceful means to settle their disputes, and shall refrain threat or use of force, they have the right of "individual or collective self-defence", if they are subjected to an armed attack (Article 51). The Constitution of India (Article 355) reflects the spirit of this provision, and may be traced back to Kautilya's 'Arthashastra' (322-298 BC), which conceptualised the justification for war and described in detail the various conditions and rationale for going to war.

However, the interpretation of UN Charter goes further. Where an attack is deemed imminent, its Article 51 may be interpreted to include 'anticipatory self-defence', a principle that emerges from *Customary International Law*, and permits pre-emptive actions in such circumstances. This legitimises the use of 'pre-emptive' force by countries to defend own territory, forces and nationals in various conditions. The US attack on Afghanistan-based Taliban in 2001 (Operation 'Enduring Freedom') is an example of 'anticipatory self-defence'.

Notably however, while international law permits 'anticipatory self-defence', it does not subscribe to 'preventive self-defence'. The notable examples of 'prevention' include the 1981 Israeli attack on Iraqi nuclear reactor at Osirak and the 1986 US air and naval strikes on Tripoli, which, as claimed by the US, were "to deter acts of *Terrorism* by Libya". Furthermore, international law does not permit the use of armed force in 'retaliation'. See *Jus in Bello*.

Jus in Bello

A Latin word, which addresses the imperative of a war being conducted justly (regardless of whether the initiation of hostilities was just). Hence, irrespective of whether the use of force is legally justifiable in any specific case, the principle beckons that international law must regulate the 'manner' in which the armed conflict is conducted. Such conduct of hostilities is, therefore, circumscribed by *International Humanitarian Law* (IHL). Essentially, it intends to place limits on the conduct of hostilities by balancing 'military necessity' and 'humanity'.

K

Knot

A unit of speed equal to one *Nautical Mile* (1852 metres) per hour. The ISO standard symbol for the knot is 'kn' (The symbol 'kt' was a common usage until the 1980s). The knot is used worldwide in maritime and air navigation, and also in meteorology. This nomenclature dates back to the days of sailing vessels, when sailors tossed a log attached to a rope knotted at regular intervals off the stern of a moving ship. (See *Ship Directions*) Sailors counted the number of knots that passed through their hands in a given time to determine the ship's speed.

Konkan (Naval Exercises)

Combined naval exercises between the Indian Navy and the Royal Navy of the United Kingdom (UK). The 'Konkan' series of bilateral exercise commenced in 2004. See *Joint and Combined.*

Kyoto Protocol, 1997

An international treaty that extends the 1992 *United Nations Framework Convention on Climate Change (UNFCCC)* committing state parties to fight global warming and attendant climate change by reducing greenhouse gas emissions. Kyoto Protocol was adopted in Kyoto (Japan) in 1997 and entered into force in 2005. The Protocol is based on the principle of common but differentiated responsibilities. It is binding only on developed countries that are historically responsible for the current levels of greenhouse gases in the atmosphere. The Protocol lists the greenhouse gases ranging from CO_2 to even the non-ozone depleting hydrofluorocarbons (HFC) used as refrigerant in air-conditioners and refrigerators (as a replacement for ozone-depleting chlorofluorocarbons or CFC regulated by the 'Montreal Protocol', 1987). There are currently 192 state parties, mostly comprising the developed countries. Notably, the United States has not ratified the Protocol.

The Protocol's first commitment period started in 2008 and ended in 2012. A second commitment period was proposed in 2012, known as the Doha Amendment, in which 37 countries (mostly mostly comprising the developed countries of Europe) have binding targets. Since 2014, negotiations are going on to agree on a post-Kyoto legal framework that would obligate all major polluters to pay for CO_2 emissions. China, India and the United States have indicated that they will not ratify any treaty that will commit them legally to reduce CO_2 emissions. See *Treaties for Protection of Ozone Layer*. See *Intergovernmental Panel on Climate Change (IPCC)* and *Lilypad.*

L

Land Attack

Among the options available for a navy to influence the outcome of a continental war is 'Land Attack'. The concept is also relevant for short-of-war scenarios such as those necessitating *Compellance, and Deterrence by Punishment.* A *Land Attack Cruise Missile (LACM)* is the key enabler of this concept. See *SLOC Interdiction* and *Amphibious Operation.*

Land Attack Cruise Missile (LACM)

LACM guidance usually occurs in three phases: launch, midcourse, and terminal. During the launch phase, a missile is guided using only the inertial navigation system (INS). In the midcourse phase, a missile is guided by the INS, updated by one or the following systems: a radar-based Terrain Contour Matching (TERCOM) system, a radar or optical system for Scene Area Correlation (SAC) and or a satellite navigation system, such as the US Global Positioning System (GPS) or the Russian Global Navigation Satellite System (GLONASS). The terminal guidance phase begins when a missile enters the target area and uses either more accurate TERCOM data or a terminal seeker, which is usually an optical or radar-based sensor. At present, very few countries possess such technology to develop LACMs with the capability of reasonably accurate targeting. LACMs can be launched from aircraft, ships or submarines. Submarines are armed with Tube-Launched Land Attack Missiles (TLAM). See *Cruise Missile* and *Precision Strike.*

Landing Craft Air Cushion (LCAC)

See *Amphibious Ships.*

Landing Ships (LCU/LST/LPD/LHD)

See *Amphibious Ships.*

Land Reclamation

It is estimated that about half the world's humankind lives in the relatively narrow coastal strip of land about 200 kilometers wide. The growth of world's population is stretching the available land resource in this part of the *Littoral* for housing, industry and recreation, among others. Hitherto, 'horizontal' expansion was not feasible, which led to 'vertical' expansion in terms of high-rise buildings. But this led to congestion and increasing stresses on public services. This led to the concept of land reclamation, which is being offered by the mushrooming dredging companies. This concept has attracted much attention of countries that are threatened by sea-level rise due to climate change. Maldives is an apt example.

See *Intergovernmental Panel on Climate Change (IPCC)*, *Kyoto Protocol 1997*, *Lilypad*, *Littoral* and *United Nations Framework Convention on Climate Change (UNFCCC).*

Law of Armed Conflict (LOAC)

See *International Humanitarian Law* (IHL).

Legal Continental Shelf (LCS)

See *Continental Shelf and Legal Continental Shelf (LCS).*

Levels of Warfare

There are four levels addressed by national and military leadership for planning and execution of warfare, including terms of the application of national resources. These are: National-Strategic, Military-Strategic, Operational and Tactical levels of war.

In India, decisions at the National-Strategic level is taken by the country's political executive through the Cabinet Committee on Security (CCS), with inputs from the National Security Council, *Intelligence* agencies, various government ministries and the Armed Forces. At this level, all resources of the nation (diplomatic, military, economic, information, technological, etc.) are directed towards attainment of national security objectives.

At the Military-Strategic level, the national military leadership, through the Chiefs of Staff Committee (COSC), determines the manner of employment of military power in accordance with the national strategic decisions, to achieve the military-strategic objectives required to achieve the political aims of the war.

The Operational level is directed by the Commanders-in-Chief of geographic theatre commands, which may be either single service or joint. The orchestration of military activities at this level is termed as 'Operational Art', which provides the link between the setting of military-strategic objectives and the tactical employment of forces.

The maritime activities at the Tactical level are orchestrated by the Fleet Commander in conjunction with other commanders, notably those directing the submarine forces or those responsible for local naval defence. The role of the Tactical commander is to ensure the most effective employment of units under his command towards accomplishment of operational objectives. See *National Strategy* and *Joint and Combined.*

Lighter Aboard Ship (LASH)

A merchant ship that carries barges loaded with cargo. The barges are towed or lifted onto the mother-ship. After the ocean passage, the barges are offloaded at the destination. The concept was developed to obviate the need for specialised port infrastructure or to pay for the *Transhipment* costs. See *Sea Barge (SeeBee) Ships.*

Lilypad

A concept of naval operations, wherein an aviation capable warship at sea is used by an aircraft (usually a helicopter) as a staging platform. The objective is to enhance the endurance of the aircraft for it to undertake distant operations, or an otherwise enduring mission, such as *Maritime Search and Rescue (M-SAR)* or *Mine Counter Measures (MCM).* Large *Amphibious Ships* like 'Landing Platform Dock' (LPD) and 'Landing Helicopter Dock' (LHD) are particularly suited for Lilypad operations. See *Amphibious Aircraft.*

The concept is also relevant to the reorientation of United States' military basing strategy, which began in 2001. In this context, 'Lilypad' refers to relatively smaller and more flexible 'forward operating bases' that are small, low-cost, secretive, inaccessible and 'small-footprint' facilities with limited numbers of troops, spartan amenities, and prepositioned weaponry and supplies.

'Lilypad' is also a name (derived from a water lily variant) given to the innovative futuristic concept of 'floating city'. The aim is to provide sustainable, alternate living environments in response to the threat of sea-level rise due to global warming. The blueprint of the 'Lilypad' floating city was demonstrated in 2008 before a panel of experts during the Oceans Symposium. Each 'Lilypad' is meant to be self-contained module providing comfortable housing for about 50,000 people. It is designed to be constantly in motion along with the ocean currents, though sited in close proximity of the coast. In this context, Lilypad supplements the emerging concept of *Land Reclamation*. See *Intergovernmental Panel on Climate Change (IPCC)*, *Kyoto Protocol 1997*, *Land Reclamation* and *United Nations Framework Convention on Climate Change (UNFCCC)*.

Limited War

A *War or Armed Conflict* fought for a limited political aim, with corresponding limitations on its scale and duration. In contrast to the aims of a 'total war', which generally include complete destruction of the enemy's military forces and its government, the aims of a Limited War fall short of total victory and unconditional surrender. The term is also applied in context of a war limited in geographical extent. Usually, in a Limited War, the limits of 'purpose' and 'geographical extent' co-exist.

Due to various reasons, present-day wars are usually limited ones. The higher risk of a war escalating beyond the nuclear threshold is among the reasons. Another one is the rationale to prevent 'horizontal escalation' in terms of involving other countries, particularly the allies of warring countries. At times, the preservation of *Balance of Power* may be an objective of war. Even in this case, a Limited War presents an alternative. Without resorting to an all-out nuclear war, or even seeking to destruct the enemy's government or its military forces, a limited war aims only to compel the adversary to 'accommodate' own critical 'non-negotiable' interests. The 'winner' must, therefore, forego a total victory, so that the 'loser' is not compelled to escalate the conflict by, for example, resorting to nuclear strikes or calling its friends to intervene. The India-Pakistan Kargil conflict is an example of a Limited War and the accompanying *Escalation* dynamics.

Line of Credit

A promise to provide loan to a government, business or an individual at a subsidised interest rate. It is effectively a source of funds that can readily be tapped at the borrower's discretion. The interest is paid only on money actually withdrawn. In government-to-government dealings, the loan is usually conditional on the recipient country using the loan amount to buy goods and services from the entities in the loan providing country. India provides lines of credit to friendly governments through the Export-Import (EXIM) Bank of India. See *Foreign Trade.*

Liquefied Natural Gas (LNG)

Natural gas—predominantly methane (CH_4)—is the third major energy source transported by sea, after crude-oil and coal. It is an environmentally friendly hydrocarbon fuel, which is converted to liquid form for ease of storage or transportation. In its liquefied form, natural gas takes up only about 1/600th of the volume in the gaseous state. Natural gas liquefies at a temperature of about minus 259 degrees Fahrenheit (minus 160 degrees Celsius) at atmospheric pressure. For transportation onboard *LNG Carriers*, it is liquefied at a shore-based liquefaction plant by reducing its temperature of about minus 2,850 degrees Fahrenheit. The liquefaction process involves removal of certain components, such as dust, acid gases, helium, water, and heavy hydrocarbons, so that the downstream product is more pure.

During transportation on a *LNG Carrier*, LNG is hazardous only to the extent of being inflammable to a limited extent—when mixed with air it is only flammable if its proportion is between 5 and 15 percent. If the proportion is less than 5 per cent, there is insufficient gas to burn. More than 15 per cent, there is too much gas and hence, not enough oxygen for it to burn. Hence, contrary to the widespread perception until a few years ago, LNG is not explosive. In the event of a spillage of LNG on water, it would merely vapourise and dissipate into the atmosphere, leaving behind no slick or residue. It is odourless, colourless, non-toxic and non-corrosive. At the destination, it is re-gassified in a *LNG Terminal.* One cubic foot of LNG expands to about 600 cubic feet of gas at atmospheric pressure.

Liquefied Natural Gas (LNG) Carrier

The transportation of *Liquefied Natural Gas (LNG)* is the most rapidly growing shipping activities. A LNG carrier—also called LNG tanker—is the most specialised of all commercial ship types. Since, LNG must be cooled to a temperature below minus 160 degrees Celsius, the refrigerated tanks of a LNG carrier are constructed of a special aluminum alloy, and segregated from the hull with the use of heavy insulation. Since the ship has no refrigeration capacity to that extent, its tanks are so well insulated that they can keep the natural gas liquefied during the entire sea transit. A typical LNG carrier has four to six such tanks located along the centre-line of the vessel.

LNG carriers began commercial operations in the early-1960s. Since then, LNG carriers have been evolving, primarily in terms of their capacity and design. Until 2006, the capacity of the largest carrier was 135,000 cubic metres. Since then, ships of over 250,000 cubic metres began to be built, particularly for new LNG exports from Qatar.

Also, in the last fifteen years, two main types of LNG carriers have been built. The older ships are based on independent spherical tanks (consisting of an insulated single wall spherical tank, supported by a vertically built skirt. The skirt is connected with the tank around the periphery of the equator). The newer ships are membrane-type LNG carriers (a tank design wherein the LNG is contained by a thin stainless steel or nickel alloy flexible membrane). Until 2000, 54 per cent of all LNG carriers were spherical, primarily because Japan—the largest shipbuilder and also the largest LNG importer—had a license for the construction of such carriers. Lately, membrane-type carriers have surpassed these. India is also seeking to build LNG carriers. A notable aspect is the compatibility of the type of LNG carrier with the *LNG Terminal.* For example, most *LNG Terminals* located in the Russian polar region are compatible with carriers with spherical tanks. See *Polar Code.*

Liquefied Natural Gas (LNG) Terminal

A structure for storage of *Liquefied Natural Gas (LNG)*, its liquefaction, or re-gasification (when brought in by *LNG Carriers*). These LNG terminals are of two types—liquefaction terminals (for LNG exports) and re-gasification terminals or receiving terminals (for LNG imports). The terminal comprises special facilities and equipment, storage tanks, port infrastructure and pipelines. Given India's growing LNG demand, LNG liquefaction terminals are necessary. The first two LNG terminals in India were built in Dahej (Gujarat) and Kochi (Kerela).

A new concept is the 'Floating Storage and Re-gasification Unit' (FSRU), which is a LNG terminal whose main structure is a special ship that is moored close to the port of the importing country. As compared to an onshore LNG terminal, setting up of a FSRU is more cost-effective. Its costs less than half of an onshore facility, and can be commissioned within two to three years, against the land-based terminal that could take as much as seven years. Resort to FSRU also eliminates the land acquisition and port management costs, besides being more environment-friendly.

India is studying a proposal to set up a FSRU that would be moored off Karnataka coast in 40 metre water depth, which can process one billion cubic feet (bcf) of gas per day, holding a storage capacity of 330,000 cubic metres of LNG onshore and the same capacity offshore.

Littoral

It is estimated that about half the world's human population lives in a coastal strip that is only 200 kilometers (120 miles) wide, and are engaged in commercial activity like shipping, port operations, fishing, oil and gas exploration, marine tourism, and so on. This zone is often referred to as the 'littoral'. Furthermore, being a geographical interface between the international medium and national space, the littoral is also used by countries for maritime *Power Projection* overseas, and even by non-state elements involved in *Maritime Crime* or *Maritime Terrorism*. There is no universally accepted dimension of sea-land stretch across the coastline constituting the littoral since it depends upon the 'context' and 'capability'. For example, although Afghanistan is a land-locked country that lies more than 500 kilometers away from sea, the Tomahawk *Land Attack Cruise Missile* (LACM) strikes by the US naval forces against the Taliban in 2001 (Operation Enduring Freedom) turned the country into a littoral.

Lloyd's Market Association (LMA) of London

See *Lloyd's Register and Lloyd's of London.*

Lloyd's Register and Lloyd's of London

Lloyd's Register Group Limited (Lloyd's Register) and Lloyd's Market Association of London (Lloyd's of London) are distinct entities, even though the main offices of both are located in the same city. Lloyd's Register Group Limited (LR) is a technical and business services organisation and a maritime classification society, wholly owned by the Lloyd's Register Foundation, a UK charity dedicated to research and education in science and engineering. The organisation dates back to 1760. Its objective is to enhance the safety of life, property, and the environment, by helping its clients to ensure the quality construction, and operation, of critical infrastructure. Historically, as Lloyd's Register of Shipping, it was a specifically maritime organisation. In the late 20th century, it diversified into other industries such as energy and rail transport.

Lloyd's Market Association of London (commonly called "Lloyd's of London") is the world's specialist insurance market that provides specialist insurance services to businesses worldwide, including commercial shipping (including "marine hull" and "marine cargo" segments) and other maritime sectors such as offshore energy. Unlike many other insurance brands, Lloyd's is not a company; it's a market where members (called "*Underwriters*") join together as syndicates to insure risks.

Much of Lloyd's business works by subscription, where more than one syndicate takes a share of the same risk. The business written at Lloyd's is largely conducted through brokers who attend to the risk needs of the client (policy-holder), and facilitate the risk transfer process between client and members. The Lloyd's Corporation oversees the efficient functioning of the insurance market. The Lloyd's of London—in conjunction with the International *Underwriting* Association (IUA) that represents insurance company markets outside Lloyd's—forms the *Joint War Committee (JWC)* that assesses insurance risks and promulgates the '*War Risk Zones*'. See *Piracy High Risk Area (HRA)*.

LNG Carrier

The transportation of *Liquefied Natural Gas (LNG)* is the most rapidly growing shipping activities. A LNG carrier—also called LNG tanker—is the most specialised of all commercial ship types. Since, LNG must be cooled to a temperature below minus 160 degrees Celsius, the refrigerated tanks of a LNG carrier are constructed of a special aluminum alloy, and segregated from the hull with the use of heavy insulation. Since the ship has no refrigeration capacity to that extent, its tanks are so well insulated that they can keep the natural gas liquefied during the entire sea transit. A typical LNG carrier has four to six such tanks located along the centre-line of the vessel.

LNG carriers began commercial operations in the early-1960s. Since then, LNG carriers have been evolving, primarily in terms of their capacity and design. Until 2006, the capacity of the largest carrier was 135,000 cubic metres. Since then, ships of over 250,000 cubic metres began to be built, particularly for new LNG exports from Qatar.

Also, in the last fifteen years, two main types of LNG carriers have been built. The older ships are based on independent spherical tanks (consisting of an insulated single wall spherical tank, supported by a vertically built skirt. The skirt is connected with the tank around the periphery of the equator). The newer ships are membrane-type LNG carriers (a tank design wherein the LNG is contained by a thin stainless steel or nickel alloy flexible membrane). Until 2000, 54 per cent of all LNG carriers were spherical, primarily because Japan—the largest shipbuilder and also the largest LNG importer—had a license for the construction of such carriers. Lately, membrane-type carriers have surpassed these. India is also seeking to build LNG carriers. A notable aspect is the compatibility of the type of LNG carrier with the *LNG Terminal*. For example, most *LNG Terminals* located in the Russian polar region are compatible with carriers with spherical tanks. See *Polar Code*.

LNG Terminal

A structure for storage of *Liquefied Natural Gas*, its liquefaction, or re-gasification (when brought in by *LNG Carriers*). These LNG terminals are of two types—liquefaction terminals (for LNG exports) and re-gasification terminals or receiving terminals (for LNG imports). The terminal comprises special facilities and equipment, storage tanks, port infrastructure and pipelines. Given India's growing LNG demand, LNG liquefaction terminals are necessary. The first two LNG terminals in India were built in Dahej (Gujarat) and Kochi (Kerela).

A new concept is the 'Floating Storage and Re-gasification Unit' (FSRU), which is a LNG terminal whose main structure is a special ship that is moored close to the port of the importing country. As compared to an onshore LNG terminal, setting up of a FSRU is more cost-effective. It costs less than half of an onshore facility, and can be commissioned within two to three years, against the land-based terminal that could take as much as seven years. Resort to FSRU also eliminates the land acquisition and port management costs, besides being more environment-friendly.

India is studying a proposal to set up a FSRU that would be moored off Karnataka coast in 40 metre water depth, which can process one billion cubic feet (bcf) of gas per day, holding a storage capacity of 330,000 cubic metres of LNG onshore and the same capacity offshore.

Long-Range Identification and Tracking (LRIT)

As amendment to the *Safety of Life at Sea (SOLAS) Convention, 1974/1988*, Long-Range Identification and Tracking (LRIT) of ships was promulgated by the *International Maritime Organisation (IMO)* in May 2006 as an international obligation of State parties to SOLAS Convention. It provides for the global identification and tracking of ships. The LRIT regulation applies to the following types of vessels engaged on international voyages:

- All passenger ships including high-speed craft.
- Cargo ships, including high-speed craft of 300 *GT* and above.
- Mobile offshore drilling units.

These ships are required to report their position to their *Flag State* at least four times a day. Other countries could request such reports as relevant to them, such as if these vessels are transiting close to their coasts or are heading for their ports. Usually, vessels make these reports through their automated ship-installed satellite communications equipment. The LRIT system also comprises communications service providers (CSPs), application service providers (ASPs), LRIT data centres, the LRIT data distribution plan and the International LRIT data exchange. LRIT is distinct from satellite-based *Automatic Identification System* (S-AIS), which is essentially a navigational aid and collision avoidance system also mandated by the *IMO*. Unlike AIS, LRIT makes it obligatory on a vessel to convey LRIT data as an indication as to whether it is involved in lawful activity, and for *Maritime Search and Rescue (M-SAR)* requirements. Nonetheless, towards this end, AIS does complement LRIT in surface picture compilation. See *Maritime Satellite Communications.*

Low Intensity Conflict (LIC)

An internal conflict environment wherein terrorists, guerrillas, insurgents and subversives active within a country's territory mount violence at a lower scale and tempo than in a conventional Armed Conflict scenario, albeit employing asymmetric means. Such activity is usually carried out by secretly organised forces operating in small groups, and employing *Small Arms* and limited quantities of explosives. LIC may be waged against symbols of State sovereignty or the common people. LIC excludes a civil war scenario. See *Asymmetric Operations* and *Low Intensity Conflict/ Maritime Operations* (*LICO/LIMO*).

Low Intensity Conflict/ Maritime Operations (LICO/LIMO)

The term Low Intensity Conflict Operations (LICO) refers to a wide range of measures taken by a State's land-based military forces in a *Low Intensity Conflict (LIC)* environment. LICO includes, but is not restricted to the application of military force. The measures encompass political, economic and informational domains.

The phase Low Intensity Maritime Operations (LIMO) refers to the measures taken by a State's *Maritime Security Forces* (navies, coast guards and other forces) to counter threats to peace and security in a *Low Intensity Conflict (LIC)* environment in the maritime and *littoral* domains. Within the State's maritime zones, LIMO operates to further its internal security, and may thus be considered as the maritime equivalent of LICO. However, in the international medium where maritime forces operate, their mandate transcends the sphere of internal security to regional security and stability. See *Asymmetric Operations.*

M

Magnetic Anomaly Detector (MAD)

See *Anti-Submarine Warfare (ASW).*

Malabar (Naval Exercises)

Combined naval exercises between the Indian Navy and the US Navy. The 'Malabar' series of bilateral exercise commenced in 1992. Notably, the proposal for *combined* naval exercises was presented by the US CINCPAC (C-in-C Pacific Fleet) to India in September 1989. After a break between 1997 and 2001, these recommenced in 2002 and began to increase in duration, scope and character. Since the 2007 edition of 'Malabar', the exercise has occasionally involved other countries, particularly Japan. See *Joint and Combined.*

Malaccamax (Ship)

See *Commercial Ship Sizes.*

MALSINDO

A coordinated naval patrol mechanism in the Straits of Malacca and Singapore involving the navies of Singapore, Malaysia and Indonesia. The trilateral initiative, launched in July 2004, is meant to safeguard the Straits against *Maritime Crimes* like *Piracy.* It has evolved from the previous bilateral coordinated patrols conducted between the littoral states. It entails the coordination of patrols by a littoral country within the area under its *Sovereign Jurisdiction* and with patrol partners in their respective areas, and with the command centred in the respective countries. See *Eyes in the Sky (EiS)* and *Regional Maritime Security Initiative* (RMSI).

Manoeuvre

The concept is employed at both Tactical and Operational *Levels of Warfare.* In context of the latter, historically, military conflict was premised on the concept of *Attrition*, which seeks to destroy the adversary's physical substance by the cumulative effect of superior firepower. Manoeuvre was developed as an alternative concept. Through manoeuvre, military forces aim to avoid the adversary's strength, and rather, seek the adversary's decapitation by disrupting its fighting system and/or break its will to fight. This is achieved by concentrating superior force against certain key elements of the adversary's fighting system, such as *Command and Control* (C^2) nodes or logistics chain. The underlying aim is to shatter the adversary's moral and physical cohesion. Manoeuvre is usually employed at the operational level of warfare.

An outstanding example of maritime manoeuvre was the landing at Inchon in 1950 during the Korean War. In September 1950, the North Korean invasion of the South had driven the UN forces far south-east to the areas around Pusan. While the UN and South Korean forces were desperately defending the Pusan perimeter, the assault by US-led maritime forces against the undefended Inchon far north-west outflanked North Korean forces, cutting their lines of communication and causing their retreat.

Notably, manoeuvre is often accompanied with 'diversion/deception'. However, the conceptual difference between the two remains, and must be understood. During the 1991 Persian Gulf War, the US forces undertook a series of diversionary *Amphibious Operations* at various locations in Kuwait and eastern Saudi Arabia. Expecting a 'likely' US amphibious assault against Kuwait, Iraq was compelled to dedicate five of its army divisions to defend the Kuwaiti coastline. This is an example of 'diversion/deception', which did not involve the concept of manoeuvre. See *Levels of Warfare*.

Mare Clausum

A policy defended by Portugal and Spain between the 15th and 17th centuries, when sailing that had been mostly coastal became oceanic. The policy asserted that ocean spaces could be proportioned for the use of a particular seafaring nation, and not generally accessible to all nations. The genesis of the policy lay in the period between 30 BC and 117 AD, when the fledging Roman Empire circumscribed the Mediterranean Sea through its control of nearly the entire adjoining coast. The Mediterranean thus began to be called 'Mare Nostrum' (Latin for 'our sea'). In those times, when the sea was considered unsafe for navigation, it used to be declared "Mare Clausum" (closed sea).

In 1609, the Dutch jurist and philosopher Hugo Grotius challenged the policy through his book '*Mare Liberum*' (Latin for 'free sea'), which asserted that the sea was international territory and all nations were free to use it for trade. England opposed the idea of '*Mare Liberum*' and claimed sovereignty over the seas adjoining the British Isles. Besides, England was also competing with the Dutch for domination of sea-trade.

In 1635, the English jurist John Seldan coined the term 'Mare Clausum', and sought to prove that the sea was as capable of appropriation as land. As conflicting claims grew out of the controversy, maritime states came to moderate their demands and base their maritime claims on the principle that it extended seawards from land. A workable formula was found in 1702 by the Dutch jurist Cornelis Bijnkershoek in his dissertation titled 'De Dominio Maris Dissertatio', wherein he proposed that that the maritime dominion of a country be limited to the distance within which, cannon range could effectively protect it. This became universally adopted and developed into the three-mile limit for a country's *Territorial Waters*. This later became the basis of negotiations during the first United Nations Conference on the Law of the Sea (UNCLOS-I). See *Freedom of the Seas*.

Mare Liberum

The theory of '*Mare Liberum*' (Latin for 'free sea') was proposed in a book of same name by the Dutch jurist and philosopher Hugo Grotius in 1609. The book was based on a contestation against Portugal's policy of '*Mare Clausum*' (Latin for 'closed sea') and its monopolisation of sea-trade with East Indies. In 'Mare Liberum', Grotius proposed the principle that the sea was international territory and all nations were free to use it. While Grotius asserted innocent passage across both 'land' and 'sea' for trade, he postulated that the 'ocean' was akin to 'air in a manner that it is not susceptible to occupation or possession, and is thus adapted for the use of all, whether for navigation or of fisheries. See *Freedom of the Seas*.

Mariculture

See *Aquaculture and Mariculture*.

Marine Biodiversity

Biodiversity refers to the variety of different types of life forms found on Earth, within or across ecosystems, which inhabit the entire planet, its particular biome (climatically and geographically contiguous areas) or even an area within the biome.

Since long, the biological diversity in the world's oceans was not fully understood. Lately, it has beginning to be realised that marine biodiversity plays a vital role, not only in maintaining the functionality and productivity of marine ecosystems, but also makes the marine habitats more resilient to environmental change. Among the most salient features of marine ecosystems is the use of sunlight and nutrients to generate plant biomass (primary productivity) that is the basic food source for all marine life, and ultimately for humans. Also critical are the coastal marine habitats and ecosystems comprising macroalgae, seagrass and corals that provide habitats for many other marine species such as molluscs, crustaceans and fish.

However, the balance among the marine species is becoming increasingly unstable due to increasing industrialisation leading to marine pollution and destruction of habitats by trawler fishing. See *Marine Pollution*, and *Anti-Fouling Systems (AFS) Convention.*

Marine Fishing Regulation Acts (MFRA)

In India, the 'Maritime Zones of India (Regulation of Fishing by Foreign Vessels) Act, 1981' regulates fishing activities (by foreign vessels) beyond the *Territorial Waters*. Fishing activities within *Territorial Waters* come under the purview of India's provincial states. The control and regulation of the fishing in this zone is undertaken through separate *Marine Fishing Regulation Acts* (MFRA) of the coastal states/union territories of India.

The Acts are based on a model piece of legislation prepared by the Ministry of Agriculture (Government of India) in 1979, in response to demand from fishermen operating unpowered fishing vessels to protect their fishing space and equipment from bottom trawlers. Some of the important management measures adopted under the MFRA are prohibitions on certain fishing gear, regulations on mesh size, establishment of closed seasons and areas, demarcations of zones for no-trawling, besides other measures such as use of turtle excluder devices, and designation of no-fishing areas. See *Maritime Zones of India (MZI) Acts* and *Sustainable Fisheries.*

Marine Pollution

The introduction by human beings, directly or indirectly, of substances or energy into the marine environment resulting in such deleterious effects as harm to living resources, hazards to human health, hindrance to marine activities including fishing and impairment of quality for use of seawater. See *Anti-Fouling Systems (AFS) Convention*, *MARPOL 73/78*, *Oil Spill*, *Oil Spill Response*, and *Particularly Sensitive Sea Area (PSSA).*

Marine Scientific Research (MSR)

The concept pertains to the conduct of marine scientific research by foreign vessels in the *EEZ* and *Continental Shelf.* Although such activity is permitted by *UNCLOS*, many coastal States are wary of the possibility of MSR being used as a cover for collection of intelligence/information of potential military value or economic gain. Hence, the *UNCLOS* stipulates that for MSR, prior consent of the coastal State must be obtained. Also, the data obtained must be shared with the coastal State.

However, this leads to an ambiguity. Since the *UNCLOS* does not address the issue of 'military survey' in these areas, a vessel may undertake such activity without prior consent. This could be justified since collection of environmental information (including *Hydrography* and *Bathymetry* data) by naval vessels may be necessary for navigational/air safety, and is in conformity with the principle of '*High Seas* freedom of navigation'.

Maritime Baseline

The baseline from which, maritime claims of a coastal State are measured. It is normally the low-water line along the coast as marked on the State's official large-scale charts. However, when the coastline is deeply indented, or due to fringing islands located in its immediate vicinity, or where the coastline is unstable due to natural conditions, the State may employ 'straight baselines', which join the prominent natural features along the general direction of the coast.

Maritime Cooperation

It involves reciprocal measures through mutual consent involving one or more countries relating to the oceanic and littoral domains. It may be divided into '*maritime Security* cooperation' and 'defence industry and technology' cooperation at the national level, and Constructive Maritime Engagement involving navies/*Maritime Security Forces* at the operational and tactical levels.

Maritime Crime

Refers to any unlawful activity in the maritime domain, which 'intentionally' contravenes either national or international law. Maritime crimes include *Piracy* and *Armed Robbery at Sea*; sea-borne trafficking of weapons, drugs and other prohibited goods, including for tax evasion; unauthorised entry into a foreign country's sovereign waters; discharging pollutants in a country's maritime zones, *Human Smuggling and Human Trafficking*; and *Illegal, Unreported, and Unregulated (IUU) Fishing.*

Maritime Domain Awareness (MDA)

An effective understanding of all activities, events, and trends within the maritime and littoral domains that bear on national security, either directly or indirectly. It enables the early identification of potential threats, planning of responses, supporting decision-making and prioritising resource allocation. It operates at three levels, viz. strategic, operational and tactical, though at each level, the nature of MDA, the ways and means to achieve it, and the application of responses differ.

At the operational and tactical levels, the initial conceptualisation of MDA related to the surface and maritime-air domains. However, the concept is being progressively expanded to encompass the undersea domain.

At the operational and tactical levels in particular, the attainment of information alone is not adequate. The information needs to be managed and shared among various agencies and geographically dispersed security forces. Primarily as a response to the emerging maritime and coastal security threats, India has developed an elaborate mechanism for information networking and management under the *National Maritime Domain Awareness (NMDA) Project*. Also see *National Command Control Communication and Intelligence Network (NC³IN), Surveillance, Reconnaissance*, Intelligence, and *Levels of Warfare.*

Maritime Exclusion Zone (MEZ)

See *Exclusion Zones.*

Maritime Identification Zone

See *Australian Maritime Identification Zone/ System (MIZ/ AMIS).*

Maritime Law

A generic term referring collectively to both *Admiralty Law* and Law of the Sea (codified in *UNCLOS*). The former is a body of laws that governs international private business or other activity involving shipping or crimes occurring in *International Waters*. The latter is a body of law between countries governing issues such as geographical extent of *Sovereign Jurisdiction* over oceans, and is thus considered as public international law.

Maritime-Military Power

It is a 'sub-set' of *Maritime Power* of a country, and refers to the capability of a *Nation-State* to exert military power at sea. Thus, it is not synonymous with *Naval Power*, since it is not restricted to the capability of the State's navy alone, but all elements of its armed forces that bear the potential to be employed in the maritime realm.

Maritime-Military Strategy

Although in common parlance, it is referred to as *Maritime Strategy*, it is in fact a 'subset' of a country's *Maritime Strategy*. It is also a part of *Military-Strategy*. It is primarily meant to be executed by the naval forces, with the other armed forces and government agencies playing supporting roles. It necessarily involves the elements of land and air forces that are tasked to operate in the maritime domain.

According to Admiral James Watkins, the former US Chief of Naval Operations (CNO), "Maritime (-Military) Strategy...does not purport to be a detailed war-plan with firm timelines, tactical *Doctrine*, or specific target sets. Instead it offers a global perspective to operational commanders and provides a foundation for advice to the National Command Authorities...".

Maritime Power

Also referred to as 'Sea Power'. It encompasses the comprehensive ability of a State to use the seas to safeguard and progress its national interests. The navy (assisted by the maritime components of the other arms of the State's military power) is the prime instrument and manifestation of the State's maritime power. This makes *Maritime-Military Power* a key subset of Maritime Power.

Maritime Power Projection

See *Power Projection.*

Maritime Rescue Co-ordination Centre (MRCC)

See *Maritime Search and Rescue (M-SAR).*

Maritime Salvage

A concept in international maritime law, which states that a person (salvor) who recovers another person's ship or cargo after peril or loss at sea is entitled to a reward commensurate with the value of the property so saved. The law pertains to 'pure salvage' or 'merit salvage, which differs from 'contract salvage' that refers to a pre-negotiated contract for salvage. The rationale of concept is that the salvor would be putting himself and his own vessel at risk to recover another, and thus should be appropriately rewarded.

The concept is closely related to the obligation of ships to go to the assistance of vessels in distress stated in *UNCLOS* and *SOLAS, 1974*, and was first codified in the *Convention of the Vessels*, 1910. Salvage Law has since been recognised nearly universally, and some of its provisions have attained uniformity through the International Convention on Salvage, 1989. While traditionally, Maritime Salvage referred only to a 'vessel', the 1989 Convention expanded its ambit to include all 'property' onboard in danger, including cargo. The salvor must bring his claim for salvage in an *Admiralty Law* court, which will award salvage based upon the merit of the service and the value of the salvaged property. The 1989 Convention does not usually apply to salvage of warships. India acceded to the Convention on 18 Oct 95. The Indian domestic legislation on Maritime Salvage is contained in the *Merchant Shipping Act, 1958*. See *Amphibious Aircraft*.

Maritime Satellite Communications

Soon after the launch of the world's first telecommunications satellite (Telstar) in 1962, the *International Maritime Organisation (IMO)* recognised the potential for satellite communications for *Maritime Search and Rescue (M-SAR)* and other 'public' services at sea. In February 1966, IMO's Maritime Safety Committee (MSC) began the study to establish a new satellite-based maritime communications system, leading to the adoption of 'Convention on the International Maritime Satellite Organisation' 1976 (*Inmarsat* Convention), which was signed by 28 countries.

The Convention established the International Maritime Satellite Organisation (*Inmarsat*) in 1979 as an inter-governmental organisation to establish and operate a satellite communications network for the maritime community. The Convention's 'Operating Agreement' set an initial capital ceiling for the Organisation of US$ 200 million. The state parties to the Convention owned varying shares of the operational business. Investment shares were determined on the basis of utilisation of the *Inmarsat* space segment. In the 1980s, in coordination with the International Civil Aviation Organisation (ICAO), the Convention was amended to include improvements aeronautical communications. Inmarsat, headquartered in London, began operations in 1982.

In 1988, the amendments to *SOLAS* incorporated the *Global Maritime Distress and Safety System* (GMDSS), which placed the responsibility upon *Inmarsat* to provide satellite-based maritime distress and safety services. It became obligatory for all seagoing ships to carry GMDSS/*Inmarsat* communications equipment for distress and safety calls, and to receive navigational warnings.

In the mid-1990s, many state parties to the *Inmarsat* Convention were unwilling to invest in improvements to *Inmarsat*'s network, especially owing to the competitive nature of the satellite communications industry. Nonetheless, there was a persisting need for an inter-governmental organisation to oversee public safety aspects of satellite communication networks. In 1999, a new satellite-based communications structure came into being, comprising two separate entities, viz. the privatised *Inmarsat* and the inter-governmental body *International Mobile Satellite Organisation (IMSO)*.

Maritime Search and Rescue (M-SAR)

Maritime (and Aeronautical) SAR is a humanitarian mission of a country's *Maritime Security Forces* and a part of the 'benign' role of navies. It is composed of two distinct phases: 'Search' and 'Rescue'. 'Search' is defined as an operation, normally coordinated by a rescue coordination centre or rescue sub-centre, using available personnel and facilities to locate persons in distress or imminent danger. 'Rescue' is defined as an operation to retrieve persons in distress, provide for their initial medical or other needs, and deliver them to a place of safety.

Maritime (and Aeronautical) SAR is meant to meet a country's international obligations that is well codified in international law. The 'International Convention on Maritime Search and Rescue, 1979' promulgated an international SAR plan, so that, no matter where an accident occurred, the rescue of persons in distress at sea would be coordinated by a specific SAR organisation and, when necessary, by co-operation among neighbouring SAR organisations. The 'International Civil Aviation Organisation (ICAO) Convention, 1944' is relevant for the aeronautical component of maritime SAR.

Following the entry into force of the Maritime SAR Convention, 1979 in June 1985, the Maritime Safety Committee (MSC) of the *International Maritime Organisation (IMO)* divided the world's oceans into 13 maritime SAR areas, in each of which the countries concerned have delimited maritime *Search and Rescue Regions (SRR)*, for which they are responsible. The Convention also provides for establishing 'Maritime Rescue Co-ordination Centres (MRCC)'. Furthermore, the obligation for ships to render assistance at sea is codified in *UNCLOS* and *Safety of Life at Sea (SOLAS) Convention, 1974/1988*. It is obligatory for all vessels (including warships) to render assistance to any person or vessel at sea in distress/danger.

After acceding to the SAR Convention in May 2001, India constituted a 'National Search and Rescue Board'. The SAR region allocated to India, called the 'Indian Search and Rescue Region' (ISRR), is an area of 4.6 million sq. Km. The Indian Coast Guard (ICG) is the designated authority for coordinating Search and Rescue in the ISRR. The ISRR is further sub-divided into three SRRs (western seaboard, eastern seaboard and off A&N Islands), with three MRCCs at Mumbai, Chennai and Port Blair, and rescue sub-centres (co-located with Coast Guard district headquarters in nine coastal states and four union territories). In February 2003, India instated an 'Indian Ship Reporting System' (INDSAR) to enable Indian maritime forces to monitor the vessels entering the Indian SRR for providing SAR assistance if required.

Notably, in Southeast Asia, only Singapore and Vietnam are parties to the SAR Convention. One reason why other regional countries have not joined the Convention is because becoming a party would bring with it the obligation to allow rescue units of other parties to enter their *Territorial Waters* on a SAR mission. See *Amphibious Aircraft*, *Global Maritime Distress Safety System (GMDSS)*, *Long-Range Identification and Tracking (LRIT)* and *Maritime Satellite Communications*.

Maritime Search and Rescue Convention, 1979

See *Maritime Search and Rescue (M-SAR)*.

Maritime Security

A subset of *National Security*. Unlike security on land, Maritime Security is a complex interplay of a country's defence, economic and foreign relations aspects of security, and the maintenance of peace, stability and lawful order in the maritime domain. It encompasses a host of issues relating to the sea under the broad constructs of national sovereignty, economic development, human security and preservation of the marine environment. The issues include security and safety of seaborne trade and commerce; *Security of Energy*; *Coastal Security*, *Coastal Defence* and *Offshore Security* against low-intensity threats; ensuring good order at sea; and the safety of its citizens engaged in maritime activities; and the delimitation and management of international maritime boundaries and the natural resources in the maritime zones.

Notably, in the context of the USA and many other western countries, the concept of 'Maritime Security' is limited to ensuring security at sea against non-traditional threats, including those posed by non-State actors. In the Indian context, however, the concept also encompasses *Seaward Defence* and *Offshore Defence* against 'military' threats.

Maritime Security Forces

Maritime Security of a country is an outcome of a complex interface among a multitude of national and provincial agencies. Among these agencies, those directly charged with operational functions and mandated by the government for the use of force are referred to as 'Maritime Security Forces'. The designation, structure and nomenclature of the maritime security forces vary from country to country. In generic terms, military security is tasked to the navy as its primary role, whereas coast-guards and their equivalents are charged with law-enforcement in the maritime zones wherein the country exercises *Sovereign Jurisdiction*. Many countries designate authorities having their own seagoing assets to enforce their customs and immigration laws. In some countries with federal government structures, the coastal provincial states exercise respective provincial laws up to the extent of the *Territorial Waters*.

In India, the three principal maritime security forces are the State Marine Police (SMP), the Indian Coast Guard (ICG) and the Indian Navy (IN). The three forces are tasked in discrete geographical layers extending seawards from India's coast as follows:

- **State Marine Police (SMP).** The SMP of each coastal (provincial) state is responsible for policing in respective stretches of the *Territorial Waters* (12 NM) in coordination with the Customs, Central Industrial Security Force (CISF) and port authorities.
- **Indian Coast Guard (ICG).** The ICG is tasked with *Maritime Security* in the entire swath of Maritime Zones of India (MZI) extending up to the 200 NM limit of the EEZ (including the 12 NM limit of *Territorial Waters*), and also the projected *Legal Continental Shelf (LCS)* beyond it. As part of India's international obligation, the force is also responsible to provide *Maritime Search and Rescue (M-SAR)* cover in the Indian Search and Rescue Region (ISRR) that extends much beyond the MZI.
- **Indian Navy (IN).** Though primarily charged with responding to the security threats of 'military' nature within the MZI and beyond—extending to India's overseas interests—the IN supports the ICG through its (secondary) constabulary and benign roles, including in the latter's *M-SAR* responsibilities in the extensive ISRR.

Maritime Silk Road (MSR)

A concept of China's economic diplomacy (albeit with significant geopolitical and even military-strategic connotations) initiated by President Xi Jinping in October 2014. It is projected as a 'reincarnation' of the ancient 'Silk Road' of Han Dynasty China (206 BC-220 AD) that was used to carry trade—predominantly silk—and cultural imprints from China to Europe. MSR seeks a partnership of key littoral countries located along the *International Shipping Lane (ISL)* stretching across the

Indo-Pacific Region to Europe. It proposes inter alia the outsourcing of Chinese manufacturing industries to the partner countries, along with China making financial investments to develop maritime-trade connectivity, ports and special economic zones in the countries. The investments are sought to be funded by China in conjunction with banks like the Asian Infrastructure Development Bank (AIDB) instituted predominantly through China's initiative and influence. See *Mausam and Spice Route* (*Projects*), and *String of Pearls*.

Maritime Strategy

As a 'subset' of *National Strategy*, Maritime Strategy can be defined as the overall approach of a country to the oceans around it, with the aim of synergising all aspects related to maritime activities, to maximise national gains. A maritime strategy would thus have economic, commercial, political, military, scientific and technological facets. The military dimension of India's maritime strategy is termed as *Maritime-Military Strategy*.

Maritime Strike

A task of a navy under its military mission, which involves deployment of naval forces at sea for delivery of ordnance against maritime and littoral targets.

Maritime Terrorism

The definition of the term is contingent upon international consensus and clarity on the term '*Terrorism*'. Nonetheless, a tentative definition may be 'the use of unlawful violence or the threat of its use against non-combatants in the maritime domain, primarily by non-State actors with the ultimate aim of meeting political or ideological objective(s). This may include violence against a sea-going vessel, including its crew, passengers or cargo; or against a littoral site, including an *Offshore Platform* or port from the sea; or even the use of a sea-going vessel to transport the instruments of terrorism. See *Sea Tigers* (*LTTE*) and *Container Security Initiative* (*CSI*).

Maritime Zones of India (MZI) Acts

The MZI Act of 1976 (titled '*Territorial Waters, Continental Shelf,*

Exclusive Economic Zone and other Maritime Zones Act, 1976') draws upon Article 297 of the Indian Constitution and the UNCLOS III deliberations leading to *UNCLOS, 1982*. The Act is an umbrella legislation to regulate resource exploration and exploitation activities in the MZI. The MZI (Regulation of Fishing by Foreign Vessels) Act, 1981 provides for the regulation of fishing by foreign vessels in MZI. See *Fishing Methods and Gear*, *Marine Fishing Regulation Acts (MFRA)* and *Sustainable Fisheries*.

MARPOL 73/78

International Convention for the Prevention of (Marine) Pollution from Ships, 1973 as modified by the Protocol of 1978. The treaty is meant to protect the marine environment by preventing pollution by dumping (of marine litter), *Oil Spill Pollution* or exhaust pollution. Since MARPOL 73/78 entered into force in October 1983, 152 countries are its State parties to the convention, representing more than 99 per cent of the world's shipping tonnage. All vessels registered in these countries are obliged to adhere to MARPOL requirements. The annexes of MARPOL 73/78 and its 1997 Protocol are as follows:

- **MARPOL 73/78 Annex I/II.** 'Prevention of pollution by oil and oily water' and 'control of pollution by noxious liquid substances in bulk'. Entered into force on 2 October 1983. 153 State parties.
- **MARPOL 73/78 Annex III.** 'Prevention of pollution by harmful substances carried by sea in packaged form'. Entered into force on 01 July 1992. 141 State parties.
- **MARPOL 73/78 Annex IV.** 'Pollution by sewage from ships'. Entered into force on 27 September 1993. 134 State parties.
- **MARPOL 73/78 Annex V.** 'Pollution by garbage from ships'. Entered into force on 31 December 1988. 141 State parties.
- **MARPOL Protocol 1997 Annex VI.** 'Prevention of air pollution from ships'. Entered into force on 19 May 2005, 80 State parties.
- **MARPOL Protocol 1997 Revised Annex VI (2008).** With significantly tightened emissions limits to prevent air pollution. Entered into force on 01 July 2010.

MARPOL designates a few sea areas as 'special areas' under Annexes I, II and V, where mandatory pollution-control provisions apply due to the *Oceanographical* and ecological conditions or the kind of shipping traffic in these areas. Under its Revised Annex VI of 1997 Protocol, MARPOL designates 'Emission Control Areas' (ECAs), wherein more stringent controls are established over Sulphur Oxide (SO_x) and Nitrogen Oxide (NO_x) emissions. It may be noted that these 'special areas' and 'ECAs' are distinct from the *Particularly Sensitive Sea Areas (PSSAs).*

Martens Clause

See *Customary International Law.*

Mausam and Spice Route (Projects)

'Mausam' is a project of the Government of India's Ministry of Culture, which was launched in June 2014 at UNESCO's 38th World Heritage Session at Doha, Qatar. Aimed at reviving India's maritime heritage, the project involves an interdisciplinary academic enquiry into the ancient sea-routes distinct to the Indian Ocean. Besides stringing together the historic past of the countries involved, it aims to understand the impact of maritime linkages on the Indian Ocean rim societies in terms of the exchange of commodities, culture, religion, ideas, values and technology.

Mausam is based on the regularly-reversing regional wind phenomenon called 'Monsoon' (derived from the Arabic word 'Mausam'). Since the beginning of the third millennium B.C., the easy predictability of 'Monsoon' facilitated sea-borne commercial and cultural linkages between the Indian sub-continent and the rest of the *Indian Ocean Region (IOR),* besides with Southeast Asia and China.

Since around the same period of the third millennium B.C., merchants involved in trade in spices (besides some other commodities like gems, metals and medicines) sailed from the Indian sub-continent to Africa, Arabia and East Asia. Eventually, the spice-trade became lucrative for the Europeans, providing an overwhelming incentive for the Dutch, the French, the Portuguese and the English to sail to the Coromandel Coast of southern India in search of these valued condiments, essential for preservation and flavouring of food and also used in ritual practices. For this reason, this coast became known as the Spice Coast. Accordingly, Project 'Spice Route' is a heritage project initiated by the south Indian provincial state of Kerela, and supported by UNESCO. It is based on the ancient 2000-year-old Spice Route that connected 31 countries. See *Maritime Silk Road (MSR).*

Medium Range Ballistic Missiles (MRBM)

See *Ballistic and Cruise Missiles.*

Merchant Ship Information System (MSIS)

A *Maritime Domain Awareness (MDA)* system developed by the Indian Navy, which fuzes and disseminates the data obtained from the *National AIS (NAIS) Network* and other sources of *Automatic Identification System (AIS)*, including open-source information on 'white shipping', feeding it into the nodal *Information Management and Analysis Centre (IMAC)*. See *White Shipping Information.*

Merchant Shipping Act, 1958

A national legislation meant to foster the development and ensure the efficient maintenance of Indian mercantile marine for the furtherance of national interests. Essentially, it seeks to regulate merchant shipping in terms of registration and certification Indian ships; collisions and accidents at sea; investigation and enquiries; liability transfers or mortgages of ships or shares; wreck and salvage; prevention of pollution; coasting trade; sailing vessels; penalties and procedure; and employment and working conditions of seafarers. The Act applies to any 'Indian ship', whether registered in India or obliged to do so under the Act. (This does not include fishing vessels and ships below 15 tons net that are employed solely in coastal navigation). The Mercantile Marine Department (MMD) under the *Directorate General of Shipping (DGoS)* administers implementation of the Act.

The Merchant Shipping (Second Amendment) Bill, 2013 proposes to amend the Merchant Shipping Act, 1958, to bring it in conformity with the International Labour Organisation's Maritime Labour Convention, 2006.

Mercosur

A sub-regional *Free Trade Area* and *Customs* union formed in 1991, which is classified as a *Common Market*. It derives its name from the Spanish phrase 'Mercado Común del Sur' (Southern *Common Market*). Its purpose is to promote free trade, including free movement of goods, people and currency, and adopting a common trade policy with non-member countries. Mercosur members are Argentina, Brazil, Paraguay, Uruguay and Venezuela. Its associate countries are Chile, Bolivia, Colombia, Ecuador and Peru. New Zealand and Mexico are observer countries.

Milan (Naval Congregation)

A biennial congregation of regional navies at Port Blair (Andaman and Nicobar Islands) instituted by the Indian Navy in 1995. 'Milan' is a hindi word for 'meeting'. It involves professional and cultural interactions. Notably, 'Milan' was originally conceived as a gathering of the Bay of Bengal navies aligned to India's 'Look East' Policy, but it gradually expanded to include countries across the *Indian Ocean Region* (*IOR*) and South China Sea littoral. In 2014, Milan witnessed the participation of 17 navies, ranging from Kenya and Tanzania in the western IOR, to Cambodia and the Philippines in the East.

Military Alliance

A result of formal agreements between two or more countries for broad, long-term defence and *National Security* objectives in various contingencies. (In contrast, a *Coalition* caters for a short-term objective). A military alliance usually involves a 'collective security' arrangement, and often has established *Doctrines, Command and Control* (*C^2*) structures and procedures. Examples of existing military alliances are *Australia-New Zealand-US (ANZUS) Security Treaty*, *Collective Security Treaty Organisation (CSTO)* and *North Atlantic Treaty Organisation (NATO).*

Military Operations Other Than War (MOOTW)

Operations that encompass the use of military forces in the *Spectrum of Conflict* from peace to *Short of War Scenarios.* For a navy, such operations are conducted in pursuit of its diplomatic, benign and constabulary roles. These military actions may complement other instruments of national power. See *Stability Operations.*

Military Strategy

As a 'sub-set' of *National Strategy*, it is the art and science of using a country's armed forces through the use or threat of use of force to achieve national objectives. The term is often used as an adjective ('Military Strategic') to qualify nouns like 'planning', '*Doctrine*' and *Levels of Warfare.* See *Maritime-Military Strategy.*

Mine Counter Measures (MCM)

Sea-mining is a potent low-cost instrument of *Sea Denial*, which is within the reach of the smallest navies and even non-State actors with modest means, and poses a major asymmetric threat (See *Asymmetric Operations*). Countering the threat is an essential prerequisite for regional security and freedom of navigation. This is sought to be achieved through MCM.

MCM incorporates the concept of layered defence encompassing all levels of war/conflict. However, the focus of MCM is usually on the operational and tactical levels. At these levels, MCM operations essentially involve three aspects: *Force Protection*, *Surveillance* and *Intelligence* operations, besides counter-mining and mine clearance operations.

MIRV and MRV

Usually, a *Ballistic Missile* carries a single warhead, either conventional or nuclear. A 'Multiple Independently Targetable Reentry Vehicle' (MIRV) refers to a *Ballistic Missile* payload (usually nuclear) comprising many warheads, each one of which is independently capable of selecting and striking different targets. An intermediate case is the 'Multiple Reentry Vehicle' (MRV) missile, which carries many warheads that are dispersed and not meant for specific targeting. See *Strategic Arms Reduction Treaty (START)*.

Missile and Rocket

In common parlance, the two terms mean the same and are often used interchangeably. Both are essentially propelled by thrust-producing systems, wherein the thrust is derived from the ejection of hot gases generated from the material carried in the system, not requiring intake of air or water.

However, in the context of military applications, a 'rocket' falls in the category of 'unguided self-propelled munitions', whereas a 'missile' is grouped under 'self-propelled precision guided munitions'. An example of a 'rocket' is an anti-submarine rocket, which does not require precision guidance. If this 'rocket' is provided with some form of 'guidance' that determines its movement (in any or all axes of movement), it is referred-to as a 'missile'. There are several ways of categorising 'missiles'. One of these is by their trajectory (flight-path), which leads to the distinction between *Ballistic and Cruise Missiles*.

Missile Technology Control regime (MTCR)

An informal political understanding among States that seeks to limit the proliferation of missiles and missile technology (relating to both *Ballistic and Cruise Missiles*), and other forms of delivery systems for all types of *Weapons of Mass Destruction (WMD)*. More specifically, the MTCR regime is meant to control the exports of goods and technologies that could make a contribution to such delivery systems (other than manned aircraft). It places particular focus on rockets and *Unmanned Aerial Vehicles (UAV)* capable of delivering a payload of at least 500 kg to a range of at least 300 km, and on equipment, software, and technology for such systems.

The MTCR regime was formed in 1987 by the G-7 industrialised countries (Canada, France, Germany, Italy, Japan, the UK, and the United States). Presently, there are 34 MTCR member countries. India is not yet a member. The MTCR is not a treaty and does not impose any legally binding obligations on its members. The MTCR Guidelines do not distinguish between exports to members and non-members. Membership of MTCR provides no entitlement to obtain technology from another member and no obligation to supply it. The members are, however, bound by a 'no-undercut' policy to consult each other before considering exports of the relevant goods and technologies. See *Hague Code of Conduct (HCoC)*.

Mobile Landing Platform (MLP)

A type of *Amphibious Ship* built for the US expeditionary forces to serve the *Sea Basing* concept, and when required, as a facilitator of ship-to-shore movement of military vehicles, stores and equipment. More specifically, the MLP is a semi-submersible deck serving as an intermediary transfer point of the hardware from a deep-draft ship (that has carried the hardware to the amphibious objective area) to the small landing craft that carries it ashore. The US MLPs have a full load *Displacement* of over 80,000 tons and can cruise at a maximum speed of 15 *Knots*. Specialised MLPs are optimised to support other naval missions such as *Humanitarian Assistance and Disaster Relief (HADR)*. Navies of some other countries—notably China—are known to be developing such capability. See *Amphibious Operation*, *Expeditionary Operation*, *Lilypad*, and *Sea Basing*.

N

Naseem-al-Bahr (Naval Exercises)

Combined naval exercises between the Indian Navy and Royal Oman Navy since 1993, under the name 'Thammar-al-Tayyib'. The exercise was renamed in 2007. See *Joint and Combined.*

Nation and Nation-State

'Nation' refers to the community of people with similar genesis, translating into a common socio-cultural, ethnic and linguistic character. The term is often used (incorrectly) as an abridged term for 'Nation-State', which refers to a sovereign political and geo-political entity. The term 'Nation-State' is more commonly referred to as 'State'. See *Sovereignty* and *Nationalism.*

National Aim

It is derived from the national Constitution and amplified through political directions. According to the 'Directive Principles of State Policy' enunciated in the Indian Constitution (Article 38), "the State shall strive to promote the welfare of the people by securing and protecting as effectively as it may a social order in which justice, social, economic and political, shall inform all the institutions of the national life". *National Aim* (combined with *National Values*) provides the basis for defining *National Interests*, and is sought to be achieved through *National Strategy.*

National Airspace

Sovereign airspace above the territory, *Internal Waters*, *Territorial Waters*, and *Archipelagic Waters* of States. See *International Airspace* and *National Waters.*

National AIS (NAIS) Network

A *Maritime Domain Awareness (MDA)* network established in India under the Directorate General of Lights and Lighthouses of the Ministry of

Shipping. It constitutes a network of shore stations installed on existing lighthouses, which track vessels equipped with *Automatic Identification Systems (AIS)*. It feeds into the *Merchant Ship Information System (MSIS)* and the nodal Information Management and Analysis Centre (IMAC). See *Coastal Surveillance Network (CSN)*, *INSPIRES*, *ISLEREP*, and *National Command Control Communication and Intelligence Network (NC³IN)*.

National Command Control Communication and Intelligence Network (NC³IN)

As the backbone of the 'National Maritime Domain Awareness' (NMDA) Project—whose blueprint was proposed by the Indian Navy in 2010—NC³IN connects 51 stations (20 naval and 31 coast-guard stations) and Joint Operation Centres (JOCs). The NC³IN is also fed by real-time information from the following sources:

- *Coastal Surveillance Network (CSN)*
- *Long-Range Identification and Tracking (LRIT)*
- *National AIS (NAIS) Network*
- *Merchant Ship Information System (MSIS)*
- Vessel and Air Traffic Management System (VATMS)—West.

The network—established in the wake of November 2008 terrorist attacks in Mumbai—feeds into the nodal Information Management and Analysis Centre (IMAC). At the IMAC, all sources (stations, centres, etc.) are connected through a high-speed computer network through the Coastal Surveillance and Decision Support software. See *Automatic Identification System (AIS)*, *INSPIRES*, *Maritime Domain Awareness (MDA)*, and *Vessel Traffic Services (VTS) and Vessel Traffic Management System (VTMS)*.

National Interests

It is shaped by a mix of *National Values* and *National Aim*. In broad terms, four fundamental interests of any *Nation-State* are security interests, economic interests, world order interests and ideological interests. The world order interests essentially relate to the maintenance of an international political and economic system in which the *Nation-State* can feel secure and in which, its citizens and commerce can operate peacefully. The ideological interests lie in the protection and furtherance of *National Values*, which the citizens of the *Nation-State* share and believe to be universally good. India's overarching national interests are expressed in the Preamble to the Constitution, and are centered on the preservation of the nation's core values from external aggression and internal subversion. These are:

- Sovereignty, unity and territorial integrity of India.
- Democratic, secular and federal character of the Indian Republic.
- Secure and stable internal and external environment that is conducive to safety, security and development of the nation and its citizens.
- Socio-cultural and economic well-being of the nation and its citizens.

In the order of their priority for national policy-makers, *National Interests* may be sub-divided into 'core', 'important' and 'other' interests. At times, countries delineate their geographical areas of national interest as primary areas, secondary areas, and so on.

Nationalism

As a key component in the making of a *Nation-State*, nationalism may be defined as 'people's sense of collective destiny through a common past and the vision of a common future'. The history of common triumphs and sufferings evokes powerful bonds of solidarity for *Nation-States*, notwithstanding their heterogeneity in terms of ethnic, cultural, linguistic and religious differences of their people.

National Maritime Domain Awareness (NMDA) Project

See *National Command Control Communication and Intelligence Network (NC^3IN).*

National Power

See *Comprehensive National Power (CNP).*

National Security

It refers to the 'physical survival' of a *Nation-State*, preservation of its 'territorial integrity', its 'political independence', besides the perpetuation of the values, patterns of social relations, life styles and varied other elements that make up the country's way of life. In a more comprehensive sense, it also encompasses the country's economic security and human security.

The National Security objectives of a country flow from its *National Interests*, and may include the following:

- Ensuring security of national territory, territorial space, citizens, resources and maritime trade routes.
- Maintaining a secure internal environment to guard against threats to national unity, core values and development.
- Strengthening co-operation and friendship with other countries to promote regional and global stability.
- Maintaining a strong and credible defence posture, and capability to safeguard the national aim and interests.

National Strategy

National Aim (combined with *National Values*) provides the basis for defining *National Interests*, and is sought to be achieved through National Strategy. Earlier referred to as 'Grand Strategy', National Strategy represents the comprehensive approach of a *Nation-State* to satiate its *National Aim* (or objectives). The means available are political, diplomatic, economic, psychological and military. National Strategy thus encompasses its constituent parts like 'Economic Strategy', *Military Strategy*, 'Informational Strategy', 'Energy Security Strategy', 'Science and Technology Strategy', and so on. The term 'National Strategy' is often used as an adjective ('National Strategic') to qualify nouns like 'planning' and '*Doctrine*'.

National Values

These evolve from a nation's culture and history. National Values (combined with *National Aim*) provide the basis for defining *National Interests.*

National Waters

Waters subject to the territorial sovereignty of coastal States. National waters include *Internal Waters*, *Territorial Waters*, and *Archipelagic Waters.*

Nationality Jurisdiction

See *Criminal Jurisdiction.*

Nautical Mile (NM)

International unit of distance equal to 1.852 kilometers. It is usually used by sea and air navigators worldwide because of its convenience when working with charts. It is the length of an arc on the Earth's surface subtended by an angle of one minute of latitude at the Earth's centre. Since the Earth is not a perfect sphere and is flattened across the polar caps, this length varies from place to place, being shortest at the Equator, and longest at the Poles. The arithmetic mean of this length measured at the Equator and that measured at the Poles is 6077 feet (1852 metres). The nautical mile differs from the land mile, which equals 5280 feet (1609 metres). See *Knot.*

Naval Base and Access Facility

A Naval (or Military) Base supports naval (or military) forces inter alia in terms of technical services and spares, ordnance services and depots, medical facilities and general logistic facilities comprising victuals, clothing, etc. A naval (military) base may be located within the country (home base) or in foreign territory (overseas base). An Overseas Base is different from an Overseas Naval Access Facility, which merely denotes a foreign location for Operational Turn Around (OTR) for forward-deployed naval forces during peace-time. Both are a result of an agreement between two countries. See *Sea Basing.*

Naval Cooperation and Guidance to Shipping (NCAGS)

As an adjunct to *SLOC Protection*, the Naval Cooperation and Guidance to Shipping (NCAGS) organisation advises the Indian Shipping companies (and potentially, all foreign-flagged vessels carrying Indian trade) on the choice of safe routes across the seas and or entry/exit from harbours, in times of *War and Armed Conflict.* It also requires monitoring and regulation of all merchant ships in Indian waters and ports, and routeing and control of all Indian merchant ships in India's areas of maritime interest. While the routing of Indian merchant ships to avoid to areas beset by low-intensity threats like *Piracy* and *Maritime Terrorism* is the responsibility of the *DGoS*, NCAGS organisation could potentially be a valuable supplement. See *SLOC Interdiction* and *Low Intensity Conflict/Maritime Operations (LICO/LIMO).*

Naval Power

It refers to the comprehensive capability of a nation's navy. In contrast with *Maritime-Military Power*, it is restricted to a single service of the nation's armed forces. See *Maritime Power*.

NAVAREA

The world's oceans are divided by the *International Maritime Organisation (IMO)* into 16 areas for dissemination of navigation and meteorological warnings. India is the coordinator for NAVAREA VIII. In India's maritime neighbourhood, South Africa, Pakistan and Australia are coordinators of NAVAREAs VII, IX and X respectively. See *Maritime Search and Rescue (M-SAR)*.

Network Centric Operations (NCO) and Network Centric Warfare (NCW)

NCO is an information-enabled concept of operations that generates increased combat power by networking sensors, decision makers, and shooters to achieve shared awareness, increased speed of command, higher tempo of operations, greater lethality, increased survivability, and a degree of self synchronisation. In essence, NCO translates information capability into combat power by effectively linking knowledgeable entities in the battle-space. *Co-operative Engagement Capability (CEC)* is among the key objectives of NCO.

A related term is 'Network Centric Warfare' (NCW). Both NCO and NCW are often used interchangeably. However, NCO applies to a much broader domain of operations across the *Spectrum of Conflict*, rather than being limited to warfare. Another difference is that unlike NCO, NCW involves disrupting the enemy's NCO processes and targeting its NCO capabilities. See *Rukmini Communications Satellite*.

No First Use (NFU)

An element of nuclear policy of a country possessing nuclear-weapons capability of not using such capability as a means of warfighting, unless it is first attacked by nuclear weapons; or in some cases, by other *Weapons of Mass Destruction*. India's nuclear *Doctrine* (1999/2003) is based on NFU principle. China has a NFU policy, albeit with some caveats. Pakistan does not have a NFU policy citing India's conventional military superiority. It may be noted that NFU is merely a declaratory policy with no obligation in terms of international law. See *Nuclear Second-Strike* and *Nuclear Deterrence.*

Non-Combatant Evacuation Operation (NEO)

An operation directed by national authority whereby non-combatant (primarily civilian) citizens are evacuated from foreign countries affected by war, civil unrest or natural disaster to safe havens since their lives are endangered. Although the primary intent is the sovereign obligation of the country to protect its citizens, evacuating citizens of a third country also falls within the ambit of NEO.

It is important to note that a country, with the various constabulary agencies and crisis-response mechanisms at its disposal, can address such insecurities to its citizens within its territory, and to an extent, even in the waters under its *Sovereign Jurisdiction.* However, to protect its citizens on foreign shores, limited national means are available. The country's diplomatic mission abroad does play an important role, but it may be unable or inadequate in case of a widespread crisis on foreign land. In such scenarios, *Strategic Airlift* and *Strategic Sealift* are the only instruments available to the country to put its citizens to safety. While *Strategic Airlift* offers a quicker NEO response, it may not be suitable for all contingencies. In a conflict scenario, for example, a suitable airfield may not be available. Also, the aircraft would be more vulnerable. See *Out of Area Contingency (OOAC) Operations* and *Remittances.*

Non-International Armed Conflicts (NIAC)

Traditionally, inter-State *Armed Conflict* has been more frequent necessitating greater global attention in terms of preventing them and their adverse effects on humanity. However, since the Second World War, the frequency of occurrence of intra-State violent conflicts has been on the increase. When the character and scope of such conflicts cross a certain 'threshold', these are termed '*Non-International Armed Conflicts*' (NIAC).

Geneva Conventions, 1949 (Common Art. 3) defines NIAC as "...an armed conflict not of an international character occurring in the territory of one of the High Contracting Parties". According to San Remo Manual, 2006, "Non-international armed conflicts are armed confrontations occurring within the territory of a single State and in which the armed forces of no other State are engaged against the central government....(However,) internal disturbances and tensions (such as riots, isolated and sporadic acts of violence, or other acts of a similar nature) do not amount to a non-international armed conflict."

Therefore, NIAC involves an armed conflict within a State between two non-State groups, or between a non-State group and the State. However, as per the 1977 Additional Protocol I to Geneva Convention, 1949, if the conflict involves "...a peoples fight against colonial domination, alien occupation or a racist regimes", it assumes the character of IAC. (India has not acceded to the Additional Protocol I).

Furthermore, in case another country intervenes to assist the government of affected country involved in NIAC against the non-State group, the conflict retains the character of NIAC. However, if the country intervenes in favour of the non-State group involved in NIAC, it becomes a IAC. See *International Criminal Court (ICC), International Humanitarian Law* (IHL) and *Human Rights Law.*

Non-Proliferation Treaty (NPT)

An international treaty signed in 1968 and effective from 1970, whose objective is to prevent the spread of nuclear weapons and related technology, to promote cooperation in the peaceful uses of nuclear energy, and to further the goal of achieving complete nuclear disarmament. Under the NPT, all countries other than the then-recognised five Nuclear Weapon States (NWS)—China, France, Russia, the United Kingdom and the United States—were prohibited from inter alia possessing, manufacturing or acquiring nuclear weapons. The treaty states that all exports of nuclear equipment and material must be regulated by safeguards laid down by the 'International Atomic Energy Agency' (IAEA).

Although India supports the objectives of the NPT, and has a proven record for nuclear non-proliferation, it has not acceded to it since it is not considered a NWS under the treaty. Also, India considers the treaty fundamentally discriminatory since it curbs the related rights of countries that do not possess nuclear weapons vis-à-vis the NWS, while making no tangible efforts towards its overarching aim of complete nuclear disarmament. Pakistan and Israel also are not parties to the NPT. See

Comprehensive Nuclear Test Ban Treaty (CTBT), Nuclear Suppliers Group (NSG) and *Zangger Committee.*

Non-Refoulement

A core principle of International Refugee Law that prohibits the government of a country to return refugees to another country wherein their lives or freedom may be threatened. This principle is a part of *Customary International Law*, and is thus a binding obligation for all countries, even if one (like India) that is not party to the 1951 Refugee Convention. See *Refuge, Refugee and Asylum.*

Non-Tariff Barriers (NTB)

A term used in economics, which refers to trade barriers—other than those based on tariffs—that restrict imports. Some common examples are anti-dumping duty and countervailing (anti-subsidy) duty. The use of NTBs has risen sharply after the *World Trade Organisation (WTO)* rules led to a very significant reduction in tariffs. Some non-tariff trade barriers are expressly permitted in very few cases when they are considered essential to protect health, safety, sanitation, or relate to depletable natural resources. In other cases, the use of NTBs is considered as a measure against global norms and rules. See *Common Market, Single Market and Unified Market, Excise Duty and Custom Duty, Foreign Trade* and *World Trade Organisation (WTO).*

North Atlantic Treaty Organisation (NATO)

A trans-Atlantic *Military Alliance* based on North Atlantic Treaty signed in 1949. Article 5 of the treaty commits the allies to collective defence in case of a military attack on any member. The alliance served to present US-Europe solidarity during the Cold War against the Soviet Union-led Warsaw Pact alliance (without any military confrontation). In 1990, shortly after the end of Cold War, the the European Community (comprising 12 European countries) and the US signed the 'Transatlantic Declaration' calling for the continued existence of NATO. The alliance later undertook its first ever military interventions in Bosnia (1992-1995) and Yugoslavia (1999), Article 5 of the Treaty was invoked for the first time after terrorist strikes in the US in 2001, leading to deployment of NATO-led 'International Security Assistance Force' (ISAF) in

Afghanistan. At present, NATO has 28 member countries. The incorporation of former Soviet republics as new members has been a cause of increased geopolitical tension between NATO countries and Russia. NATO has an integrated *Command and Control* structure, and is headquartered in Brussels, Belgium.

Nuclear Attack Submarine (NATO Designation: SSGN/SSN)

Nuclear propulsion for submarines was developed by the United States and the erstwhile Soviet Union after the Second World War. The UK, France and China followed suit. A nuclear attack submarine is much larger than a *Conventional Submarine (SS/SSG)*. It is capable of very high speeds. Its larger internal space accommodates a better outfit of sonar and other sensors. It is, however, important to note that since a 'nuclear' submarine is actually propelled by 'steam' turbines, it is much noisier than a diesel-electric *Conventional Submarine (SS/SSG)*.

Western countries use a nuclear attack submarine as an anti-submarine escort for a *Carrier Battle Group (CBG)*. Its nearly unlimited power, endurance and virtual 'omni-presence' confers it the ability to exercise *Sea Control.* A SSGN is similar to a SSN, except that it is also armed with guided cruise missiles. Both the SSN and SSGN can also perform roles such as anti-shipping, distant *Sea Denial*, insertion of forces for *Special Operations*, intelligence gathering, shadowing of enemy *Ballistic Missile Submarine (SSBN)* and escorting friendly SSBNs.

Nuclear Deterrence

A subset of *Strategic Deterrence*. It is essentially based upon the possession of capabilities of nuclear weapons and their delivery appropriate to a country's nuclear *Doctrine*, and its political posture. The credibility of nuclear deterrence is extremely critical for the effectiveness of such deterrence. Being most survivable of land and air-based nuclear weapons, a nuclear-armed missile submarine is considered the most 'credible' and thus, also most effective of all nuclear arsenals. It also contributes to arms control stability that is best achieved at the lowest arsenal levels. At times, countries use nuclear 'signalling' or 'posturing' to reinforce nuclear deterrence, which could involve 'brinkmanship'. See *Ballistic Missile Submarines (SSBN)*, *Deterrence* and *Counterforce and Countervalue Targeting* and *No First Use (NFU)*.

Nuclear Second-Strike

A concept of nuclear strategy. Refers primarily to a nuclear retaliation by a country that has been first attacked through nuclear weapons. A nuclear second-strike capability is a country's assured ability to respond to a nuclear attack with a forceful punitive nuclear retaliation. Such capability is critical for a country that professes a *No First Use (NFU)* doctrine. The credibility of such capability is vital for *Nuclear Deterrence*, so as to prevent the potential adversary into believing that it could win a nuclear exchange by undertaking a pre-emptive decapitating nuclear strike against the country's nuclear weapons capability for it to retaliate. A capability based on a nuclear weapons triad is essential for a country to disperse and diversify its nuclear arsenals towards attaining an assured second-strike capability. The underwater dimension based on *SSBN*s is considered the most 'survivable' element of the triad, and is, therefore, also a critical enabler for a nuclear *Doctrine* of *No First Use (NFU)*. See *Counterforce and Countervalue Targeting.*

Nuclear Suppliers Group (NSG)

A multinational group of nuclear supplier countries set up in 1974 with the objective to counter nuclear proliferation by controlling exports and other transfer of materials applicable for development of nuclear weapons through the implementation of guidelines for nuclear exports and nuclear-related exports.

Although at that time, the nuclear *Non-Proliferation Treaty (NPT)* was already in force, NSG was considered necessary for a more inclusive approach to nuclear non-proliferation, primarily to bring in non-*Zangger Committee* countries. The inclusion of France—a non-signatory to *Zangger Committee* at that time—was considered particularly necessary. Initially, seven countries formed the NSG, viz. Canada, West Germany, France, Japan, the USSR, the UK, and the US. In the subsequent years, many other countries—mostly in Europe, and some successor States of erstwhile-USSR joined the group. In 2014, the NSG had 48 members, including China, which joined in 2004. India has lately received a wide-based support from the NSG to be included in the group.

NSG guidelines forbid nuclear trade with a country which has not signed the NPT. As per the guidelines, the identified materials can be exported to non-nuclear States only if certain safeguards stipulated by the 'International Atomic Energy Agency' (IAEA) have been met or some other exceptional circumstances exist. In 1994, the NSG adopted the 'Non-Proliferation Principle', whereby a supplier, notwithstanding other provisions in the NSG Guidelines, authorises a transfer only when satisfied that the transfer would not contribute to the proliferation of nuclear weapons. This seeks to cover the rare cases where adherence to the NPT or to a *Nuclear Weapon Free Zone (NWFZ)* treaty may not by itself be a guarantee that a country will actually further the spirit of such treaties.

In September 2008, to enable India to progress its nuclear deal with the US, the NSG agreed to grant India a waiver from its rules, based on a formal pledge by India stating that it would not share sensitive nuclear technology or material with others and will uphold its voluntary moratorium on testing nuclear weapons. NSG is also referred to as the 'London Suppliers Group' since the initial meetings to formulate NSG guidelines were held in London.

Nuclear Weapon Free Zone (NWFZ) and Nuclear Free Zone

A Nuclear Weapons Free Zone (NWFZ) refers to a geographic area, wherein a group of countries have entered into a treaty banning the use, development or deployment of nuclear weapons, and which is recognised by the UN General Assembly. The nuclear *Non-Proliferation Treaty (NPT)*, which entered into force in 1970, affirms the right of countries to establish specified zones free of nuclear weapons. The UN General Assembly reaffirmed that right in 1975 and outlined the criteria for such zones. Within these nuclear-weapon-free zones, countries may use nuclear energy for peaceful purposes. Presently, five NWFZ exist worldwide. The treaties establishing these zones are the Treaty of Tlatelolco (1967) covering Latin America and the Caribbean, the Treaty of Rarotonga (1985) covering the South Pacific, the Bangkok Treaty (1995) covering Southeast Asia, the Treaty of Pelindaba (1996) covering Africa and the Treaty of Semipalatinsk (2006) covering Central Asia. (It is important to note that other than the treaties establishing NWFZ, there exist other international treaties banning the deployment of nuclear weapons in Antarctica, Mongolia, on the seabed, and in outer space.) Each NWFZ treaty includes a protocol for the five Nuclear Weapon States (NWS) recognised under the NPT to accede to it, and thereby affirm that they would not use or threaten to use nuclear weapons against any country in the zone. See *Nuclear Suppliers Group (NSG)* and *Southeast Asia Nuclear Weapons Free Zone (SEANWFZ)*.

A Nuclear Free Zone is an area where nuclear weapons (and sometimes also nuclear power plants) are banned by domestic legislation, rather than being a result of an international treaty. In 1987, for example, New Zealand passed an Act making the country a Nuclear Free Zone. (The ban, however, does not apply to nuclear power stations). The national legislation bans the entry of nuclear weapons and nuclear-propelled vessels into its *Territorial Waters*. It also bans dumping of radioactive waste, and prohibits its citizens and residents to "manufacture, acquire, possess, or have any control over any nuclear explosive." It may be noted, however, that nuclear free zones do not prohibit the medical usages of radioactive material. Many sub-national authorities worldwide have also declared themselves as "nuclear-free". (e.g. Brisbane in Australia and Vancouver in Canada). However, such declarations are symbolic, if these are not supported by national legislation.

O

Oceanography and Oceanology

Traditionally, 'Oceanography' referred to recording or describing the physical, chemical and biological characteristics of the ocean. (The Greek term 'graphia' means 'the act of recording'). In the later years, however, the term was replaced by 'Oceanology', which was considered to be better to describe the complex sciences relevant to study of ocean. (The Greek term 'ology' means 'the science of').

In common lexicon currently in use, the terms 'Oceanography' and 'Oceanology' are used interchangeably as synonyms, with the former being used more often. In the scientific lexicon, however, Oceanography (also called Marine Sciences) is the branch of Earth Sciences involving the study of the Earth's ocean realm, which comprehensively covers a wide range of aspects pertaining to the oceans, ranging from marine life to ocean currents, and from geology of the sea bottom to the physical and chemical properties of seawater. It also involves the compilation of scientific data pertaining to the oceans.

On the other hand, 'Oceanology' has emerged as a branch of 'Oceanography' that studies only the economic geography (physical and biological aspects) of the ocean. It is, therefore, a science concerned with the resource-oriented application of 'Oceanography'. Among the other branches of 'Oceanography' are *Bathymetry and Hydrography.*

India established the Department of Ocean Development (DOD) in 1981 as the government's nodal department for oceanographic research and development. In 1982, India issued its 'Ocean Policy Statement' for management and utilisation of marine resources and the development of relevant technologies (the temporal coincidence with *UNCLOS*, 1982 may be noted). The envisaged objectives of the policy statement are being met by various institutions such as the National Institute of Oceanography (Goa), the National Institute of Ocean Technology (Chennai) and the National Centre for Antarctic (Polar) and Ocean Research, Goa. See *Amphibious Aircraft.*

Offshore Defence

See *Offshore Security and Offshore Defence.*

Offshore Development Area (ODA)

The abbreviation ODA is sometimes expanded as 'Oilfield Development Area'. The concept of ODA were introduced in 1980 as an advice to commercial shipping to avoid transit through specific areas in the maritime zones of coastal countries due to the high levels of activity associated with the establishment of *Offshore Platforms* for exploitation of mineral resources, particularly hydrocarbons. These supplement the 500 metre *Safety Zones* provided for in the *UNCLOS*. Notably, unlike *Safety Zones*, the promulgation of ODAs places no legal obligation upon the mariners to avoid sailing through these areas.

Nearly half of India's domestic crude-oil production and two-thirds of its natural gas production is sourced from ODAs. The exploitation of mineral resources in Indian maritime zones is regulated by 'the Offshore Areas Mineral (Development and Regulation) Act, 2002', which came into force in January 2003. The *Directorate General of Shipping (DGoS)* issues periodic advisories (MS Notices) for the vessels navigating in the vicinity of the Indian ODAs. See *Vessel Traffic Management System (VTMS).*

Offshore Platform

Also called Oil Platform or Oil Rig, it is a large structure with facilities to drill wells, to extract and process crude oil and natural gas, or, or to temporarily store the product until it can be brought to shore for refining and marketing. In many cases, the platform contains facilities to house the workforce as well. Depending on the circumstances, these platforms could be 'bottom supported' or 'floating' rigs.

A 'bottom supported platform' could be among the following:

- **Gravel Islands.** Artificial islands may be used in water depths of up to 50 feet to support large drilling rigs. Many tons of gravel are placed on the seafloor to create the island. When completed, the islands may be left to erode naturally or dredged to a depth that allows for vessel navigation.
- **Steel Jacket.** Typical fixed steel platforms consist of large pipe legs and a tubular steel cross bracing that form a 'jacket'. The jacket is

supported by piles driven into the seafloor to transmit wave, wind and current force into the ground. It is used in depths up to 1,400 feet.

- **Gravity-Based Structures.** These platforms made of steel or concrete take advantage of their mass to support heavy drilling rigs and production equipment in depths of up to 1,000 feet. They function similarly to gravel islands and jacket structures, but can be used in deeper waters than gravel islands.
- **Compliant Towers.** In waters as deep as 1,000 to 3,000 feet, small steady waves cause fatigue on the fixed structure. Compliant towers are slender and so flexible that they sway with the waves to avoid fatigue at such depths.

A 'floating rig' could be among the following:

- **Tension Leg Platform (TLP).** Similar to Compliant Tower except that the hull is floating, and moored to seafloor with 'vertical' tension legs that dampen movements due to wind and sea. It can be used in depths up to 6,000 feet.
- **Semi-Submersible.** A deck supported by four columns and connected underwater by four pontoons. Unlike TLP, its floating hull uses a 'lateral' mooring system of steel cables connected to subsea wells via flowlines to keep the platform in position.
- **Spar.** The rig is supported by a floating, hollow cylinder (spar) containing extra weight in the bottom. Like the TLP and Semi-Submersible, it is moored to the seafloor, but with a 'vertical-cum-lateral' mooring system. Ninety per cent of the spar is underwater to provide stability in waters as deep as 10,000 feet.
- **FPSO.** A Floating Production Storage and Offloading (FPSO) vessel can operate in depths up to 10,000 feet, and is best suited for catering to lack of underwater pipeline to transport oil to shore. FPSO can process the oil or gas produced from a reservoir, separating the oil and gas and storing the oil until it can be offloaded to tankers for transportation.

Offshore Security and Offshore Defence

India's *Sovereign Rights* (or *Sovereign Jurisdiction*) extends beyond *Territorial Waters* up to the 200 nautical mile *Exclusive Economic Zone (EEZ)*. Such jurisdiction is likely to be extended up to 350 nm when the delineation of the *Legal Continental Shelf (LCS)* is completed. India has the right to regulate all maritime activities in this area related to the exploration and production of natural resources, ocean research and fishing. The protection of all natural resources, assets and people engaged in maritime activities in this area constitutes 'offshore security'.

Offshore Defence pertains to the defence of offshore infrastructure and vessels in the *Exclusive Economic Zone (EEZ)* against military threats in wartime. See *Offshore Development Area (ODA)*, *Safety Zones*, and *Sovereignty and Sovereign Rights*.

Offshore Support Vessel (OSV)

Also called 'Platform Support Vessel' (PSV), OSV is a vessel specially designed to support the activities of *Offshore* (oil and gas) *Platforms*. These vessels range from 50 to 100 meters in length. Their primary function is logistic support and transportation of goods, tools, equipment and personnel to and from the *Offshore Platforms*. Some OSVS are equipped for fire-fighting and *Oil Spill Response*. See *Offshore Development Area (ODA)*.

Oil Spill

The term is usually used in context of the maritime environment (marine oil spill) involving release of crude oil, or petroleum products into the sea or coastal waters from *Oil Tankers* or *Offshore Platforms*.

At the global level, the law on vessel-based marine oil-spills is laid down in the 'International Convention for Prevention of Pollution from Ships' (1973), as modified by its additional protocol of 1978 (*MARPOL 73/78*), and various MARPOL protocols and amendments (such as of 2003 pertaining to *Oil Tankers*) and *UNCLOS*. The *UNCLOS* provides a three-party concurrent jurisdiction in terms of their rights and obligations, as summarised below.

- **Flag State Jurisdiction**. The ship's *Flag State* can establish laws and regulations to set anti-pollution standards, but which must conform to the accepted international rules and standards. In case of a violation, it needs to institute legal proceedings, keeping the requesting country and the *International Maritime Organisation (IMO)* informed.

- **Coastal State Jurisdiction.** The coastal State can establish laws and regulations to set anti-pollution standards for its *Territorial Waters* in conformity with international standards; and for its *Exclusive Economic Zone (EEZ)* in conformity with international law. The coastal State can physically inspect a foreign-flagged vessel in its maritime zones, and institute legal proceedings, if required.
- **Port State Jurisdiction.** Introduced by *UNCLOS* the first time, it confers the authority to the port State to set unilaterally its own requirements with regard to ship construction and crew standards for foreign-flagged ships entering the port. The port State can physically inspect a foreign-flagged vessel in its ports and if the ship is unworthy, it may detain it until it is repaired in the nearest repair yard.

See *Marine Pollution*, *Oil Spill Response,* and *Particularly Sensitive Sea Area (PSSA).*

Oil Spill Response

The preparedness for responding to *Oil Spills* is usually addressed by categorising these into a three-tiered system based on the size and location of the spill, which indicate its severity and response capacity required. Tier 1 spills are relatively small, occurring at or near an operator's own facilities, as a consequence of its own activities. The individual operators are expected to respond with their own resources. Tier 2 spills are much larger, typically up to 10,000 tons that extends beyond the remit of the Tier 1 response area, where more stakeholders are affected and external resources are needed to respond. Tier 3 spills are widespread—typically above 10,000 tons—that, due to its scale and likelihood to cause major area-wide impact, calls for substantial augmentation of regional resources.

Oil spill response at the national level is laid down in 'National Oil Spill and Disaster Contingency Plan' (NOSDCP). The Indian Coast Guard (ICG) is the central coordinating agency for implementation of the NOSDCP. The ICG conducts exercises with various agencies to simulate oil spill contingencies. In 2010, the ICG began inducting three specialised Pollution Control Vessels (PCV) with the aim of increasing its *Oil Spill* response capacity to Tier-3. The first PCV inducted in August 2010 was CGS 'Samudra Prahari'. Each PCV has the capacity to recover and store 300 tons of spilled oil from the sea, as also to continuously recover and transfer oil through floating barges. See *Marine Pollution*, MARPOL 73/78, and *Particularly Sensitive Sea Area (PSSA)*.

Oil Tanker

A ship designed to carry oil in bulk in tanks. Tankers load their cargo by gravity from ashore or by shore pumps, and discharge using own pumps. See *Ultra Large Crude Carrier (ULCC)* and *Very Large Crude Carrier (VLCC)*.

In December 2003, the Marine Environment Protection Committee (MEPC) of the *International Maritime Organisation (IMO)* adopted amendments to *MARPOL 73/78* Convention. Aimed at preventing *Oil Spills* from oil tankers, this made it obligatory for the older single-hull tankers carrying heavy fuel oil to meet a new set of deadlines for phase-out or conversion to double hulls. Specifically, it implied that single-hull oil tankers more than 23 years old must be phased out or converted to double hulls if they are above 20,000 tons *DWT* and carry crude oil, fuel oil, heavy diesel oil or lubricating oil, and above 30,000 tons *DWT* if carrying other oils. The rule applies only to pre-MARPOL *Oil Tankers* that do not comply with the requirements for protectively located segregated ballast tanks. The MARPOL amendments came into force in April 2005. Warships, naval auxiliary ships and other government vessels are exempt from the phase-out. See *Oil Spill Response*.

Operational Art

See *Levels of Warfare*

Operational Level of Warfare

See *Levels of Warfare*

Operational Logistics

Although warships are inherently self-contained, their extended or distant operational deployments necessitate logistic support, not only in terms of fuel and victuals, but also maintenance support, and even ordnance stores. This could be achieved either through sea-based logistic support integral to the *Task Force* in the form of Fleet Support Ships (FSS), or though replenishment in an overseas facility, as a government-to-government understanding. The process of replenishing the warship in such a facility is called 'Operational Turn Around' (OTR). See *Lilypad, Mobile Landing Platform (MLP), Naval Base and Access Facility* and *Sea Basing.*

Operational Turn Around (OTR)

See Operational Logistics.

Organisation for the Prohibition of Chemical Weapons (OPCW)

See *Chemical Weapons Convention (CWC).*

Organisation of Petroleum Exporting Countries (OPEC)

A multilateral organisation comprising 12 countries that are major exporters of petroleum (crude oil and natural gas), viz. Algeria, Angola, Ecuador, Iran, Iraq, Kuwait, Libya, Qatar, Saudi Arabia, the UAE and Venezuela. The OPEC was established in 1960 with the objective of coordinating and unifying their petroleum-related policies for providing stability to the oil markets for both consumers and producers, and also for the investors in petroleum industry. The OPEC sets production targets for its member countries to regulate global oil prices.

Out of Area Contingency (OOAC) Operations

Military missions conducted beyond a country's territorial frontiers and maritime zones. These include inter alia *UN Peace-Support Operations* (UNPSO), *Non-Combatant Evacuation Operations* (NEO), security assistance to friendly countries, distant *Low-Intensity Maritime Operations* (LIMO), missions to ensure good order at sea and *Humanitarian Assistance and Disaster Response* (HADR) operations.

Over the Horizon (OTH) Operations

The technological evolution of war-fighting has lately enabled maritime-military forces to cause an effect on the adversary forces that may be located at distances beyond the 'line-of-sight'. Such operations that seek to achieve this are commonly referred to as OTH Operations. Such operations constitute a key enabler for *Manoeuvre* warfare. The concept is usually used in the context of OTH Targeting and OTH *Amphibious Operation.* See *Anti-Surface Warfare (ASuW).*

P

P&I (Protection and Indemnity) Clubs

It refers to an international group of thirteen *Underwriting* member clubs, who, among themselves, provide insurance liability cover (protection and indemnity) for approximately 90 per cent of the world's ocean-going shipping tonnage. The liabilities include personal injury to crew, passengers and others onboard, cargo loss and damage, oil pollution, wreck removal and dock damage. Operating in a group provides distinct opportunities, such as the following:

- Pooling of resources to cater for relatively high monetary claims.
- Formulation of common policies.
- Collective 'voice' at international fora, and while interacting with inter-governmental organisations (like the *International Maritime Organisation*) and national governments.
- Exchange of information and analyses, particularly on *Maritime Security*.

See *Joint War Committee (JWC)*, *War Risk Insurance*, *War Risk Zones*, and *Wreck Removal Convention (WREC)*.

Panamax (Ship)

See *Commercial Ship Sizes*.

Particularly Sensitive Sea Area (PSSA)

An area established in consonance with *UNCLOS* Article 211 (Pollution from Vessels), paragraph 6, which needs special protection through action by the *International Maritime Organisation (IMO)* because of its significance for recognised ecological or socio-economic or scientific reasons, and which may be vulnerable to damage by international shipping and other maritime activities. When PSSA is designated, an appropriate Associated Protective Measure (APM) is adopted as stipulated by the *IMO*. The Maritime Environment Protection Committee (MEPC) of the *IMO* identifies the PSSAs in conjunction with coastal countries. At present, 14 PSSAs have been designated worldwide.

PSSA is among the rare cases when coastal countries can impose and enforce their national environmental and navigation regulations on foreign ships passing through their waters. The concerned coastal country cannot bar a foreign ship's entry into their PSSA, but it is permitted to promulgate specific regulations such as avoiding certain specific areas, the use of compulsory routes, banning discharging of ship-borne waste and compulsory reporting. See *Marine Pollution, MARPOL 73/78, Oil Spill and Oil Spill Response.*

Passage Exercise

Refers to a *Combined* exercise between two navies that is not structured, but ad hoc and merely incidental to passage of a foreign warship in the vicinity of the port of another country. Such exercises are often conducted when a warship departs a foreign port on completion of a port call, when it is customary for it to be escorted for some distance by the warship of the host country.

Passive Deterrence

See *Conventional Deterrence.*

Passive Personality Jurisdiction

See *Criminal Jurisdiction.*

Patrol

See *Search and Patrol.*

Peace Enforcement Operations (PEO)

PEO are the application of military force, or threat of its use, normally pursuant to international authorisation, to compel compliance with the resolutions or sanctions designed to maintain or restore peace and order. Although 'Peace Enforcement' finds no mention in the UN Charter, these operations are generally undertaken under Chapter VII (threat to international peace and security) of UN Charter, when the consent of any of the major parties to the conflict is uncertain. Due to the UN's limited *Command and Control* (C^2) resources, the command of large-scale PEO is increasingly being delegated to military alliances such as *NATO*, or to *Coalitions* based on a 'lead' nation.

PEO may be sub-divided into 'partial' PEO involving imposition of the solution by force, and 'impartial' PEO involving consent of the host country. The examples of the former are the Korean War (1950-53) and the first Gulf War (1990-91). UN operations in Somalia in 1993-94 (UNOSOM II) and deployment of the NATO-led 'Implementation Force' (IFOR) in Bosnia and Herzegovina in 1995-96 are examples 'impartial' PEO. 'Impartial' PEO, while potentially involving combat, does not amount to full-scale warfare on a sustained basis against a State, and falls conceptually between 'partial' PEO and traditional *Peacekeeping Operations (PKO)*. Being mandated by Chapter VII, none of the two types of operation require consent as a legal condition, but 'impartial' PEO seeks and attempts to achieve and maintain consent, or at least acquiescence, from the relevant parties whenever possible.

Some legal experts consider 'partial' PEO under a separate head called 'Enforcement Operations', as distinct from (impartial) 'Peace Enforcement Operations'. It is, however, important to note that such 'Enforcement Operations' (Article 42 of UN Charter) are distinct from *Enforcement of Sanctions* (under Article 41 of the UN Charter).

Peacekeeping Operations (PKO)

Military operations undertaken with the consent of all major parties to a dispute, aimed to monitor and facilitate the implementation of a peace agreement and support diplomatic efforts to reach long term political settlement. Although the UN Charter makes no specific mention of 'Peacekeeping', such operations are generally undertaken under Chapter VI of UN Charter. Not all peacekeeping forces are mandated by the UN. The Indian Peace Keeping Force (IPKF) in Sri Lanka from 1987-90 was deployed as per an agreement between the two States. Also see, *Peace-Making*.

Peace-Making

The concept involving a 'negotiated settlement' evolved in the late 1980s. Its aim is to help the parties implement a comprehensive settlement after a certain process of negotiation. It involves not only military arrangements, but also wide ranging socio-political and economic ones. See *Peacekeeping Operations (PKO).*

Pelagic Fish

Fish that live in zones neither close to the bottom nor near the shore. See *Fishing Methods and Gear* and *Demersal Fish.*

Permanent Court of Arbitration (PCA)

See *International Arbitration.*

Permissive RoE

See *Rules of Engagement (RoE).*

Persuasion and Dissuasion

Persuasion is convincing another country, by diplomatic means and without the threat of force, or use of force, to 'carry out' certain action(s) that are in own interests, by emphasising the benefits of the action to that country. (This is distinct from *Coercion* that involves threat of use of force, and *Compellance* that involves demonstration of force).

In similar vein, Dissuasion uses the same means to convince another country to 'desist' from carrying out certain action(s) that are inimical to own interests, by indicating its disadvantages to that country. Given its inherent attributes of versatility and flexibility, naval power is ideally suited for Persuasion and Dissuasion. Building maritime partnerships with friendly countries is a valuable instrument to achieve Persuasion and Dissuasion. See *Deterrence.*

Pilot and Pilotage

Pilot is a person who is qualified to assist the Captain of a ship to navigate in restricted waters, mostly while entering or leaving a port. Pilotage is the act of the Pilot, or the fee payable for the services of a Pilot. In most ports, pilotage is compulsory.

Piracy

Any illegal act of violence, detention or plundering, committed for 'private ends' by the crew or passengers of a private ship against another ship in *International Waters* (simplified and paraphrased definition of *UNCLOS*

Art 101). According to *Customary International Law* (codified in *UNCLOS*), 'Piracy' is considered as 'Crime Jure Gentium' (Crime Against Humanity), and thereby provides for a maritime force from any country to seize a pirate ship in *International Waters*. (See *Criminal Jurisdiction.*) However, if the crime is committed in *Territorial Waters* of a country, it is not termed '*Piracy*', but 'Armed Robbery at Sea', wherein only the law-enforcement agencies of the concerned coastal State have the authority to act. See *Private Maritime Security Companies (PMSC)*. See *Anti-Piracy and Counter-Piracy, International Maritime Bureau (IMB), Piracy: Activity, Approach, Attack, Hijack, etc.* and *Piracy High Risk Area (HRA).*

Piracy: Activity, Approach, Attack, Hijack, etc.

- **Suspicious Approach.** An unexplained close proximity of an unknown vessel.
- **Piracy Approach.** An aggressive approach by pirates against a vessel involving weapons clearly seen on display as a show of force or threat against the vessel, but weapons have not yet been discharged against the vessel.
- **Piracy Attack.** The vessel has been subjected to an aggressive approach by a pirate craft, and weapons have been discharged at or towards a vessel.
- **Suspicious Activity.** Any piracy related event that is suspicious enough to warrant consideration and sharing with the merchant shipping community, but does not have sufficient weight to constitute an approach or attack.
- **Attempted Boarding.** A close approach by pirate boat on to a vessel or a hull-to-hull contact with it, wherein boarding paraphernalia were employed or visible in the approaching boat. The piracy attack has been repelled by the vessel's crew. The pirates have not succeeded in boarding the vessel.
- **Illegal Boarding.** Unauthorised boarding of a vessel by persons not part of its complement without successfully taking control of the vessel's propulsion and steerage. The Command remains with the Master.
- **Hijack.** Where pirates have boarded and taken control of a vessel's propulsion and steerage against the crew's will. (Naval forces often

refer to a 'pirated' vessel rather than a 'hijacked' vessel, but the meaning is the same).

- **Hostage-Taking.** Where pirate have taken control the vessel's crew or passengers for seeking attainment of their demands.
- **Kidnapping.** An unauthorised forcible removal of persons belonging to the vessel from it.
- **Robbery.** A theft from a vessel or from persons aboard the vessel.

Piracy High Risk Area (HRA)

Refers to a maritime area wherein commercial ships are prone to encounter pirate attacks. The geographical extent of the areas are promulgated by the shipping industry represented by the *International Chamber of Shipping (ICS)*, based on periodic analyses of pirate activity and/or attacks and the related threat assessments. The *War Risk Zones* designated by the *Joint War Committee (JWC)*—a part of the Lloyd's (Insurance) Market Association of London—also influences the geographical extent of such areas. The 'piracy high risk areas' are promulgated through (anti-piracy) *Best Management Practices (BMP)* guidance booklets published by the ICS, which are circulated by the Maritime Safety Committee (MSC) of the *International Maritime Organisation (IMO)*.

The designation of 'piracy high risk areas' is accompanied with significant implications, not only for the affected littoral countries but also for the entire chain of sea-borne commerce. For example, listing of an area as such may require shipping to be re-routed to avoid entering the area, thereby increasing shipping costs. Otherwise, the *ship-operator* may be required to pay higher insurance premium, with the additional cost passed on to the *shippers* in the form of additional freight cost. This would translate into a higher price that the consumer has to pay to buy the product. The designation of 'piracy high risk areas' also bears significant implications for *ship-owners* and *ship-operators*, such as in terms of compensation to seafarers.

The *International Bargaining Forum (IBF)* Warlike Operations Areas Committee and the *International Transport Workers' Federation (ITF)* draw upon the 'piracy high risk areas' promulgated by ICS in BMP-4 to designate various areas like 'Warlike Operations Area, 'High Risk Area (HRA)' and 'Extended Risk Zone (ERZ)'. These are graded according to the level of risk of pirate attacks. For each of these sub-categories, specific proviso for seafarers are stipulated. These include the bonus (in addition to the basic wage), compensation on death and disability and the right to refuse sailing. The IBF are ITF promulgations vary slightly, and the applicability of one or the other depends upon the agreement relevant to a particular vessel. See *Private Maritime Security Companies (PMSC)*.

Polar Code

The 'International Code for Ships Operating in Polar Waters' adopted by the Maritime Safety Committee (MSC) of *International Maritime Organisation (IMO)* in November 2014 for the safety for ships operating in polar waters of the Arctic and Antarctic, and the prevention of ship-based pollution in the waters. The Code is premised on the fact that the vessels operating in polar environment are exposed to a number of unique risks due adverse weather conditions taking its toll on men and material, and other challenges ranging from meagre *hydrographic* survey to paucity of navigation and communication aids, and the attendant 'inaccessibility' of the area to *Search and Rescue (SAR)* efforts. The environmental fragility of the polar regions is a major driver. Some environment regulations have lately been implemented in Antarctica, notably the 2010 amendment to *MARPOL 73/78* adopted by the Marine Environment Protection Committee (MEPC) of the *IMO* against ship-sourced pollution by heavy-grade oils. However, no such regulation applies to the Arctic region.

The Polar Code is a proposed binding international framework based on two existing treaties—*Safety of Life at Sea (SOLAS) Convention, 74/ 88* and *MARPOL 73/78*. It is intended to encompass the entire gamut of issues, ranging from the design, construction and equipment-fit of vessels meant to operate in polar regions, to their *Search and Rescue (SAR)* and environmental protection matters. The draft provisions for protection of the environment include the prevention of pollution by oil, noxious liquid substances and sewage.

The Polar Code and its related *SOLAS* amendments are likely to enter into force on 01 January 2017, and will apply to new ships constructed after that date. Ships constructed before 01 January 2017 will be required to adhere to the Polar Code by the first intermediate survey (every 2-3 years) or renewal survey every (every 5 years) after 01 January 2018. See

Arctic Council, Arctic Economic Council (AEC), Arctic Marine Strategic Plan (AMSP), Marine Pollution, Oil Spill and *Oil Spill Response.*

Porus Maritim Duniya

A concept initiated by Indonesia's President Joko Widodo in November 2014, which means 'global maritime axis (fulcrum)'. It postulates that concurrent to the 'rise' of Asia, the sea would assume immense salience for the archipelagic country that is geo-strategically located at the crossroads of the *Indo-Pacific Region*. The concept seeks to transform Indonesia into a maritime power, and envisions Jakarta's pivotal role in shaping security in the region. The concept is intended to be fructified through roadmap articulated in a new Maritime *Doctrine* at the *National-Strategic* level. It encompasses five key elements: rebuilding Indonesia's maritime culture, harnessing marine resources, enhancement of economic connectivity through development of maritime infrastructure, cooperation through maritime diplomacy, and capacity building of *Maritime Security Forces.*

Power Projection

At the *National Strategic* level, it is the ability of a country to apply all or some of its elements of national power—politico-diplomatic, economic, informational, or military—to meet national objectives beyond its territorial frontiers. Hence, Power Projection constitutes the projection of either 'hard' or 'soft' power.

The genesis of the concept lies in the writings of Sir Julian Corbett (1854-1922) on the ability of a country's navy to "forward military action ashore". Although it bears a narrower 'maritime-military' connotation, this facet of Power Projection continues to be relevant. In this context, Power Projection missions comprise inter alia *Land Attack, Amphibious Operation* and strategic nuclear strike. Furthermore, at the *Joint* level, land-based aircraft and missile strikes against the enemy territory also constitute power-projection.

The country's *Maritime-Military Power* remains the key enabler of Power Projection, in peacetime, in *Short-of-War Scenarios* or during *Armed Conflict*; and projection of both 'hard' and 'soft' power. In peace-time, maritime power projection could range from presence missions, benign diplomacy and cooperative endeavours to military coercion (often called 'Gunboat Diplomacy). During wartime, maritime Power Projection is the key method to influence a continental war 'directly'. This, however, necessitates littoral *Sea Control.* See *Aircraft Carrier*, *Carrier Battle Group (CBG) and Carrier Task Force (CTF)*, *Land Attack* and *Sea Control.*

Pre-Arrival Notification (PAN)

As per the *International Ship and Port Security (ISPS) Code*, all vessels of more than 500 *GT* on international voyages must provide to the next port of call at least 24 hours advance notice with a completed proforma detailing the security status of the vessel and previous ports of call. This is called Pre-Arrival Notification (PAN). PAN is sometimes referred to as Pre-Arrival Notification of Security (PANS). The information to be provided through PAN includes the following:

- Particulars of ship and contact details of agent.
- Details of port entry.
- Geographic location and last port of call.
- Security compliance by ship.
- Details of cargo/passengers carried by the ship.

The regulations for PAN notices for entry into Indian ports are promulgated through notices issued by the *Directorate General of Shipping (DGoS)* of the Ministry of Shipping. As per the prevailing regulations, the PAN is required to be submitted by a vessel 96 hours prior to its arrival at any Indian port. If the voyage is shorter than 96 hours, PAN is required to be submitted within two hours of its departure from the last port. This also applies to vessels trading in coastal waters or coasting between Indian ports. See Private *Maritime Security Companies (PMSC)*, and *Vessel Traffic Services (VTS) and Vessel Traffic Management System (VTMS).*

Precision-Guided Munitions

See *Precision Strike.*

Precision Strike

See *Land Attack.*

Private Maritime Security Companies (PMSC)

Defined by *International Maritime Organisation (IMO)* as "private contractors employed to provide security personnel, both armed and unarmed, on board for protection against piracy". 'Private Contracted Armed Security Personnel' (PCASP) are defined as "armed employees of PMSC".

The practice of employing PCASP onboard commercial ships gained widespread ascendency following the increasing incidents of piracy in the western Indian Ocean since 2005. However, the practice is not governed by any international law. In 2015, the *IMO*, in conjunction with the shipping industry and *Flag States* promulgated ISO 28007-1:2015 guidelines to standardise the practice and regulate PMSCs. The regulations—that are primarily meant for ships transiting the *Piracy High Risk Area (HRA)* in the western Indian Ocean—address the command relationship between the master and PCASP, *Rules of Engagement (RoE)* and questions of liability. However, many other legal issues such as the use of force against persons on board foreign-flagged ships and carriage of weapons in foreign *Territorial Waters* and ports ('Floating Armouries') remain unaddressed.

In India, the guidelines for employment of PMSCs on merchant ships are issued by the Ministry of Shipping and promulgated through circulars issued by the *Directorate General of Shipping (DGoS)* of the Ministry of Shipping. The existing guidelines require ships to provide information on armed security guards to the Indian Navy, the Indian Coast Guard and Customs. *See International Ship and Port Security Code (ISPS), Piracy, Pre-Arrival Notification (PAN), Vessel Protection Detachment (VPD).*

Prize Courts

Prize Courts are established during *War and Armed Conflict* by belligerent countries to dispose the captured enemy merchant ships and cargos. These are constituted under the national laws and promulgated by the governments. In India, the High Courts at Kolkata, Mumbai and Chennai having *Admiralty Law* jurisdiction have been declared Prize Courts by the Naval Prize Act, 1864. The Naval and Aircraft Prizes Act, 1971 provides for adjudication of cases by the Prize Courts. See, *Contraband*, and *Visit, Board, Search and Seizure (VBSS) Operations.*

Proliferation Security Initiative (PSI)

An initiative of the United States launched on 31 May 2003 as an ad hoc coalition of 11 States meant to prevent illegal trafficking of cargo related to *Weapons of Mass Destruction (WMD)* transiting through land, sea or air routes. The PSI was driven by the concern that WMDs and their means of delivery may fall into the hands of terrorists through some States with doubtful credibility, if not used by these States themselves, the implicit reference being to countries like North Korea and Iran. The original 11 PSI participants have since been joined by many more, taking the total number to about 107. The US and its partners have since continued to conduct *Combined* naval exercises to further the objectives of PSI.

The PSI's primary focus is the maritime domain—interception of any vessel 'suspect' of such illegal transportation through *Visit, Board, Search and Seizure (VBSS) Operations*, irrespective of the vessel's nationality or geographical position in terms of the legal maritime regime. This is to be enabled by the coordinated naval action among member-States and guided by their combined intelligence effort. The legality and legitimacy of PSI in terms of the law of the sea and laws regarding use of force in international relations had triggered a debate worldwide. In September 2003, however, the US issued the PSI's *Statement of Interdiction* (SOI) *Principles*, which clarified that actions would be restricted to legal confines and interdiction of foreign vessels in international waters would only be undertaken with consent of the vessel's *Flag State*. For this, the US entered into bilateral boarding arrangements with countries that offer *Flags of Convenience (FoC)* registrations to commercial vessels and thereby flag a major part of global shipping.

Protective Jurisdiction

See *Criminal Jurisdiction*.

R

Radar

A system using beamed and reflected radio-frequency (RF) energy for detecting objects and measuring their distance or altitude, for various purposes including navigation, targeting and directing. The functioning of radar is based on calculating the time interval between transmission of the RF energy and the reception of the reflected energy, which establishes the range of an object in the beam's path. The term *RADAR* was coined in 1940 as an acronym of 'RAdio Detection And Ranging'. The term 'radar' has since entered English and other languages as a common noun, losing all capitalisation. See *Electronic Warfare (EW)*.

ReCAAP-06

Regional Cooperative Agreement against Piracy (ReCAAP-06). Initiated by Japan, this arrangement came into force on September 04, 2006. It aims to facilitate intelligence exchange through its *Information Sharing Centre* (ISC) at Singapore. India ratified the ReCAAP in June 2006. Notably, Indonesia and Malaysia have not ratified ReCAAP-06.

Reconnaissance

See *Tracking and Reconnaissance.*

Refuge, Refugee and Asylum

Refuge implies a 'temporary' sanctuary provided to any person, regardless of nationality, who may be in imminent physical danger for the duration of that danger. International law and norms have long recognised this as a lawful humanitarian act. As extension of a *Flag State's* territorial sovereignty in foreign or *International Waters*, warships and merchant ships may provide refuge to foreign nationals, but not to those escaping from law of the coastal State, whether such person is national of the coastal State or not.

Asylum may be defined as the protection and sanctuary granted by a country within its territorial jurisdiction to a foreign national who applies for such protection because of persecution or fear of persecution on account of race, religion, nationality, membership in a particular social group, or political opinion. An individual granted Asylum is commonly referred to as a 'Refugee'. One who has left the country of origin and has applied for grant of 'refugee' status in another country, but the same has not been decided yet is an 'Asylum-seeker'. Asylum-seekers are normally entitled to remain on the territory of the country of asylum until their claims have been decided upon and should be treated in accordance with basic *Human Rights Law* (*HR Law*).

International law recognises the right of a State to grant 'political' asylum to foreign nationals already present within or seeking admission to its territory. Its legal underpinning is derived from the principle of *Non-Refoulement*, which forbids the rendering a true victim of persecution to his/her persecutor (State/Government). The international regime governing asylum and refugees is the UN Convention Relating to the Status of Refugees (CRSR), 1951, which defines who is a refugee and who is not (e.g. war criminals), and lays down their rights and the responsibilities of countries that grant asylum.

It is important to note that for *Asylum*, international law characterises 'political' ends as legitimate, but not the 'economic' ends. Hence, while people involved in *Illegal Immigration* due to financial deprivation may be '*Asylum*-seekers', they do not have any legal right to be granted *Asylum* (or the status of *Refugee*) by the host country. However, in reality, it is sometimes difficult to distinguish between the 'political' and 'economic' dimensions since in many *Fragile States*, poverty and unemployment are often linked with political instability and persecution.

India is not party to the 1951 Refugee Convention or its 1967 Protocol, but it hosts a large number of refugees premised on the principle of *Non-Refoulement*. India's policy on granting asylum is based on two fundamental rights enshrined in the Constitution of India (articles 21 and 14). These rights give any resident in India the right to life, equality and justice.

Warships, owing to their immunity from the territorial sovereignty of the foreign State in whose waters they may be present, may lawfully provide asylum. However, such actions are also guided by the tenets of domestic law and policy, politico-diplomatic considerations, and the prevailing circumstances. Warships and merchant ships are usually not authorised by their governments to embark asylum seekers. See *Human Smuggling and Trafficking.*

Regional Maritime Security initiative (RMSI)

In April 2004, the US launched the RMSI, wherein it was envisaged to deploy US Marines and *Special Operations* Forces on high-speed vessels in the Malacca Straits. While the initiative was acceptable to Singapore, it was rejected by Indonesia and Malaysia since these States have traditionally been sensitive over issues of national sovereignty. See *MALSINDO.*

Remittances

A term used in economics, which refers to the transfer of money by a foreign worker to the home country. Money sent home by the migratory work-force constitutes one of the largest financial inflows to the developing world, particularly to the labour-exporting countries. Remittances from *Diaspora* overseas is considered more stable than other capital inflows, which makes it a reliable financial resource to tide over financial crises and economic downturns. Remittances also enhance recipient country's sovereign credit rating, thus lowering borrowing costs and lengthening debt maturity. Global rating agencies have lately begun factoring remittances in a country's credit rating. In recent years, India has been topping the global remittance chart. In 2014, it drew a remittance of US$ 70.38 billion, which constituted 3.7 per cent of its US$ 2 trillion GDP. See *Non-Combatant Evacuation Operations (NEO).*

Registration of Ships

A process whereby the functional existence of a commercial ship is formally recognised and documented. Registration also accords the ship a nationality, enabling it to undertake international voyages. The object of registration is also to ensure that the *Flag State* is able to provide protection to the ship and the individuals onboard. The *Flag State* exercises legal and regulatory control over the ship and—in accordance with the State's international obligations—is obliged to ensure that it maintains international standards with regard to maritime safety and security.

The 'registry' refers to the organisation authorised by the *Flag State* to register the ship, which may be a government or a private agency. A registry that is open only to ships of its own nation is known as a 'national registry'. Registries that are open to foreign-owned ships are known as 'open registries', leading to the concept of *Flags of Convenience (FoC)*.

The broader guidelines for registration of Indian ships is laid down in the *Merchant Shipping Act, 1958*, and the Merchant Shipping (Registration of Indian Ships) Rules, 1960, as amended in 1966, 1970, 1994 and 1997. The detailed procedures are amended occasionally and promulgated through *Directorate General of Shipping (DGoS)* circulars. The ships eligible to fly the Indian flag are those that are owned by an Indian citizen or by a company based in India. The ships that qualify are required to be registered only at Indian ports of Mumbai, Kolkata, Chennai, Kochi and Mormugao that are designated as 'ports of registry'. The principal officers/surveyors in these ports are designated as the 'Registrars'. The registration process involves application from owner, submission of documents as per check list, verification of documents, plans and drawings of the vessel, assessment of the suitability of the vessel to fly the Indian flag and establishing the ownership and credentials of owner. The 'Registrars' are required to maintain a complete record of 'ships on register'. A central register is also maintained by the *Director General of Shipping (DGoS)*. See *Indian Register of Shipping (IRS)*.

Responsibility to Protect (R2P)

A concept that is founded on the obligations of the governments of sovereign States to protect their citizens, as also imposing the responsibility on the international community to protect a population that is suffering serious harm, as a result of internal conflict, repression or State failure, when the State is unwilling or unable to address it. The 2001 Report of the International Commission on Intervention and State Sovereignty (ICISS) notes that the responsibility to protect encompasses inter alia the responsibility "to respond to situations of compelling human need with appropriate measures, which may include coercive measures like sanctions and international prosecution, and in extreme cases military intervention".

The concept of R2P also draws upon the responsibility of the UN Security Council under Article 24 of the UN Charter for the maintenance of international peace and security, specific legal obligations under *International Humanitarian Law (IHL), Human Rights Law (HR Law)* and other human protection instruments, and national law, as well as in the evolving practice in countries and regional organisations. However, the concept of R2P bears a potential to be misused by major powers to satiate their self-interest in the guise of R2P. This concept is thus still evolving, and has not yet been able to garner adequate consensus to be embodied into international law. See *Fragile State and Failed State, Low Intensity Conflict (LIC), Spectrum of Conflict,* and *War Crimes, Crimes against Humanity and Genocide.*

Restrictive RoE

See *Rules of Engagement (RoE).*

RIMPAC Exercises

The 'Rim of the Pacific Exercise' (RIMPAC) is the world's largest multi-nation maritime exercise conducted biennially (every even year) by the US Navy's Pacific Fleet and hosted by Honolulu, Hawaii. Also involving the US Marine Corps, the US Coast Guard and local Hawaii National Guard, RIMPAC solicits participation of maritime forces of countries largely of the Pacific rim, but also and a few others. The first exercise held in 1971 involved naval units from only five countries (Australia, Canada, New Zealand, the UK and the United States). In 2014, the participation (involving naval units) grew to 22 countries, including China, India and Norway for the first time. (Russia and Thailand had participated in RIMPAC 2012, but dropped out in 2014). In addition, six countries, including Bangladesh, Brazil and Germany, sent observers to RIMPAC 2014. See *CARAT Exercises* and *West Pacific Naval Symposium (WPNS).*

Roll-on/Roll-off (RO-RO) Ship

Freight ship or ferry with facilities for vehicles to drive on and off (roll-on and roll-off); a system of loading and discharging a ship whereby the cargo is driven on and off on ramps. The large openings at the ship's bow and stern (and sometimes on the side) provide easy access, including fully loaded trucks or trailers carrying *containers,* which are accommodated on the ship's deck.

Rotterdam Rules (Shipping)

See *Carriage of Goods at Sea (Laws and Rules)*.

Rukmini Communications Satellite

A communications satellite (GSAT-7) meant exclusively for military use by the Indian Navy. It was placed in geosynchronous orbital position at 74 degree east longitude 36,000 km above the Earth in August 2013. Developed by the Indian Space Research Organisation (ISRO), GSAT-7 is an advanced communication satellite capable of providing wide spectrum multi-band (UHF, S, C and Ku bands) services ranging from low bit rate voice to high bit rate encrypted data communications in the *Indian Ocean Region (IOR)* and beyond. Earlier, India's over-the-horizon naval communications were based on *Immarsat* and HF links. The Rukmini-based communication facility has led to a quantum increase in the Indian Navy's capability to undertake *Network Centric Operations (NCO)*.

Rules of Engagement (RoE)

A set of rules factoring provisions of international law and political directives meant to authorise and guide operational commanders with regard to the freedom to initiate or continue combat, and extent of use of military force in a specified scenario.

As per the traditional definition, RoE are "the directives that the 'highest national authorities' establish to authorise subordinate Commanders to employ military force. These delineate the circumstances and limitations under which the naval, ground, and air forces under their command will initiate and/or continue combat engagement with enemy forces. "In present times, however, the scope of RoE has widened to cater for the increasing involvement of military forces in *Low-Intensity Conflict* and other operations.

Hence, RoE apply to the entire '*Spectrum of Conflict*', and to the full range of situations in which military forces may be called upon to operate, ranging from stable peace to nuclear war. Also, the RoE are generally being promulgated by the higher authorities in the military chain-of-command, albeit on behalf of the national government. In this regard, the Indian Maritime Doctrine, 2009 states that the RoE lie at the apex of maritime *Command and Control* (*C^2*) functions. Furthermore, while standing RoE cover generic contingencies and scenarios, temporary RoE are derived from these for specific operations as required.

It is important to note that peace-time RoE are distinct from those applicable during *War and Armed Conflict*. The distinction needs to be understood on the basis of the fundamental difference between war and peace-time operations. The primary difference is that in war, diplomatic efforts have failed, and a military solution is sought through the application of decisive combat power. Hence, the RoE are usually 'Permissive'. On the other hand, in peace-time, since diplomatic solutions are sought through negotiation or mediation, the use of force is restrained. The RoE are, therefore, more 'Restrictive' in peace operations, making them more politically sensitive as well.

Rules of the Road (RoR)

See *COLREGS and Rules of the Road.*

S

SAARC

The South Asian Association for Regional Cooperation (SAARC) is an economic and geopolitical organisation established in 1985 comprising eight member countries—Afghanistan (added as a member in 2007), Bangladesh, Bhutan, India, Maldives, Nepal, Pakistan and Sri Lanka. Notably, India shares borders with all SAARC members except Afghanistan. Beyond India, only two SAARC members—Pakistan and Afghanistan—share a common border. The SAARC Secretariat was established in Kathmandu (Nepal) in January 1987.

The SAARC aims to accelerate economic welfare and self-reliance among its members, and promote socio-cultural development in the sub-region. Countries with observer status include Australia, China, the EU, Iran, Japan, Mauritius, Myanmar (interested in attaining membership), South Korea, and the US. Whereas Russia and Turkey have applied for observer status, South Africa has participated in SAARC meetings.

Safety of Life at Sea (SOLAS) Convention, 1974/1988

The 'International Convention for the Safety of Life at Sea (SOLAS) 1974' is the primal international treaty-based legal instrument pertaining to maritime safety. It requires a *Flag State* to ensure that their ships comply with minimum safety standards in construction, equipment and operation. India ratified SOLAS in June 1976, and the Convention entered into force in May 1980. SOLAS, 1974, makes it obligatory for a vessel of any nationality in the vicinity to respond to a distress call and render assistance to another vessel in distress. (See *Maritime Search and Rescue.*) The Convention has undergone many amendments since 1974 to keep it contemporary, the notable being the 1988 SOLAS Protocol and various resolutions adopted by the 'Maritime Safety Committee' (MSC) of the *International Maritime Organisation (IMO)* or during conferences of the state parties to SOLAS, 1974.

See Global *Maritime Distress Safety System (GMDSS), International Ship and Port Security Code (ISPS), Long-Range Identification and Tracking (LRIT), Maritime Satellite Communications* and *Maritime Search and Rescue (M-SAR).*

Safety Zone

As per international law (*UNCLOS*), coastal States may establish 'Safety Zones' to protect installations, structures and artificial islands located in their *Internal Waters, Archipelagic Waters, Territorial Waters* and *EEZ*, and on their *Continental Shelves*. Such installations largely refer to the *Offshore Platforms* installed for extraction of hydrocarbons. In case these are established beyond sovereign waters (*Internal Waters* and *Territorial Waters*), such zones cannot exceed beyond 500 metres from the outer edges of the facility (installation/structure/artificial island). See *Offshore Development Area (ODA)*, and *Security Zones*.

Sagar Mala (Port Project)

'Sagar Mala' (hindi term for 'ocean garland') is a *National Strategic* initiative of the Government of India first enunciated by the former Prime Minister Atal Bihari Vajpayee in August 2003. Involving a model of port led development, the project seeks transform the existing Indian seaports into modern world-class ports and develop new ones based on the requirement. These ports are meant to be integrated with industrial clusters and hinterland through efficient and seamless transport connectivity involving road, rail, inland and coastal waterway-based freight corridors. It is envisaged that these measures would make exports more competitive due to reduced logistics costs, and the ports would become the drivers of economic activity in the coastal areas.

The Sagar Mala Project aims to align with and support the other national priorities of the Indian government such as the development of 'smart cities', the 'Ganga water-way' program and 'Make in India' initiative. The concept and institutional framework of the Project received the 'in-principle' approval of India's Union Cabinet in March 2015.

Salvage

See *Maritime Salvage*.

Scouting Operations

See *Search and Patrol*, and *Tracking and Reconnaissance.*

Sea Barge (SeeBee) Ships

A large barge-carrying merchant ship similar to *Lighter Aboard Ship (LASH)*, but much larger. It uses rollers to embark the relatively large self-propelled barges (carrying *Containers*) on to the Sea Barge.

Sea Basing

A naval capability to undertake military missions overseas of expeditionary nature without reliance on land-based *Operational Logistics* and *Command and Control* (*C^2*) infrastructure, either of home bases or the overseas bases. The concept has been developed by the US expeditionary forces, largely due to the increasing constraints to maintain overseas military bases, besides the emerging concepts of amphibious warfare such as '*Over-The-Horizon (OTH)* operations', 'Ship-To-Objective Manoeuvre (STOM)' and '*Vertical Envelopment*'. See *Amphibious Operation*, *Expeditionary Operation*, *Lilypad*, *Mobile Landing Platform (MLP)*, and *Naval Base and Access Facility.*

Seabed Mining

Also referred to as 'Deep Seabed Mining'. In general, the term 'seabed' (or 'deep seabed') refers to the area beyond the (geological) *Continental Shelf.* In the context of international law, the concept refers to the exploitation of the resources of ocean floor at depths beyond the *Legal Continental Shelf.* This area is codified in *UNCLOS* as lying beyond the limits of national jurisdiction, and accepted as the '*Common Heritage of Mankind*'.

Detailed surveys by some countries indicate that the seabed area bears a high concentration of base metals and noble metals, and has thus potentially become a storehouse of resources for manufacturing industries world-wide. These minerals occur in the following forms:

- **Polymetallic (Manganese) Nodules.** Constituting a variety of metals like manganese, iron, copper, nickel, cobalt, lead and zinc, these potato-sized nodules are dispersed on the seafloor of the abyssal plains, and are known (since the 19th century) to have been formed over millions of years by the accumulation of metallic particles from seawater, supplied from continental run-off, and volcanic, hydrothermal and atmospheric sources.

- **Polymetallic Sulphides.** Rich in copper, iron, zinc, silver and gold, these deposits are sited at tectonic plate boundaries of ocean ridges at depths of about 2,000 metres, and are formed over millennia through hydrothermal activity, emanating from the fault-lines of the Earth's crust.
- **Cobalt Crusts.** Containing iron, manganese, nickel, cobalt, copper and rare metals (including rare earths), these deposits are formed at 400-7,000 metre depths on the flanks and tops of seamounts through precipitation of minerals from seawater.
- **Phosphorite/Phosphates.** These are cumulations of calcium phosphates, a commodity that is used as fertiliser in agriculture throughout the world.

The mid-ocean ridges in the central and south western Indian Ocean are known to be particularly rich in seabed minerals comprising metals like copper, lead, zinc as well as noble metals like gold, silver, palladium and platinum. The exploration of these resources beyond national jurisdiction is regulated by an international regime overseen by the Jamaica-based *International Seabed Authority* (ISA). At the moment, no country is permitted to mine the seabed areas, but the ISA issued contracts to allow for prospecting and exploration for seabed resources.

India seeks to carry out the exploration in the seabed mining area of 150,000 square kilometres allotted to it in the central Indian Ocean. But extraction from depths of 6,000 metres would be an engineering challenge. Environmental issues also exist. The Indian government's Ministry of Earth Sciences (MOES) has designated the Goa-based 'National Centre for Antarctic and Ocean Research (NCAOR)' as the lead agency for seabed mining programme.

Sea Control

It denotes a condition where one is able to use a defined sea area, for a defined period of time, for one's own purposes, and at the same time deny its use to the adversary. Sea control is synonymous with dominance of the maritime battle-space, which allows own maritime-military power to be used to advantage. It finds its genesis in the concept of 'Command of the Seas' propounded by Admiral AT Mahan in 1890. While the concept of 'Command of the Sea' was unqualified by time and space, this state is rarely achievable. Hence, any control would per force be limited in time and space, and for a given mission.

Attrition of enemy's maritime forces is among the means to achieve Sea Control. Since an *Aircraft Carrier*-based *Task Force* is able to dominate all dimensions of maritime war—air, surface, sub-surface, electromagnetic spectrum and cyber space—the *Aircraft Carrier* is critically necessary for achieving and maintaining Sea Control. Sea Control is the central concept around which the Indian Navy is structured.

Sea Control is never an end in itself, but an essential pre-requisite for undertaking a follow-on maritime-military mission ranging from *SLOC Interdiction* to *Power Projection*. Depending upon the kind of the follow-on mission, it is sub-divided into 'mid-ocean Sea Control' and 'littoral Sea Control'.

Sea Denial

Sea Denial is exercised when one party denies another the ability to control a maritime area without either wishing or being able to control that area himself. Classic means of achieving it are to lay a minefield or to deploy submarines to threaten enemy surface forces; a more recent method, particularly appropriate in littoral operations, is to mount surface to surface missile batteries along the coast to pose an unacceptable level of risk to enemy surface units. It is important to note that *Sea Denial* and *Sea Control* operations are not mutually exclusive. The former represents *Attrition*, which is also inherent in the latter.

Sealift and Sealift Capacity

Usually used in context of 'Strategic Sealift', which refers to the ability of a country to undertake an *Amphibious Operation* or (in case of a major power) an *Expeditionary Operation* using its strategic sealift platforms, particularly the naval *Amphibious Ships*. In the Indian context, despite their obvious limitations, State-owned commercial vessels—such as those belonging to the 'Shipping Corporation of India' (SCI)—can supplement Indian Navy's sealift capacity. These are referred to as 'Ships Taken Up From Trade' (*STUFT*). See *Sukoon (Operation)* and *Airlift and Airlift Capacity*.

Sea Lines of Communication (SLOC)

SLOC differs from *International Shipping Lanes* (ISL). During war, while quick access to strategic commodities arriving from overseas is important, commercial/economical factors are not overriding, and hence States determine the routing of the shipping carrying strategic commodities based on the envisaged areas where naval operations are likely to occur and the military risks involved. Hence, SLOCs are usually specific to a particular State, which may or may not overlap with *International Shipping Lanes (ISLs)*. Some old books refer to SLOCs as "Sea Lanes of Communication", or simply, "Sea Lanes". However, after UNCLOS, 1982 came into force in 1994, it became necessary to shift to the term 'Sea Lines' to avoid confusion with 'Archipelagic Sea Lanes', which was a new concept introduced in *UNCLOS*. Interestingly, military doctrines for war-fighting on land have always referred to 'Lines of Communication'.

Sea Power

See *Maritime Power*.

Search and Patrol

Both are tasks undertaken by naval forces (surface ships, submarines or aircraft) under their 'Scouting' mission. A search is the systematic investigation of a particular area, for the purpose of locating or confirming the absence of an object known or suspected to be somewhere in that area.

A patrol is the systematic and continuing investigation along a line known as the 'barrier line' to prevent a moving object from crossing it undetected. Instead of searching an area where the enemy is believed to be, the scout traverses over the same geographical tracks, or patrols in such a manner that it will be able to give warning if the object attempts to cross those lines.

Essentially, therefore, Search and Patrol are distinct on two counts. First, in a Search, the scout goes out to find the object being searched for, whereas in a patrol the scout waits for the object to approach. Second, surface ships, submarines and aircraft on Patrol are normally capable of attacking the expected enemy, but this capability is not essential when they are engaged in a Search. See *Tracking and Reconnaisance.*

Search and Rescue (SAR)

See *Maritime Search and Rescue (M-SAR)*.

Search and Rescue Region (SRR)

An area of defined dimensions, associated with rescue coordination centre within which *Maritime Search and Rescue (M-SAR)* services are provided. These regions are delineated based on global SAR Plan promulgated by the *International Maritime Organisation (IMO)*. The aeronautical SRRs are depicted in the Regional Air Navigation Plans (RANPs) promulgated by the International Civil Aviation Authority (ICAO).

Seaward Defence

Among the salient military missions of a navy that necessitates deployment of its forces to prevent and counter an offensive mission by hostile forces against the country from seawards. A particular emphasis is laid to protect the country's critical infrastructure and assets in the littoral areas. It usually involves a layered defence, and may involve the employment of the country's air forces in maritime role. See *Coastal Security and Coastal Defence*.

Security Zones

Unlike in case of *Safety Zone*, international law does not stipulate any 'Security Zone'. However, international practice has led to promulgation of such zones. The inherent right of self defence stipulated in *Customary International Law* and codified in the UN Charter (see *Jus Ad Bellum*) legitimizes the promulgation of such zones such as *Air Defence Identification Zone (ADIZ)* and *Maritime Exclusion Zone (MEZ)*.

Shanghai Cooperation Organisation (SCO)

A Eurasian political, economic and military organisation founded in 2001 in Shanghai by the leaders of China, Kazakhstan, Kyrgystan, Russia, Tajikistan and Uzbekistan. The genesis of SCO lies in the 'Shanghai Five' (the current members excluding Uzbekistan), who signed a couple of pacts on military *Confidence-Building Measures (CBM)* in 1996 and 1997. In June 2002, the members signed the SCO Charter, which formally articulates the SCO's objectives, principles, structure and form of operation. The SCO secretariat is located in Beijing.

In 2003, the SCO defence forces began conducting combined

exercises. (These include the large-scale China-Russia biennial 'Peace Mission' war games since 2005). In 2015, India and Pakistan were admitted as SCO members. Afghanistan, Iran and Mongolia are SCO observers. Most observers have applied for SCO membership. A few other countries like Bangladesh, Nepal and Sri Lanka have applied to become SCO observers. Belarus, Sri Lanka and Turkey are currently SCO dialogue partners. Notably, since 2014, the member countries are debating the idea to merge the SCO with the *Collective Security Treaty Organisation (CSTO).*

Ship Directions

There is a long list of terms that describe directions in respect of a seagoing vessel, which have historical origins. The salient ones are described below.

- **Bow (and Stem).** Bow is the forward part of a vessel. Stem refers to the forward-most structure of the vessel's hull (body).
- **Aft (and Stern).** Aft is the rear part of the vessel. Stern refers to the structural part of the vessel in the aft.
- **Amidships.** The portion of vessel between the Stem and the Stern.
- **Port Side.** The left hand side of the vessel, facing forward (opposite of 'starboard'). The term originates from the erstwhile practice of tying up a ship in port with its rudderless (left hand) side against the wharf.
- **Starboard Side.** The right hand side of the vessel, when facing forward (opposite of 'port'). It is a distortion of the word 'Steer board', which referred to the right hand side of a ship where the tiller was located to steer the ship. Some say that 'Starboard' referred to a board fixed on the right hand side of the ship that was used to track stars for night navigation.
- **Aloft.** The stacks, masts, rigging, or other area above the vessel's highest solid structure.
- **Windward.** The vessel's side on to which, the wind blows (opposite of 'leeward').
- **Leeward.** The vessel's side that is away from the wind (opposite of 'windward').
- **On board.** Somewhere on the vessel.
- **Outboard.** Attached outside the vessel, such as an 'outboard motor' to propel the vessel.

Shipment, Ship-owner, Ship-operator, Shipper and Carrier

- **Shipment.** A separate identifiable number of goods (cargo) transported under the terms of a *Bill of Lading*, irrespective of the quantity or number of containers or packages. Also called 'Consignment'. See *Cargo Manifest.*
- **Ship-owner.** Simply, it refers to the person who owns the commercial vessel. In legal terms, it is the person(s) officially registered in the vessel's certificate of registry.
- **Ship-operator.** A ship operator is either the ship-owner or the (legal) person—usually a technical management position within a shipping company—responsible for the actual management of the vessel and its crew. The role of the ship-operator is to ensure that all technical tasks in relation to the operation of a vessel are performed in accordance with the company's procedures.
- **Shipper.** The party responsible for initiating a shipment, and who may also bear the freight cost. Also called 'Charterer' or 'Consignor'. ('Consignee' is the party shown on the *Bill of Lading*, to whom the shipment is consigned). The shipper signs a contract (called 'Charter Party') with the ship-owner, and thus hires or leases a vessel or a part of its capacity.
- **Carrier.** The party (company or person representing a company) that undertakes to transport goods (shipment). The Carrier is responsible for any possible loss of the goods during transport.

See *Cargo Manifest*, and *Carriage of Goods at Sea (Laws and Rules).*

Ship-operator

See *Shipment, Ship-owner, Ship-operator, Shipper and Carrier.*

Ship-owner

See *Shipment, Ship-owner, Ship-operator, Shipper and Carrier.*

Shipper

See *Shipment, Ship-owner, Ship-operator, Shipper and Carrier.*

Short of War Scenarios

A conflict scenario between two countries that could potentially escalate into a *War or Armed Conflict.* See *Spectrum of Conflict* and *Escalation.*

Short-Range Ballistic Missile (SRBM)

See *Ballistic and Cruise Missiles.*

Signal Intelligence (SIGINT)

See *Electronic Warfare (EW).*

SIMBEX (Naval Exercises)

Combined naval exercises between the Indian Navy (IN) and the Republic of Singapore Navy (RSN). SIMBEX is an acronym for 'Singapore-India Maritime Bilateral Exercise'. The 'SIMBEX' series of bilateral exercise commenced in 1994 as IN-RSN *Anti-Submarine Warfare (ASW)* Training Exercise 'Lion King'. See *Joint and Combined.*

Single Market

See *Common Market, Single Market and Unified Market.*

SLINEX (Naval Exercises)

Combined naval exercise between the Indian Navy (IN) and the Sri Lankan Navy (SLN) instituted in 2005. See *Joint and Combined.*

SLOC Interdiction

A concept of *War and Armed Conflict* at sea, which enables naval power to be able to affect the outcome of a continental war through 'commodity denial' against the enemy. The interdiction of enemy's *Sea Lines of Communication (SLOC)* is based on the traditional belligerent right of 'guerre de course' or 'trade warfare'.

According to the view of some experts, the legal underpinnings of SLOC Interdiction is reinforced by the traditional belligerent right of *Blockade*, which provides the legal justification of SLOC interdiction, even though as 'distant blockade'. The *Law of Armed Conflict (LOAC)* provides this 'leeway' to a belligerent by stating that "the force maintaining the blockade may be stationed at a distance determined by military requirements". It is, however, important to note that the provisions of Law with regard to *Blockade* must be observed. Also, it is necessary for the government to publish '*Contraband* List' that specifically includes the commodities that could sustain the adversary's war effort. SLOC interdiction may be supplemented by promulgation of *Exclusion Zones.*

Although submarines—with their ability to operate with stealth and relative invisibility—have been traditionally employed for SLOC Interdiction, these platforms are highly constrained to positively confirm the identity of the target and cater for the safety of the crew as required by international law. Hence, the preferred means to interdict enemy *SLOCs* is through *Visit, Board, Search and Seizure (VBSS) Operations* undertaken by surface forces and their integral air elements. See *Power Projection.*

SLOC Protection

A concept of *War and Armed Conflict* at sea, which entails the responsibility upon a country's naval power to be able to preserve its warfighting potential by protecting its sea-borne trade, and particularly the supply of strategic commodities via its *Sea Lines of Communication (SLOC).* This can be done by deploying a balanced fleet, use of convoys, routeing, and by gaining broader *Sea Control* in the main areas of *SLOC* vulnerability. See *SLOC Interdiction.*

Small Arms and Light Weapons (SALW)

A term used in context of arms control protocols, besides *Low Intensity Conflict/Maritime Operations* (*LICO/LIMO*) to refer to two broad weapon categories:

- **Small Arms.** Hand-held small-calibre manual, semi-automatic and fully automatic firearms like handguns, rifles, shotguns and man-portable machine-guns.
- **Light Weapons.** Medium-calibre guns and explosive ordnance in anti-personnel, anti-tank or anti-aircraft role, including man-portable and vehicle-mounted systems firing rockets, missiles, grenades and land-mines.

SALW are used by all armed forces, including internal security forces, for inter alia, self-protection or self-defence, close or short-range combat, direct or indirect fire, and against tanks or aircraft at relatively short distances. In broad terms, 'Small Arms' are meant for personal use, whereas 'Light Weapons' constitute a collective weapon of a group of personnel.

Sonar

The principal means of detecting and tracking a submerged submarine, and thus the critical enabler of a navy's military task of *Anti-Submarine Warfare (ASW)*. Sonar refers to the technique that uses (usually) underwater sound propagation for submarine navigation, targeting, and communications. Whereas a 'passive' sonar is 'listens' for the sound made by other vessels, an 'active' sonar emits sound pulses and listens for the echoes. The sonar finds its genesis to the concept of ASDIC developed by the Royal Navy sometime during the First World War. Later, the term SONAR began as an acronym for 'SOund Navigation And Ranging', which has since entered English and other languages as a common noun, losing all capitalisation.

Although the detection ranges have been increased by using more powerful sonar sets, the Variable Depth Sonar (VDS) and towed array sonars, the vagaries of the maritime medium in terms of attenuation and refraction of sound waves still inhibit the efficacy of detection.

Southeast Asia Nuclear Weapons Free Zone (SEANWFZ)

In 1997, following the entry into force of the SEANWFZ Treaty (1995)—also referred to as the Bangkok Treaty—Southeast Asia became the third NWFZ. The treaty requires each state party not to "develop, manufacture or otherwise acquire, possess or have control over nuclear weapons; station or transport nuclear weapons by any means; or test or use nuclear weapons." As per the treaty provisions, the term "zone" refers to the area comprising the territories of the states and their respective *Exclusive Economic Zones (EEZ)* and *Continental Shelves*. It bans the dumping of radioactive waste or materials in the zone. It, however, permits each State party to decide individually whether to allow foreign nuclear-powered or nuclear-armed ships or aircraft to visit or transit through their *Territorial Waters* or *National Airspace*.

SEANWFZ Treaty included the protocol seeking the five 'de jure' Nuclear Weapon States (NWS) to accede to it, committing the NWS "not to use or threaten to use nuclear weapons against any State Party to the (SEANWFZ) Treaty." None of the five powers has signed the Protocol due to various ambiguities inter alia with regard to freedom of navigation in Southeast Asian waters and the visits by foreign warships—nuclear-propelled and nuclear-armed—to Southeast Asian ports. See *Nuclear Weapon Free Zone (NWFZ) and Nuclear Free Zone.*

Sovereign Jurisdiction

See *Sovereignty and Sovereign Rights.*

Sovereignty and Sovereign Rights

'Sovereignty' is a key ingredient of the concept of *Nation-State.* In 1576, the French political thinker Jean Bodin defined it as "a State's supreme authority over citizens and subjects", which continues to be largely valid today. The concept of 'Sovereign Rights' or 'Sovereign Jurisdiction' differs from 'Sovereignty'. For example, a State could exercise its 'Sovereignty' to formulate and enforce laws upon its citizens within its territory. However, in its *Exclusive Economic Zone (EEZ),* the State possesses only 'limited' 'Sovereign Rights' or 'Sovereign Jurisdiction' for exploiting the natural resources.

Special Economic Zone (SEZ)

A term that refers to any promulgated area within a country's national borders, wherein business and trade laws differ from the rest of the country. In the SEZ, the government provides concessions on taxes such as income tax, *Excise Duty, Customs Duty* and sales tax; provides subsidised services such as water and electricity; and relaxes its regulations with regard to investments and labour. The key objectives are to enhance trade (particularly exports), facilitate overseas investment and generate infrastructure development and employment opportunities. Such privileges are usually stipulated for a limited period, typically a decade. A SEZ can be sector-specific or have multi-product structure. The generic term SEZ includes similar concepts such as Free/Foreign Trade Zone (FTZ), Export Processing Zones (EPZ), industrial parks and *Duty Free Ports.*

The concept of SEZ originates from the erstwhile 'entrepôts' ('trading posts') sited along maritime trade routes. During the days of the sailing ships, merchandise was imported into these 'entrepôts', stored and—based on the prevailing wind pattern—re-embarked on ships for export. The concept prevailed, leading to the emergence of the concept of '*Duty Free Port*' (including airports), as a special *Customs* area, wherein re-export trade is subject to no *Customs Duty* or *Transhipment* control. Eventually, the relaxation of national regulation expanded deeper into the port's hinterland.

See *Common Market, Single Market and Unified Market, Foreign Trade, Free Trade Agreement (FTA) and Free Trade Area, Non-Tariff Barriers (NTB)*, and *World Trade Organisation (WTO)*.

Special Operations

Actions conducted by specially organised, trained and equipped military forces called Special Operations Forces (SoF) in hostile, denied, or politically sensitive areas, to achieve military, political, economic or psychological objectives through non-conventional means. Special Operations serve to bridge the asymmetry between own conventional forces and the unconventional means that the adversary may employ, which would otherwise permit him to act with impunity against own interests. In addition to their applicability across the *Spectrum of Conflict*, Special Operations are usually meant to cause an effect at *national-strategic, strategic* or *operational* levels, but may also be used at the *tactical* level of war, usually in support of conventional forces. The Marine Commando Force (MARCOS) is the Indian Navy's SoF. In the past, the MARCOS has been employed against the Tamil Tigers in Sri Lanka (1987-88) and for interdicting suspect ships at sea. Also see, *Clandestine and Covert Operations*, and *Visit, Board, Search and Seizure (VBSS) Operations.*

Spectrum of Conflict

The range of scenarios that the security environment of a country encounters at any given time, from stable peace and internal conflict to *Armed Conflict*, and even a nuclear war.

Stability Operations

Military operations undertaken by a country that seek to manage a political, socio-economic or security crisis beyond its territorial frontiers. Such operations form a part of the concept of *Military Operations Other Than War (MOOTW).*

India's *Maritime-Military* forces may be required to undertake Stability Operations in response to a request for assistance from a friendly nation or to meet its international obligations by contributing to UN *Peacekeeping Operations (PKO).* In 1988, for example, Indian armed forces quelled a coup attempt by Tamil mercenaries against the Maldivian President (Operation *Cactus*). Between 1987 and 1990, the Indian Navy supported the Indian Peacekeeping Force (IPKF) in Sri Lanka to enforce a negotiated settlement following the civil war (Operation *Pawan*). India is well known to be among the largest contributors to UN *Peacekeeping Operations (PKO)*. In 1994, the Indian Navy supported Indian peacekeepers in Somalia (UNOSOM II), wherein it undertook de-induction of troops in a hostile environment.

Strategic Airlift

See *Airlift and Airlift Capacity*.

Strategic Arms Limitation Talks (SALT)

Strategic Arms Limitation Talks (SALT) were two rounds of talks between the United States and the erstwhile Soviet Union on limiting strategic weapons, which led to two agreements SALT I and SALT II. SALT I negotiations began in 1969, and led to freezing the number of strategic ballistic missile launchers at existing levels and the *Anti-Ballistic Missile (ABM) Treaty*. SALT II negotiations (1972-1979) sought to reduce strategic nuclear weapons, and concluded with an agreement, but the United States did not to ratify the treaty in response to the Soviet invasion of Afghanistan. The agreement expired in 1985. SALT led to *Strategic Arms Reduction Treaty (START)*.

Strategic Arms Reduction Treaty (START)

A series of bilateral treaties between the United States and Russia on reducing strategic weapons. These were a follow-up of the US-USSR *Strategic Arms Limitation Talks (SALT)* of the Cold War era. START I—signed in July 1991, entered into force in December 1994, and implemented in 2001—capped the nuclear warheads on each side to 6,000 and *Inter-Continental Ballistic Missiles (ICBM)* to 1,600. It expired in December 2009.

START II, signed in January 1993, agreed to ban the use of *Multiple Independently Targetable Reentry Vehicles (MIRV)* on *ICBMs*, but it never entered into force. Although both countries ratified it, Russia withdrew from the treaty in response to the US withdrawal from the *Anti-Ballistic Missile (ABM) Treaty* in 2002. In lieu of START II, the '*Strategic Offensive Reductions Treaty (SORT)*' came into force in June 2003, which reduced strategic warheads on either side to 1,700-2,200. SORT was superseded by a 'New START' treaty signed in April 2010. It stipulated a reduction of strategic nuclear missile launchers to half. New START is expected to remain in force for at least 10 years after coming into force in January 2011.

Strategic Communication

As an element of *National Strategy*, it is a way of persuading the target audience to accept one's ideas, policies or courses of action. It is essential enabler of 'perception management' to support a country's national-strategic *Doctrine*. It includes the coordination of statecraft, public affairs and public diplomacy. It roots lie in the classic military concept of 'propaganda', which has evolved to become a more encompassing concept relevant to contemporary times. In the military-strategic context, it operates through 'information operations'. 'Think tanks'—though their academic writings and 'track-two' interactions—constitute a valuable instrument for a country for furthering strategic communication. See *Deterrence* and *Military Strategy*.

Strategic Deterrence

It is an element of a State's *National Strategy* that synergises and effectively leverages all elements of national power—diplomatic, economic, informational, soft-power and military. The term is often used incorrectly as a synonym for '*Nuclear Deterrence*'. However, since Strategic Deterrence constitutes any form of deterrence that operates at the national-strategic level, it includes *Nuclear Deterrence*, but is not necessarily restricted to it. Building strategic partnerships with friendly countries is an instrument to develop Strategic Deterrence against a potential adversary. See *Deterrence* and *Dissuasion*.

Strategic Level of Warfare

See *Levels of Warfare*

Strategic Offensive Reductions Treaty (SORT)

See *Strategic Arms Reduction Treaty (START)*.

Strategic Petroleum Reserves (SPR)

Crude oil inventories (or stockpiles) held by the government of a particular country, as well as private industry, for the purpose of providing economic and national security during an energy crisis. There are five types of storage facilities—surface tanks, underground concrete tanks, underground salt cavern, underground rock cavern and floating tanks. Compared to surface storage, underground storage is considered to be safe and also makes more effective use of land.

In January 2004, the Indian government approved construction of strategic crude oil reserves in two phases. While the first phase was completed in 2014, the second phase is planned to be completed by 2020. India presently maintains SPR at three locations—Visakhapatnam in Andhra Pradesh (1.33 million tonnes capacity), Mangalore in Karnataka (1.5 million tonnes) and Padur in Karnataka (2.5 million tonnes), which are roughly equivalent to 14 days of consumption. More are being added (such as at Bikaner, Rajkot, Padur and Chandikhol). It is planned to increase the SPR capacity to 18 million tonnes (132 million barrels) by 2020. The SPR project in India is implemented by 'Indian Strategic Petroleum Reserves Ltd' (ISPRL), which was established in 2004.

Strategic Sealift

See *Sealift and Sealift Capacity*.

Strategy

May be understood as connection between the 'Ends' (objective) to the 'Ways' and 'Means'. While the word 'Ways' refers to the 'method', 'Means' refers to the instruments at one's disposal to adopt the chosen 'method' to achieve the desired 'Ends'. The term applies to the national-strategic level (*National Strategy*) to the military-strategic level (*Military Strategy*). In the military domain, *Strategy* is often confused with *Doctrine*, with the latter (incorrectly) used to denote the former.

String of Pearls

First used in a 2005 report by Booz-Allen-Hamilton titled 'Energy Futures in Asia' prepared for US Defense Secretary, the term refers to China's 'nodes' of influence in the Indo-Pacific Region, where maritime infrastructure is being developed through Chinese assistance, Although these facilities are ostensibly for civilian/commercial use, their 'dual-use' nature cannot be ignored. Potentially, such facilities could be invaluable to sustain distant Chinese naval operations.

STUFT

Acronym for 'Ships Taken Up from Trade', a term that largely applies to *Amphibious Operation* and *Out of Area Contingency* (*OOAC*) *Operations. See Sealift and Sealift Capacity.*

SUA Convention

The Convention for Suppression of Unlawful Acts against the Safety of Maritime Navigation (SUA Convention) is meant to curb acts of violence against ships at sea. It was a result of a resolution adopted by the *International Maritime Organisation (IMO)* that directed its Maritime Safety Committee (MSC) to develop a legal instrument on the lines of one instituted by the International Civil Aviation Organisation (ICAO) for aviation security. SUA Convention, along with a Protocol relating to security of fixed platforms at sea, was signed at Rome in 1988 and entered into force in 1992. The Convention lays down the types of offences including seizure of ships by force, endangering the safety of passengers and crews and placing devices on board a ship that will destroy or damage the ship. The Convention applies to vessels operating beyond *Territorial Waters.* It also applies when the (alleged) offender is found in the territory of a country that is party to the Convention. All countries acceding to the Convention need to ensure that the offences committed under it are punished appropriately. For this, the Convention sets out the principle of 'aut dedere aut judicare'—that the countries that have acceded to the Convention must either prosecute the alleged offender, or extradite the offender to another State that is willing to undertake the prosecution. The Convention does not apply to warships.

India is state party to the SUA Convention and its Protocol of 1988, and has incorporated the provisions in its domestic legislation through enactment of the SUA Act, 2002.

Submarine

See *Conventional Submarine* and *Nuclear Submarine.*

Submarine-Launched Ballistic Missile (SLBM)

See *Ballistic Missile Submarine (SSBN).*

Submarine Rescue

In the event of an accident onboard a dived submarine, the vessel is immediately brought to the sea surface. But if it sinks, the crew members are trained to escape from the disabled submarine either on their own (through the submarine's torpedo tube) or through external assistance, depending upon the depth of water and the nature of the vessel's disability. A free ascent by the crew to the surface can usually be undertaken from up to depths of about 120 metres, but this may not be possible due to damage to the submarine.

In any case, if the water is deeper, free ascent cannot be resorted to due to the risk of decompression sickness (a condition arising from dissolved nitrogen in blood-stream bubbling out due to sudden de-pressurisation). Hence, external assistance is provided through a 'Deep Submergence Rescue Vehicle (DSRV)' or a rescue chamber. The DSRV or rescue chamber is locked on the submarine's escape hatch, and the crew transferred to it, which surfaces and shifts the crew to the submarine support ship equipped with recompression and medical facilities.

Some submarines (like the German-designed Indian Shishumar class) have their own 'rescue sphere' as an integral part of the submarine. The 'rescue sphere' is released with the entire crew in it, without any external aid. Once it pops up on the sea surface, the crew can be rescued.

Suezmax (Ship)

See *Commercial Ship Sizes.*

Surveillance

The word comes from a French phrase that denotes 'watching over something' ('sur' means 'from above' and 'veiller' is a verb for 'to watch'). It is an essential enabler for *Maritime Domain Awareness* (MDA), which is essential for various missions. Surveillance by warships, submarines and maritime reconnaissance/patrol aircraft is primarily undertaken through their integral sensors like radars (including early warning radars) and *Electronic Support Measures (ESM)*. These are supplemented by other means like space-based systems and *Unmanned Aerial Vehicles (UAV).*

Sustainable Fisheries

A concept pertaining to the exploitation of fish resources in a given water-body at a sustainable rate, where the fish population does not decline over time because of prevalent fishing practices.

The concept largely stems from the growing concerns of the global community of two types of overfishing in the world's oceans—'growth overfishing' and 'recruitment overfishing'. Growth overfishing occurs when the fish is harvested at an average size that is smaller than the size that would produce the maximum yield. Recruitment overfishing occurs when the mature adult fish population is depleted to a level where it no longer has the reproductive capacity to replenish itself. These practices result in a significant loss of potential yield, and the fish stocks erode to the point where it loses diversity and resilience to environmental fluctuations. In the longer term, it also leads to permanent damage to the marine ecosystem.

Sustainable fishery involves a thorough study of the theoretical disciplines like fish population dynamics, combined with practical measures to avoiding overfishing through formulation of appropriate laws and policies, techniques like promulgation of fishing quotas, areas and seasons, curtailing destructive and illegal fishing practices, setting up protected areas, restoring collapsed fisheries, incorporating all externalities involved in harvesting marine ecosystems into fishery economics, educating stakeholders and the wider public, and developing independent certification programs. See *Blue Economy*, *Fishing Methods and Gear*, *Illegal, Unreported, and Unregulated (IUU) Fishing*, and *Marine Fishing Regulation Acts (MFRA)*.

T

Tactical Ballistic Missiles

See *Ballistic and Cruise Missiles.*

Tactical Level of Warfare

See *Levels of Warfare*

Tactical Nuclear Weapons (TNW)

A nuclear weapon designed to be used for military warfighting at the *Operational* or *Tactical* levels of warfare, rather than as a national-strategic (political) weapon of last resort. TNW include not only short-range *Cruise Missiles*, but also bombs, artillery shells, mines, torpedoes and depth charges armed with a nuclear warhead. For TNW, there is no precise definition of the 'tactical' in terms of their effective ranges or the yield of nuclear warhead. Although the yield is lower than that of strategic nuclear weapons, some TNW could be more destructive than those used against Japan in the Second World War. The development of TNW by some countries represents a major deviation from the established norms for use of nuclear weapons at the *National Strategic* level, whether employed for *Counterforce* or *Countervalue Targeting*. Also, the use of such weapons against nuclear-capable adversaries carries a significant danger of *Escalation*.

Tactics

In the maritime-military context, 'Tactics' is the science and art of organising a force up to the Fleet or *Task Force* level, and employing appropriate techniques to combine and use the units of the force and their weapon systems, to attain the desired military objectives at the tactical level of warfare. See *Levels of Warfare*.

Task Force

A composite formation of individual units established to undertake a single defined task or activity. In the naval context, a 'task force' usually comprises one or more 'task groups', which in turn, is composed of one or more 'task units'. Such 'task' organisation is essential for operational flexibility. As an ad hoc arrangement, it differs from a more permanent 'type' organisation that usually comprises fleets, flotillas, squadrons and divisions. A task force can be assembled using ships from different divisions and squadrons, without requiring a formal and permanent reorganisation, and can be easily dissolved following completion of the operational task. See *Carrier Battle Group (CBG) and Carrier Task Force (CTF).*

Territorial Jurisdiction

See *Criminal Jurisdiction.*

Territorial Waters

An area of waters adjacent to a coastal state over which it exercises sovereignty, subject to the right of *Innocent Passage*. Every state has the right to establish the breadth of its territorial waters up to a limit not exceeding 12 *nautical miles* (NM), measured from the *Maritime Baseline.* The 12 NM limit has evolved over decades from the erstwhile three NM limit, including through deliberations during the United Nations Conferences on the Law of the Sea, which is now codified as a legal tenet in *UNCLOS*, 1982. See, *Mare Clausum*, *Innocent Passage* and *Internal Waters.*

Terrorism

While there is no consensus on its precise definition, the concept of 'terrorism' usually refers to acts intended to create a dramatic effect of fear, primarily through death and destruction involving civilian populace, for furtherance of a politico-economic or ideological (secular or religious) objectives. Very often, terrorist activity and effects are transnational. Even when terrorism is resorted to by a sub-national group, the crucial need for extra-national support reinforces its trans-national linkages. At times, countries use terrorism as a proxy to further their national strategic objectives against another country. See *Maritime Terrorism* and *Weapons of Mass Destruction (WMD).*

Thousand Ship Navy (TSN)

A concept defined by the US Navy's Chief of Naval Operations (CNO) Admiral Mike Mullen at the October 2005 International Seapower Symposium at the Naval War College. He referred to it as "a global maritime partnership that unites maritime forces, port operators, commercial shippers, and international, governmental and non-governmental agencies to address mutual concerns". The TSN concept emerged from the realisation that the US naval power was stretched thin due to its growing global commitments, which the US could offset by enhancing cooperation with regional navies. The concept was showcased as an initiative aimed at obtaining the cooperation of "friendly navies", primarily through information exchange, to enhance *Maritime Domain Awareness (MDA).*

The TSN concept later began to be referred to within the US Navy as 'Global Maritime Partnership' (GMP) Initiative. The same was articulated in the US maritime strategy document of 2007, which stated that the initiative "seeks a cooperative approach to *Maritime Security*, promoting the rule of law by countering Piracy, *Terrorism*, weapons proliferation, drug trafficking, and other illicit activities". The US Maritime Strategy document of 2015 furthers the appeal for the partnership—re-phrased as "global network of navies"—and effectively communicates to the potential partners the rationale for such "plug and play" cooperation with the US forces sans "commitment".

Tidal Wave Energy

A form of hydropower that refers to harnessing the energy of tides (or the consequent tidal flow) into electricity. The concept has not yet been implemented on a commercial scale mainly due to relatively high costs involved, besides some other reasons such as the limited availability of suitable sites with sufficiently high tidal ranges and environmental considerations. Nonetheless, it holds immense promise as a source of renewable energy, particularly because tides are more predictable than wind and solar power. Recent developments suggest that technological improvements may soon overcome the commercial non-viability of the tidal energy. These developments are represented by four options:

- **Tidal Stream Generator.** These utilise the moving water's kinetic energy to turn the blades of a power turbine, similar to wind turbines. The turbine may be placed horizontally, vertically, or in a ducted manner, based on the geophysical circumstances.
- **Tidal Barrage.** These utilise mainly the potential energy latent in the difference in height high and low tides leading to hydraulic pressure. With the rising tide, the potential energy is captured into a large basin behind a specialised dam. With the receding tide, this energy is converted into mechanical energy as the water turns the turbines to generate electrical power.
- **Dynamic Tidal Power.** An untried but technologically feasible method that seeks to harness the interface between potential and kinetic energies in tidal flows. It involves constructing long dams of 30 to 50 km in length into the sea that introduces a tidal phase difference between the sea areas on its either side. This triggers a strong oscillating tidal currents along the coast (perpendicular to the dam) whose energy is harnessed by use of special turbines.
- **Tidal Lagoon.** It involves building circular structure with retaining walls that are equipped with turbines to harness the tidal energy. The reservoir is similar to a tidal barrage, except that the location is artificial and does not contain a pre-existing ecosystem.

Given India's emerging energy needs, the resort to renewable energy in the form of tidal wave energy presents an attractive potential alternative to fossil-fuels. The project is being overseen by the Indian government's 'Ministry of New and Renewable Energy', which has identified the areas—particularly on India's western coast—with significant tidal energy potential. Although tidal power potential in India is lesser relative to more northern and southern latitudes, preliminary estimates indicate that the total available potential of wave energy along the entire Indian coast is about 40,000 megawatts.

Torpedo

A self-propelled weapon with an explosive warhead, launched above or below the water surface, propelled underwater towards a target, and designed to detonate either on contact with its target or in its proximity.

Historically, a torpedo has been a principal weapon of a *Submarine* to destroy enemy warships and merchant vessels. While a torpedo continues to be among the weapons for *Anti-Surface Warfare (ASuW)*, it has become the principal weapon for *Anti-Submarine Warfare (ASW)*. It may be launched directly from a torpedo tube of a submarine, or launched by a ship or from fixed-wing aircraft or helicopter.

Total Exclusion Zone (TEZ)

See *Exclusion Zones.*

Total War

See *Limited War.*

Tracking and Reconnaissance

Both are tasks undertaken by naval forces (surface ships, submarines or aircraft) under their 'Scouting' mission. Tracking is the observation of a mobile objective for the purpose of regularly reporting its composition, location, movement and any other relevant information. Once an objective has been located by a scout either by a *Search* or a *Patrol*, own forces may or may not be in a position to take any action at the time. The objective, therefore, needs to be tracked till a more opportune time. Tracking is therefore often a sequel to a *Search* or *Patrol.* Reconnaissance is meant to obtain information by visual observation or other means, about the activities and resources of a (potential) adversary, or about the meteorological, hydrographic, or geographic characteristics of a particular area of interest. See *Search and Patrol.*

Traffic Separation Scheme (TSS)

In busy and confined maritime passageways, such as in straits or around capes, the *International Maritime Organisation (IMO)* makes it necessary for the coastal country to promulgate a traffic-management system comprising a Traffic Separation Scheme (TSS). Essentially, a TSS is a one-way lane for vessels plying in such 'restricted' waters. The TSS rules are incorporated in the International Regulations for Preventing Collisions at Sea, 1972 (*COLREGS*) (under rule 10).

The traffic-lanes indicate the general direction of the ships in that zone; ships navigating within a TSS all sail in the same direction, and cross the lane in an angle as close to 90 degrees as possible. The TSS often has an unregulated 'inshore traffic zone' between the traffic-lanes and the coast, which is meant only for local traffic, fishing and small craft. The body of water between two opposite lanes is also required to be avoided by vessels transiting across the TSS except in unavoidable circumstances such as emergencies, or for fishing activities. In the TSS, coastal radar stations monitor the traffic movement, and provide necessary guidance to the vessels, if required.

In the separation lanes of the English Channel, all eastbound traffic uses a lane off the French coast, whereas all west-bound vessels use the lane off the coast of England. In 1967, the Dover Strait/Détroit du Pas de Calais became the first *IMO*-approved TSS in the world. The other well-known TSS locations are the Singapore Strait and Cape Horn. See *COLREGS and Rules of the Road.*

Transatlantic Trade and Investment Partnership (T-TIP)

A proposed *Free Trade Agreement (FTA)* between the European Union and the United States, which could boost overall trade between the two parties by 50 per cent. Notably, the proposal was first mooted in 1990, when the European Community (comprising 12 European countries) and the US signed the 'Transatlantic Declaration'. Economic barriers between the two sides are relatively low, largely due to their coherence flowing from the Bretton Woods institution of the *World Trade Organisation (WTO)*, supplemented by the 2007 agreements of EU-US 'Open Skies' and Transatlantic Economic Council. However, disagreements on protectionism are conspicuous, due to which the proposed 'Transatlantic Free Trade Area' (TAFTA) proposed in 1990, and again in 2006 by Germany could not fructify.

Together with *Trans-Pacific Partnership (TPP)*, T-TIP is an arrangement through which the United States seeks to be a part of a near-worldwide *Free Trade Zone* covering two-thirds of the global economy. See *Common Market, Single Market and Unified Market*, and *World Trade Organisation (WTO).*

Transhipment and Transhipment Ports

The term 'Transhipment' refers to the *shipment* of merchandise trade to an intermediate destination, before reaching its final destination. This is done at 'transhipment ports', usually to combine small shipments into a large shipment, or some other reasons. For example, if a *container* shipment destined for ports in the United States has originated from a port that does not have an automated security screening system in compliance with the US *Container Security Initiative (CSI)*, the shipment would need to be routed through a CSI-compliant 'transhipment port'.

The 'transhipment ports' are usually *Duty Free Ports*, where no customs checks or duties apply. Most of the world's busiest 'transhipment ports' are located in Asia. These include Busan (South Korea), Colombo (Sri Lanka), Dubai (UAE), Hong Kong (China), Kaohsiung (Taiwan), Klang (Malaysia), Shanghai (China), Singapore and Tanjung Pelepas (Malaysia). See *Special Economic Zone (SEZ)*.

Transit Passage (International Straits)

See *International Straits*.

Trans-Pacific Partnership (TPP)

A regional economic grouping proposed to be established through 'Trans-Pacific Strategic Partnership Agreement', as a form of *Free Trade Agreement (FTA)*. As of 2014, twelve countries of the Asia-Pacific region have joined in the TPP negotiations—Australia, Brunei, Canada, Chile, Japan, Malaysia, Mexico, New Zealand, Peru, Singapore, the US and Vietnam. More economies like South Korea and Taiwan are potential members. The negotiations have still not concluded due to lingering contentions on issues such as agriculture, intellectual property, and services and investments.

The genesis of TPP lies in the negotiations launched in 2002, which initially included three countries (Chile, New Zealand and Singapore) to institute a 'Pacific-Three Closer Economic Partnership' (P3 CEP). In the later years, the proposed partnership added more countries and assumed various other nomenclatures. Although the US joined the negotiations only in 2009, TPP has eventually turned out to be a potential US-led trade bloc, and is being seen as a counter to the China-dominated 'ASEAN Plus Three' economic forum. See *Association of Southeast Asian Nations (ASEAN)*.

Trawling

See *Fishing Methods and Gear.*

Treaties for Protection of Ozone Layer

Two international environmental agreements address the global issue on the protection of the earth's ozone layer. The 'Vienna Convention for the Protection of the Ozone Layer' 1985 entered into force in 1988. It was aimed to protect the ozone layer by phasing out substances responsible for it. However, it did not include legally binding reduction goals for the use of Chlorofluorocarbons (CFCs), the main chemical agents causing ozone depletion. This void was sought to be addressed through the follow-on 'Montreal Protocol on Substances that Deplete the Ozone Layer' 1987, which entered into force in 1989.

As a result of these international agreements, the ozone hole in Antarctica is slowly recovering. Climate projections indicate that the ozone layer will return to 1980 levels between 2050 and 2070. Due to its widespread adoption and implementation the two treaties represent exemplary international co-operation. The two treaties have also been ratified by 197 parties, making them the first universally ratified treaties in the history of the United Nations.

Notably, although CFCs are greenhouse gases, the two treaties are motivated by the need to counter ozone depletion rather than global warming. Lately, however, the international community is seeking to amend Montreal Protocol to address the issue of global warming. It is considering the long-standing demand of developed countries to bring non-ozone depleting Hydrofluorocarbons (HFC)—used as a replacement for ozone-depleting CFC for refrigeration—under the purview of the Montreal Protocol. See *Intergovernmental Panel on Climate Change (IPCC)*, *Kyoto Protocol 1997*, *Lilypad* and *United Nations Framework Convention on Climate Change (UNFCCC).*

Trilateral Maritime Cooperation (India-Maldives-Sri Lanka)

A forum for *Maritime Security* cooperation among India, Sri Lanka and Maldives, which was launched in October 2011 during the first NSA-level 'Trilateral Meeting on *Maritime Security* Cooperation' held in Maldives. The broader objective of the forum is to enhance *Maritime Security* in the *Indian Ocean Region (IOR).*

At the second meeting in Colombo in July 2013, the three countries agreed on a roadmap for cooperation in *Maritime Security* through various measures and activities, particularly the enhancement of *Maritime Domain Awareness (MDA)* and *Capacity Building*. The former involves inter alia the use of *Long Range Identification and Tracking (LRIT)* and *Automatic Identification System (AIS)* mandated by the *International Maritime Organisation (IMO)* and data sharing, and information exchange on maritime crime. *Capacity Building* involves various activities such as development of technological means of MDA including *Merchant Ship Information System (MSIS)* for exchange of data on 'white shipping', *Combined Exercises*, enhancing the capacity (hardware and training) of maritime forces for *Search and Rescue* and *Oil Spill Response*, and developing policy and legal coherence to respond to *Piracy*.

The three countries have since been holding NSA-level meetings, occasionally involving the government representatives of Mauritius and Seychelles as 'guest countries'. These are interspersed with more frequent meetings among senior official and at the technical level. Working/ technical level groups have also been formed to progress the identified areas of *Maritime Cooperation*. Other potential areas of cooperation being discussed include *Hydrography*, training for *Visit, Board, Search and Seizure (VBSS) Operations*, cadets training on board Indian Sail Training Ships, track-two (think-tank) interactions and combined maritime adventure activities. See *White Shipping Information*.

Tropical Cyclone

Generically called Tropical Revolving Storm (TRS), it refers to a storm system, wherein high-speed winds exceeding 65 km per hour spiral from high-pressure to low-pressure areas, accompanied by thunderstorms and heavy rain. Depending on its location, a TRS is referred to by names such as 'cyclone' (in the Indian Ocean, and southwest Pacific Ocean), 'hurricane' (in the Atlantic and eastern Pacific oceans) or 'typhoon' (in the western Pacific Ocean). When the wind-speed reaches 65 km per hour, it is called a 'tropical storm'. If the wind-speed exceeds 120 km per hour, it is called a 'cyclone', 'hurricane' or 'typhoon'.

The adjective 'tropical' refers to the geographical origin of the storm system. TRS always occurs in a band that lies roughly between the tropics of Cancer and Capricorn (between approximately 5° and 30° latitudes).

The intense low pressure areas form almost exclusively in tropical latitudes over large bodies of relatively warm water through the water's evaporation and re-condensation into clouds (when moist air rises and cools to saturation). While releasing the 'latent heat' during re-condensation, water vapour acts as the 'fuel' for the storm. (This heat energy was absorbed by water vapour during evaporation). This phenomenon incrementally provides the energy to the storm system.

The term 'cyclone' refers to its spiralling nature. Based on the 'Coriolis Effect' (the angular momentum imparted by the Earth's rotation, in this case), rather than transiting directly from areas of high pressure to low pressure, the winds tend to deflect to the right of their direction of travel in the Northern Hemisphere, and fail to arrive at the low pressure centre, but instead circulate around it in a counter-clockwise spiral. Similarly, the winds are deflected to the left of their direction of travel in the Southern Hemisphere, leading to a clockwise spiral. As the winds converge toward the low-pressure core, they spiral upwards, sending more warm moist air upwards. As this air rises, it cools and releases more latent heat into the atmosphere to add further energy to the storm. The winds spiralling around this central core create the eye of the storm.

The storm typically weakens rapidly over land where it is cut off from its primary energy source. However, the high-speed storm pushes the sea in front of it, leading to temporary but a significant sea-level rise. Hence, the littoral areas are particularly vulnerable to damage from a tropical storm, particularly during high tide. See *Humanitarian Assistance and Disaster Relief (HADR)*.

Tsunami and TWS

Derived from the Japanese term meaning 'harbour wave', it is also called a 'seismic sea wave' or a 'tidal (a misnomer) wave', and usually refers to a series of waves in an ocean caused by the displacement of a large volume of water due to seismic activity, rather than the wind or tide system. Hence, while a Tsunami may initially resemble a rapidly rising tide (leading to the misnomer), Tsunami waves do not resemble normal sea waves in terms of their much longer 'wavelength', 'time period' (ranging from minutes to hours), and 'amplitude' (wave height of tens of metres). The Indian Ocean Tsunami of 2004 was among the deadliest natural disasters in human history with at least 230,000 lives lost in 14 littoral countries of the *Indian Ocean Region (IOR).*

A Tsunami Warning System (TWS) is used to detect Tsunamis in advance and issue warnings to prevent loss of life and damage. The TWS adopts a two-pronged approach. Firstly, a combination of sensors comprising shore-based tide gauges and sea-based DART (Deep-ocean Assessment and Reporting of Tsunamis) buoys are deployed to detect Tsunamis. The second prong constitutes a communications infrastructure is to issue timely alarms to enable speedy evacuation of in forecasted coastal areas. The effectiveness of the two-pronged approach is premised on the complementary nature of international and regional (local) TWS. Following the UN 2005 UN Conference held in Kobe (Japan), an international TWS for the Indian Ocean was installed in 2006. It incorporates 25 seismographic stations and 6 DART buoys relaying information to 26 national tsunami information centres. See *Humanitarian Assistance and Disaster Relief (HADR).*

Tube-Launched Land Attack Missile (TLAM)

See *Land Attack Cruise Missile (LACM).*

U

Ultra Large Crude Carrier (ULCC)

As the largest commercial vessel type, it is a super-tanker of 320,000 to 550,000 *Dead Weight Tonnage (DWT)*, with standard dimensions of 415 meters length, 63 meters width and 35 meters draught (underwater section). ULCCs cannot cross the Suez Canal, and therefore need to be routed via the Cape of Good Hope. These ships can carry up to 3.7 million barrels of crude oil, but need special oil-discharge terminals. See *Very Large Crude Carrier (VLCC).*

United Nations Convention on the Law of the Sea (UNCLOS)

UNCLOS is an international treaty signed in 1982, and currently in force since 1994 on the regulation of the use of the oceans. UNCLOS is also referred to as Law of the Sea (LOS) Convention and UNCLOS, 1982. The treaty resulted from the Third UN Conference on the Law of the Sea (UNCLOS-III) held from 1973 to 1982. UNCLOS-III is sometimes incorrectly used as a synonym for UNCLOS (or UNCLOS, 1982). Currently, 166 countries and the European Union (EU) are state parties to UNCLOS. It is important to bear in mind that countries that have not acceded to the Convention are still bound by most of its provisions that represent *Customary International Law*. See *Freedom of the Seas.*

Underwriting

A term commonly used in economics, which refers to signing for acceptance of liability, and thereby guaranteeing financial payment in case of a unforeseen loss or damage. The service of underwriting is provided by large financial service providers such as banks, investment companies or insurers. See *International Underwriting Association (IUA), Joint War Committee (JWC), Lloyd's Register and Lloyd's of London, P&I (Protection and Indemnity) Clubs*, and *War Risk Insurance.*

Unified Market

See *Common Market, Single Market and Unified Market.*

United Nations Framework Convention on Climate Change (UNFCCC)

It is currently the overarching international treaty on climate change. The treaty came into being in 1992 at the UN Conference on Environment and Development (UNCED) held in Rio de Janerio, which is commonly referred to as the 'Earth Summit'. It entered into force in 1994. The overarching aim of the treaty is to regulate the concentration of greenhouse gases in the atmosphere to prevent global warming and climate change induced by human activity. Towards this objective, the member countries were required to establish their respective levels of greenhouse gas emissions as a datum for further treaties to limit such emissions.

At present, UNFCCC is effectively the only global treaty on climate change with a near-universal membership (196 state parties) and acceptance. Notably, however, it does not bind State parties to cap their greenhouse gas emissions. See *Kyoto Protocol 1997*, *Lilypad*, and *Treaties for Protection of Ozone Layer.*

Universal Jurisdiction

See *Criminal Jurisdiction.*

Unmanned Aerial Vehicles (UAV)

An aircraft without a human pilot aboard, commonly called a drone. A UAV is usually remotely piloted, but could also be flown under autonomous control. It is usually deployed for military operations, but also used in a growing number of civil applications. In the maritime-military context, a UAV is invaluable for *Surveillance.* The various UAV types range from the US 'Phantom' High Altitude Long Endurance (HALE) to the hand-held Micro-UAV (also called MAVs) that the US Navy employs to assist in *VBSS Operations.* Such vehicles designed for combat are called Unmanned Combat Air Vehicle (UCAV). The export of UAVs or technology capable of delivering a payload of at least 500 kg to a range of at least 300 km is restricted by the *Missile Technology Control regime (MTCR).* See *Unmanned Underwater Vehicles (UUV).*

Unmanned Underwater Vehicles (UUV)

A submersible without a human operator aboard, commonly called an underwater drone. These vehicles may be divided into two categories, Remotely Operated Underwater Vehicles (ROVs), which are controlled by a remote human operator, and Autonomous Underwater Vehicles (AUVs), which operate independently of direct human input. UUVs are generally employed for undertaking tedious or risky underwater tasks such as searching for sunken objects or mine-clearance. See *Unmanned Aerial Vehicles (UAV).*

V

Varuna

A term emanating from Hindu mythology meaning 'God of the Oceans'. The motto of the Indian Navy is 'Shano Varuna', which means, 'May the Lord of the Oceans be auspicious unto us'.

Varuna (Naval Exercises)

Combined naval exercises between the Indian Navy and the French Navy. Exercises between the two navies began in 1983. However, following the 2001 agreement between France and India to establish a strategic partnership, the *combined* exercises were named 'Varuna'. See *Joint and Combined.*

Vertical Envelopment

A tactical *Manoeuvre* wherein military troops are air-dropped or air landed. In the maritime context, the concept applies to amphibious assaults, where 'vertical envelopment' is critical element of seizing the initiative. See *Amphibious Operation.*

Very Large Crude Carrier (VLCC)

A supertanker of 160,000 to 320,000 *Dead Weight Tonnage (DWT)* with standard dimensions of 300-330 meters in length, 58 meters in breath and 31 meters draft (underwater portion). A VLCC can carry about 2 million barrels of crude oil. VLCCs cannot cross the Suez Canal, and therefore need to be routed via the Cape of Good Hope. See *Ultra Large Crude Carrier (ULCC).*

Vessel Protection Detachment (VPD)

A team of government security personnel embarked onboard commercial ships to protect them from pirate attacks. VPD being composed of uniformed personnel is fundamentally distinct from 'Private Contracted

Armed Security Personnel' (PCASP) employed by *Private Maritime Security Companies (PMSC)*. VPD personnel are subject to regular processes of military discipline and authorised to act in furtherance of the State monopoly on the use of force. Many European countries have preferred to employ VPD on board their merchant ships, rather than resorting to *Private Maritime Security Companies (PMSC)*. See *Piracy* and *Flag Follows Trade*.

Vessel Traffic Services (VTS) and Vessel Traffic Management System (VTMS)

Vessel Traffic Services (VTS) is a concept that involves monitoring of maritime traffic by port authorities, similar to Air Traffic Control (ATC) by airport authorities. VTS is meant to improve the safety and efficiency of navigation, ensure safety of life at sea and protect the marine environment. VTS is governed by *Safety of Life at Sea (SOLAS) Convention, 1974/1988* Chapter V Regulation 12 together with the IMO Resolution A.857(20) on 'Guidelines for Vessel Traffic Services' adopted in November 1997.

VTS involves adherence to laid down procedures specific to the VTS area such as approach procedures, pilotage, and arrival and departure reports. VTS is enabled by the Vessel Traffic Management System (VTMS), which integrates surveillance information obtained from port radars, *Automatic Identification System (AIS)*, Direction Finding (DF) system, CCTV, VHF communications and other systems. Similarly, Air Traffic Control (ATC) is enabled by the Air Traffic Management System (VATMS).

In India, the surveillance information from port radars is integrated in a VTMS system, and relayed to the Indian Navy and Indian Coast Guard. The information obtained in the Offshore Development Areas (ODA) is integrated in the Vessel and Air Traffic Management System (VATMS)—West system, coordinated by the Indian Navy. See *Pre-Arrival Notification (PAN)*.

Visit, Board, Search and Seizure (VBSS) Operations

Operations undertaken by naval forces involving boarding a suspect vessel at sea to check the nature of the activity it is involved. The term VBSS originated from the historical right of belligerents during war to the 'right to visit' and 'seizure' of vessels destined for enemy ports. Wartime VBSS is the means by which a belligerent warship may determine the true character of merchant ships (whether 'enemy' or 'neutral'), the manner of their employment ('innocent' or 'hostile'), and the nature of goods the ships are carrying ('*Contraband*' or 'Free Goods'). All warships and neutral vessels engaged in government non-commercial service are not subject to VBSS. The seizure of a merchant vessel carrying *Contraband* is exercised by taking over the vessel and its cargo as prize for adjudication in a *Prize Courts*. See, *Blockade* and *SLOC Interdiction*.

VBSS is also undertaken as part of constabulary role of navies during peacetime to confirm that the vessel is not involved in unlawful activity. The VBSS team may board the vessel using a boat or a helicopter. The boarding operation may be 'opposed', 'non-compliant' or 'compliant'. Compliant boarding is one wherein the master and crew of the vessel cooperate. Non-compliant boarding is one wherein an agreement to board has not been obtained. Opposed boarding is one wherein the master or crew has made it clear that steps will be taken to prevent the boarding. *Special Operations* Forces (like MARCOS) are trained to undertake 'opposed' and 'non-compliant' boarding. In the past, MARCOS have undertaken VBSS operations against MV Nafis-1 (2011) and during counter-piracy operations in the Gulf of Aden since 2008.

An essential difference between war-time and peace-time VBSS Operations is notable. For peace-time missions, collection of evidence is necessary to prove the crime in court of law. In contrast, war-time VBSS does not require any evidence. Once the boarding unit's commander has confirmed that it is carrying *Contraband*, the vessel could be seized.

Voyage Charter

A term used in commercial shipping industry. It is a contract whereby the *ship-owner* places his ship at the disposal of the 'Charterer' for one or more voyages, with the *ship-operator* being responsible for the operation of the ship.

W

War and Armed Conflict

In its traditional sense, 'War' refers to fighting between two or more States. 'War' is one that is formally declared; otherwise it is an 'Armed Conflict'. It is important to note that the *Hague Conventions, 1907* states that hostilities should not commence 'without previous and explicit warning, in the form either of a declaration of war, giving reasons, or of an ultimatum with conditional declaration of war'. Even in this Convention, however, there was no provision to impose any period of delay between the issue of notification and the beginning of hostilities. Even in 1939, Germany attacked Poland and declared war simultaneously.

Codified law does not provide any definition of the term 'Armed Conflict'. Nonetheless, some guidance is provided by judicial writings and past cases. It may be said that an 'Armed Conflict' exists whenever there is a resort to armed force between States or protracted armed violence between governmental authorities and organised armed groups within a State.

In contemporary times, countries rarely resort to formal declaration of 'War'. Even if a country initiates the use of military force against another, it could assert that it is merely acting in legitimate self defence, and thus deny the existence of a state of war. It is in these situations that the expression of 'Armed Conflict' comes in use since international law applies similarly to both 'War' and 'Armed Conflict'. *Geneva Conventions, 1949* states that the law applies to "all cases of declared war or any other armed conflict which may arise between two or more of the High Contracting Parties, even if the state of war is not recognised by one of them." See *Human Rights Law (HR Law)*, *International Armed Conflicts (IAC)*, *International Criminal Court (ICC)*, *Non-International Armed Conflicts (NIAC)* and *International Humanitarian Law (IHL)*, *Short of War Scenarios*, and *War Crimes, Crimes against Humanity and Genocide*

War Crimes, Crimes against Humanity and Genocide

Whereas 'War Crimes' are violations of the *Law of Armed Conflict (LOAC)*, 'Crimes against Humanity' refers to murder, extermination, rape, torture, enslavement, enforced disappearances and similar systematic inhumane acts committed against civilian population, and meant to cause widespread suffering, serious mental or bodily injury. The authoritative definition of the term is derived from the Statute of the *International Criminal Court (ICC)*. However, it is important to note that unlike 'War Crimes', the law governing 'Crimes against Humanity' is not codified in any international convention, but is underpinned by *Customary International Law*. Also, it is difficult to identify the precise elements that distinguish such crimes from those that are subject to sovereign national laws.

'Genocide' refers to persecutions on political, racial or religious grounds, with the objective of destroying a national, ethnic, racial or religious group. It includes killing members of the group and imposing measures to prevent procreation. The international law governing genocide is also derived from *Customary International Law*, but codified in the 'Convention on the Prevention and Punishment of the Crime of Genocide' of December 1948. It applies in times of both peace and war, and is thus not strictly a component of the *Law of Armed Conflict (LOAC)*, but the awareness of its provisions is necessary because genocide is often committed by armed forces during wars. The treaty has 142 State parties, including India. Notably, Article 9 of the Convention says that any country can refer a dispute on the responsibility of another country for genocide to the International Court of Justice (ICJ). However, while ratifying the treaty, India declared that while doing so, "...the consent of all the parties to the dispute is required in each case." See *Amnesty*, and *War and Armed Conflict*.

War Risk Insurance

Insurance that covers adversities due to *War and Armed Conflict*, which includes various acts of non-state violence. Some insurance policies also accept the liability for the effects of use of *Weapons of Mass Destruction (WMD)*. War risk insurance is common for trans-national commercial interactions by sea and air. Such insurance has two main components. The first is 'War Risk Liability' that covers the crew, passengers and cargo, and is based on the indemnity amount. The second is the 'War Risk Hull' that covers the platform/craft, and is calculated based on its value. The premium is based on the expected risk in the area through which the platform/craft would transit. See *Joint War Committee (JWC)*, *P&I (Protection and Indemnity) Clubs*, *Underwriting*, and *War Risk Zone*.

War Risk Zone

'War Risk Zones' are designated by the *Joint War Committee (JWC)*, which is part of the Lloyd's (Insurance) Market Association of London. The risks pertain to those from *War*, *Piracy*, *Terrorism* and related perils. The 'war risk zones' designated by the JWC strongly influences the promulgation of *Piracy High Risk Areas*. See *Joint War Committee (JWC)*, *Lloyd's Register and Lloyd's of London*, *P&I (Protection and Indemnity) Clubs*, and *War Risk Insurance*.

Wassenaar Arrangement

The 'Wassenaar Arrangement on Export Controls for Conventional Arms and Dual-Use Goods and Technologies' is a multilateral export-control regime established in 1996 at Wassenaar, the Netherlands to promote transparency and greater responsibility in transfers of conventional arms and dual-use goods and technologies, thus prevent global and regional instabilities arising from such accumulations. The participating countries agreed to tailor their national policies to ensure that transfers of these items do not undermine the aims of the arrangement, while also affirming that it will not be directed against any State or group of States and will not interfere with their rights to acquire legitimate means of self-defence as bestowed by Article 51 of the UN Charter.

The Wassenaar Arrangement is the successor to the Cold War-era 'Coordinating Committee for Multilateral Export Controls' (COCOM). Like its predecessor, it is not a treaty and thus not legally binding, but is less stringent than COCOM, and it does not grant veto power to individual member countries over organisational decisions. It mainly focuses on the transparency of national export control regimes with regard to transfers of certain items identified and laid down in the 'Control Lists'. Every six months, member countries voluntarily exchange information on conventional arms transfers to non-Wassenaar countries. The 'Control Lists' are broadly sub-divided into the 'Dual-Use Goods and Technologies' (Basic List) and the 'Munitions List'. The former comprises ten categories such as electronics, computers, sensors, navigation and aerospace. The latter is further sub-divided into eight broad categories of weapons, such as armoured vehicles, artillery, military aircraft, warships, missile systems and *Small Arms and Light Weapons (SALW)*.

The Wassenaar Arrangement has 41 participating countries. Two major arms exporters China and Israel are not members, although they have aligned their export controls with Wassenaar 'Control Lists'. The Secretariat is located in Vienna, Austria.

Weapons of Mass Destruction (WMD)

A nuclear, radiological, chemical, biological or other weapon that can kill and bring significant harm to a large number of humans or cause great damage to human-made structures (e.g. buildings), natural structures (e.g. mountains), or the biosphere. The scope and application of the term is of evolving nature, driven more by political rather than technical factors. See *Australia Group, Biological Weapons Convention (BWC), Chemical Weapons Convention, Comprehensive Nuclear Test Ban Treaty (CTBT), Non-Proliferation Treaty (NPT), Proliferation Security Initiative (PSI), Terrorism.*

West Pacific Naval Symposium (WPNS)

A voluntary grouping of maritime forces of the countries that are littorals of the Pacific Ocean region. It was inaugurated in 1988 to establish a forum where leaders of regional navies could meet to discuss cooperative initiatives. Under the WPNS, member countries convene biennially to discuss regional and global maritime issues. Twenty one countries are WPNS members, whereas four (Bangladesh, India, Mexico and Pakistan) are observers. See *Indian Ocean Naval Symposium (IONS)* and *RIMPAC Exercises.*

White Shipping Information

Surface picture compilation on position and movement of merchant ships obtained from open sources (like World Register of Shipping database and Lloyd's List Intelligence) and information-sharing arrangements with friendly countries. In India, the information is collated by the Indian

Navy and fed into the *Merchant Ship Information System (MSIS)*. See *Coastal Surveillance Network (CSN)*, *INSPIRES*, *ISLEREP*, and *National Command Control Communication and Intelligence Network (NC^3IN)*.

World Bank

An *International Financial Institution (IFI)*, borne out of the Bretton Woods Conference in 1944. Then known as the International Bank for Reconstruction and Development (IBRD), it was meant to help in the restoration of economies disrupted by the Second World War by facilitating the investment of capital for productive purposes and to promote the long-range balanced growth of international trade. The World Bank is the world's largest source of development assistance. Along with financial assistance, the Bank uses its trained staff and its knowledge base to provide technical advice to the developing countries.

The World Bank's functions are undertaken collectively inter alia by three legally and financially distinct affiliates, as follows:

- **International Bank for Reconstruction and Development (IBRD).** World Bank's original lending arm established in 1945 to function as a self-sustaining business and to provide loans to middle-income and credit-worthy developing countries. It raises money by tapping the world's capital markets.
- **International Development Association (IDA).** It was established in 1960, to provide developmental assistance to the world's poorest countries. It provides concessional financing (interest-free loans or grants), usually with sovereign guarantees. Its funds are largely drawn from the rich member governments.
- **International Finance Corporation (IFC).** Established in 1956, it is a private-sector arm of World Bank that offers investment, advisory, and asset management services to encourage private sector development in developing countries.

Together, the three entities forming the 'World Bank Group' have interrelated functions of lending funds, providing advice and serving as a catalyst to stimulate investments by others. In the process, financial resources are channelled from developed to developing countries to enable the latter to use such assistance to progress their economies to the extent that these begin contributing to the development process of the least developed economies. Japan is an apt example. Formerly a borrower, it later became a major lender to these three organisations. Presently, 194 countries are members of the World Bank Group, which is headquartered in Washington DC. The US holds the maximum shareholding in the Group.

World Trade Organisation (WTO)

A global inter-governmental organisation formed in 1995, which deals with the rules of trade among countries. The WTO evolved from the 1948 General Agreement on Tariffs and Trade (GATT). At its heart are the WTO agreements—covering goods, services and intellectual property—entered into by a majority of the world's trading countries (161 at present). The agreements spell out the principles of liberalisation, and the permitted exceptions. They include individual countries' commitments to lower *Customs* tariffs and other trade barriers, and to open and keep open services markets. They also set procedures for settling disputes.

The WTO agreements are not static. These are renegotiated from time to time and new agreements forged. The Doha Development Round is the current trade-negotiation round of the WTO, which commenced in 2001 with the objective of enhancing global trade through further lowering trade barriers. However, the negotiation has reached a stalemate on various issues, particularly over the demand by developed countries for retention of agricultural subsidies against the demand of the developing countries for fair trade on agricultural products. WTO is headquartered in Geneva (Switzerland). See *Excise Duty and Custom Duty, Foreign Trade, Free Trade Agreement (FTA) and Free Trade Area*, and *Non-Tariff Barriers (NTB).*

Wreck Removal Convention (WREC)

The International Convention on the Removal of Wrecks was adopted at an international conference held in Nairobi (Kenya) in May 2007, and entered into force in April 2015. The Convention requires all ships of over 300 *Gross Tonnage* (including fishing vessels and commercial yachts) to have in place insurance to cover the location, marking and removal of a wreck in the maritime zones of the countries that are party to the Convention. It makes it obligatory upon all ships to carry insurance and Wreck Removal certificates on board, and provides for State Parties to have a right of direct action against insurers. India has ratified the Convention.

The Convention provides a legal basis for States Parties to remove, or have removed, wrecks that pose a hazard for navigation or are harmful for the marine environment, or impinge upon the other interests of member countries. The Convention also applies to a ship that is about to sink or to run aground. It fills a gap in the existing international legal framework by providing a set of uniform rules for the prompt and effective removal of wrecks located in a country's *Exclusive Economic Zone (EEZ)*. See *P&I (Protection and Indemnity) Clubs*, and *Underwriting*.

Z

Zangger Committee

Also called the 'Nuclear Exporters Committee', it was derived from Article III (paragraph 2) of the *Nuclear Non-Proliferation Treaty (NPT)*, which states that all exports of nuclear "equipment or material" must be regulated by safeguards laid down by the 'International Atomic Energy Agency' (IAEA). It was established in 1971 soon after the NPT came into force. Between 1971 and 1974, a group of 15 nuclear supplier countries held informal meetings at Vienna. Chaired by Professor Claude Zangger of Switzerland (and hence, later referred to as the 'Zangger Committee'), the group sought to reach a consensus on the definition of the "equipment or material" relating to "use or production of special fissionable material", and lay down the rules governing their exports, so as to meet non-proliferation obligations, while ensuring fair commercial competition. The decisions of the Committee were not meant to be legally binding upon its members.

Presently, 39 countries are members of the Committee. The Committee maintains an updated list of equipment or material that cannot be exported without safeguards being applied to the receiving facility. The list is called the 'Trigger List' because such exports trigger the need for safeguards. The Committee also serves as a platform for members to coordinate issues relating to nuclear exports, and facilitate discussions at the *Nuclear Suppliers Group (NSG)*.

SOURCES

Primary Sources

A Cooperative Strategy for 21st Century Seapower, US Maritime Strategy documents released in October 2007 and March 2015

Arctic Marine Strategic Plan 2015-25, Arctic Council, April 2015

Australian Defence Doctrine Publication (ADDP) 00.1 (Command and Control), 27 May 2009, Department of Defence, Canberra ACT

"BMP4: Best Management Practices for Protection against Somalia Based Piracy", *International Chamber of Shipping*, Version 4, August 2011.

Charter of the United Nations, San Francisco, 1945

Commander's Handbook on the Law of Naval Operations, (US) Naval Warfare Publication (NWP) 1-14M, (Jul 07), and its Annotated Supplement (1997).

Constitution of India, Government of India, Ministry of Law and Justice, New Delhi, 01 December 2007 *(As modified up to that date).*

Convention for the Suppression of Unlawful Acts against the Safety of Maritime Navigation, 1988

Customs Manual 2011, Central Board of Excise and Customs (CBEC), Department of Revenue, Ministry of Finance (Govt of India)

'Department of Defense Dictionary of Military and Associated Terms', Joint Publication (JP) 1-02, US Joint Chiefs of Staff, 08 November 2010 (Amended through 15 January 2015)

Glossary of Shipping Terms, Maritime Administration, US Department of Transportation, May 2008

Guidelines on the Use of Foreign Military and Civil Defence Assets in Disaster Relief (Oslo Guidelines), May 94 (Updated Nov 07)

Guidelines on the Use of Military and Civil Defence Assets to Support UN Humanitarian Activities in Complex Emergencies', Mar 03

Indian Maritime Doctrine (INBR 8), August 2009, *Integrated Headquarters,*

Ministry of Defence (Navy)/Maritime Doctrine and Concept Centre (MDCC), Mumbai.

International Plan of Action to Prevent, Deter and Eliminate Illegal, Unreported and Unregulated Fishing (IPOA-IUU), Food and Agriculture Organisation (FAO) of the United Nations, Rome, 2001

'India's Maritime Security Strategy', *Integrated Headquarters, Ministry of Defence, (Navy)*, October 2015

'Freedom to Use the Seas: India's Military Maritime Strategy', *Integrated Headquarters, Ministry of Defence, (Navy)*, May 2007

National Maritime Search and Rescue Manual, *National Maritime Search and Rescue Board*, NMSARB PUB 1 – 10 (Revised Edition), August 2010

NATO Glossary of Terms and Definitions, NATO AAP-06

Naval Prize Act, 1864 and Prize Courts Act, 1894

'Responsibility to Protect', Report of the *International Commission on Intervention and State Sovereignty* (ICISS), 2001

San Remo Manual on International Law Applicable to Armed Conflicts at Sea, *International Institute of Humanitarian Law*, 12 Jun 94.

San Remo Manual on the Law of Non-International Armed Conflict, *International Institute of Humanitarian Law*, 2006

San Remo Handbook on Rules of Engagement, *International Institute of Humanitarian Law*, November 2009

'Special Operations', Joint Publication (JP) 3-05, US Joint Chiefs of Staff, 18 April 2011

The Arbitration and Conciliation Act, 1996

The Asia-Pacific Maritime Security Strategy: Achieving U.S. National Security Objectives in a Changing Environment, July 2015

United Nations Peacekeeping Operations: Principles and Guidelines, 2008

United Nations Convention on the Law of the Sea, 1982 (UNCLOS)

Books

James D Watkins. *The Maritime Strategy* (1986: US Naval Institute Press, Annapolis)

Encyclopedia Britannica 2013, (September 2012: Focus Multimedia Ltd, Staffordshire, the UK)

GM Hiranandani. *Transition to Eminence: The Indian Navy 1976 to 1990* (2005: Lancer Publishers, New Delhi)

Gurpreet S Khurana. *Maritime Forces in Pursuit of National Security: Policy Imperatives for India* (2008: IDSA/Shipra Publications, New Delhi)

Jane's Fighting Ships 2013/2014, 21 Jul 13

John W Spanier. *Games Nations Play* (1987, 6th edition: Congressional Quarterly Inc., USA)

Julian S Corbett. *Some Principles of Maritime Strategy* (1911: London)

Kevin Stephens. *Glossary Chartering & Shipping Terms* (2007: Hamburg) Project Professionals Group (www.ppgprojects.com)

Vijay Oberoi (ed.) *Special Forces: Doctrine, Structures and Employment Across the Spectrum of Conflict in the Indian Context* (2006: CLAWS/Knowledge World, New Delhi)

Net Security Provider: India's Out of Area Contingency Operations (October 2012: Magnum Books Pvt Ltd./IDSA Military Affairs Centre, New Delhi)

PR Franklin. *Submarine Operations* (2010: NMF/Knowledge World, New Delhi)

Relief Web Glossary of Humanitarian Terms, August 2008

SS Byce and RK Tiwari. *Anti-submarine Warfare* (2006: NMF/Anamaya Publishers, New Delhi)

Journals

Journal of Conflict & Security Law, Oxford University Press

Newport Papers, Naval War College, Newport, Rhode Island

Research Papers and Other Sources

Basic Fishing Methods, 'Seafish', Fisheries Development Centre, Seafish Flume Tank, Manchester Street, Hull, April 2005

Global Ocean Commission. *Strengthening Deep Seabed Mining Regulation* (November 2013: Policy Option Paper No 5)

OP Sharma, Various writings on Law of the Sea

Personal notes of the author (unclassified)

Sudarshan Y Shrikhande, 'India's Search for a Cogent Maritime Military Strategy: Continuing Relevance of Mahan and Corbett', M.Phil Dissertation submitted to the University of Mumbai, 2014

Vijay Sakhuja, 'Asymmetric Warfare and Low Intensity Maritime Operations: Challenges for Indian Navy', *ORF Occasional Paper* No.5, August 2006

Internet Sources

Websites of the Arctic Council, Arms Control Association, African Union (AU), APEC, Arab League, ASEAN, Fund for Peace, Government of India (various ministries), International Hydrographic Organisation (IHO), International Chamber of Commerce (ICC), International Chamber of Shipping (ICS), Global Security, Gulf Cooperation Council (GCC), Indian Coast Guard, Indian Navy Marine Insight, Maritime Connector, Maritime Terrorism Research Center, National Oceanic and Atmospheric Administration (NOAA), OPEC, Ports and Ships, Saro Associates (Chennai), United Nations (including its various agencies and bodies), US Center for Strategic and Budgetary Assessments, US Department of Homeland Security, US Department of State, US Maritime Liaison Office (MARLO) Bahrain, Wassenaar Arrangement, Wikipedia, World Bank, World Ocean Review and Your Article Library.

ABOUT THE AUTHOR

Captain Gurpreet S Khurana is a serving Indian Navy officer with 27 years of commissioned service, and a PhD in Defence Studies. A missile specialist and ship's diver, he has participated in all major naval operations since IPKF operations (1987-90) and has held the Command of two warships, including the commissioning Command of a Fast Attack Craft at Port Blair (2002).

During his Research Fellowship at the IDSA (2003-8), he authored the book titled *Maritime Forces in Pursuit of National Security* (2008). He was commended by the Chief of Naval Staff for reviewing and editing the Indian Maritime Doctrine, 2009 (INBR-8). He also compiled the Navy's *Handbook on the Law of Maritime Operations*, 2013 (INBR-1652).

He represents India at the Search and Rescue (SAR) Working Group of the Council for Security Cooperation in the Asia-Pacific (CSCAP). He is currently the Executive Director at National Maritime Foundation, New Delhi.